Samsung® Galaxy Note® 3

FOR DUMMIES®

A Wiley Brand

Samsung® Galaxy Note® 3

FOR DUMMIES®

A Wiley Brand

by Dan Gookin

FOR DUMMIES®
A Wiley Brand

Samsung® Galaxy Note® 3 For Dummies®

Published by: **John Wiley & Sons, Inc.,** 111 River Street, Hoboken, NJ 07030-5774, www.wiley.com

Copyright © 2014 by John Wiley & Sons, Inc., Hoboken, New Jersey

Published by John Wiley & Sons, Inc., Hoboken, New Jersey

Published simultaneously in Canada

For general information on our other products and services, please contact our Customer Care Department within the U.S. at 877-762-2974, outside the U.S. at 317-572-3993, or fax 317-572-4002.

For technical support, please visit www.wiley.com/techsupport.

Wiley also publishes its books in a variety of electronic formats and by print-on-demand. Not all content that is available in standard print versions of this book may appear or be packaged in all book formats. If you have purchased a version of this book that did not include media that is referenced by or accompanies a standard print version, you may request this media by visiting http://booksupport.wiley.com. For more information about Wiley products, visit us www.wiley.com.

Library of Congress Control Number: 2014935510

ISBN 978-1-118-92011-4 (pbk); ISBN 978-1-118-92028-2 (ebk); ISBN 978-1-118-92012-1 (ebk)

Manufactured in the United States of America

10 9 8 7 6 5 4 3 2 1

Contents at a Glance

Introduction 1

Part I: What Is This Thing? 7

Chapter 1: A Note for You...9
Chapter 2: On, Off, and Configuration 23
Chapter 3: Rule the Galaxy Note 35
Chapter 4: Text Creation and Editing 57

Part II: Phone Duties 71

Chapter 5: Phone 101 73
Chapter 6: Super Phone 85
Chapter 7: Voice Mail and Beyond 99

Part III: Keep in Touch............................. 107

Chapter 8: The People in Your Galaxy 109
Chapter 9: Message for You!..123
Chapter 10: Galactic E-Mail 133
Chapter 11: It's a World Wide Web We Weave....................147
Chapter 12: Your Digital Social Life 157
Chapter 13: I See What You're Doing There 167

Part IV: Incredible Tasks and Amazing Feats 179

Chapter 14: There's a Map for That.....................................181
Chapter 15: Everyone Say "Cheese" 195
Chapter 16: Listen to the Music 211
Chapter 17: What Else Does It Do? 223
Chapter 18: The Apps Chapter 241

Part V: Nuts and Bolts 255

Chapter 19: Wireless Wizardry 257
Chapter 20: Sync, Share, and Store......................................271
Chapter 21: Take It Elsewhere...281
Chapter 22: Customize Your Phone 289
Chapter 23: Keep It Running...307

Part VI: The Part of Tens **321**

Chapter 24: Ten Tips, Tricks, and Shortcuts...323

Chapter 25: Ten Things to Remember 335

Index **341**

Table of Contents

Introduction *1*

About This Book 1
How to Use This Book 2
Foolish Assumptions 3
How This Book Is Organized 3
    Part I: What Is This Thing? 4
    Part II: Phone Duties 4
    Part III: Keep in Touch 4
    Part IV: Incredible Tasks and Amazing Feats 4
    Part V: Nuts and Bolts 4
    Part VI: The Part of Tens 4
Icons Used in This Book 5
Where to Go from Here 5

Part I: What Is This Thing? *7*

Chapter 1: A Note for You **9**

Out of the Box 9
Phone Assembly 11
    Removing the rear cover 11
    Installing and removing the battery 11
    Installing the SIM card 13
    Adding and removing a MicroSD card 13
    Reattaching the phone's rear cover 15
Charge the Battery 15
Explore the Galaxy Note 16
    Identifying important things 16
    Using earphones 19
    Adding other accessories 19
A Home for Your Phone 20
    Toting your Galaxy Note 20
    Storing the phone 21

Chapter 2: On, Off, and Configuration **23**

Hello! 23
    Turning on your phone for the first time 24
    Turning on the Galaxy Note 25
    Unlocking the phone 27

Account Setup..28
  Obtaining a Google account 28
  Setting up with AT&T Ready2Go 29
  Adding other accounts 30
Goodbye!..31
  Locking the phone 31
  Controlling the automatic screen lock....................................31
  Turning off the phone..32

Chapter 3: Rule the Galaxy Note 35

Basic Operations 36
  Manipulating the touchscreen 36
  Exploring the navigation icons..37
  Setting the volume...38
  "Silence your phone!"...39
  Enjoying the accelerometer..39
Home Screen Chores 41
  Examining the Home screen 41
  Accessing the Home screen panels 43
  Reviewing notifications...43
  Using Quick Actions 45
The App Galaxy..46
  Starting an app 46
  Quitting an app...46
  Working a widget 46
  Browsing the Applications screen..47
  Switching apps 48
  Playing with Multi Window 49
  Using common icons 51
The Magical S Pen...53
  Understanding the S Pen...53
  Using Air Command 54
  Doing some S Pen tricks..55

Chapter 4: Text Creation and Editing 57

Behold the Onscreen Keyboard 57
Everybody Was Touchscreen Typing..59
  Typing one character at a time...59
  Accessing special characters 60
  Typing quickly by using predictive text 61
  Activating Keyboard Swipe...63
  Writing text with the S Pen 64
Voice Typing and Dictation...65
  Activating voice input 65
  Talking to your phone 65
  Uttering b**** words 67

Text Editing 67
> Moving the cursor.. 67
> Selecting text 68
> Cutting, copying, and pasting text 69

Part II: Phone Duties 71

Chapter 5: Phone 101 73

I Just Called to Say 73
> Making a phone call... 74
> Dialing a contact 78
> Calling a favorite 78

Ring, Ring, Ring 78
> Receiving a call.. 79
> Rejecting a call with a text message... 80
> Dealing with a missed call 82

The Call Log.. 82

Chapter 6: Super Phone..85

Super Dialing Tricks 85
> Configuring speed dial.. 85
> Adding pauses when dialing a number 87

Captain Conference Call 88
> Putting someone on hold.. 88
> Receiving a call when you're on the phone................................. 88
> Juggling two calls 89
> Making a conference call 91

Calls Sent Elsewhere 92
> Forwarding phone calls... 92
> Rejecting incoming calls 94
> Managing the reject list... 95

Intergalactic Ringtones 95
> Choosing the phone's ringtone.. 95
> Setting a contact's ringtone... 96
> Creating your own ringtones 97

Chapter 7: Voice Mail and Beyond 99

Plain Old, Boring Carrier Voice Mail 99
> Setting up carrier voice mail 100
> Retrieving your messages.. 101

Wonderful Google Voice 101
> Configuring Google Voice 102
> Adding a second line to Google Voice.. 103
> Using the Google Voice app.. 104

Part III: Keep in Touch 107

Chapter 8: The People in Your Galaxy 109
The Digital Address Book 109
    Accessing the address book 110
    Searching contacts 112
Some New Friends 112
    Adding a contact from the call log 113
    Creating a new contact from scratch 114
    Importing contacts from your computer 114
    Mixing in social networking contacts 115
    Finding a new contact by location 116
Address Book Management 117
    Making basic changes 118
    Adding a contact picture 118
    Making a favorite 120
    Linking identical contacts 120
    Unlinking a contact 121
    Removing a contact 121

Chapter 9: Message for You! 123
Life in Less Than 160 Characters 123
    Composing a text message 124
    Receiving a text message 127
    Forwarding a text message 127
Multimedia Messages 128
    Attaching media to a text message 128
    Saving media from a text message 130
Text Message Management 130
    Removing messages 130
    Setting the text message ringtone 131
Text Messaging Alternatives 131

Chapter 10: Galactic E-Mail 133
E-Mail on the Galaxy Note 133
    Setting up an e-mail account 134
    Adding more e-mail accounts 136
You've Got Mail 137
    Getting a new message 137
    Checking the inbox 138
    Reading e-mail 139
Make Your Own E-Mail 140
    Writing a new electronic message 141
    Sending e-mail to a contact 142
Message Attachments 142

E-Mail Configuration...143
    Creating a signature..144
    Setting the default e-mail account 145
    Configuring the server delete option 145

Chapter 11: It's a World Wide Web We Weave 147

Web Web Web..148
    Visiting a web page...149
    Browsing back and forth..150
    Working with bookmarks..150
    Managing multiple web page windows 151
    Searching the web...152
    Finding text on a web page...152
    Sharing a web page..152
That Downloading Thrill..153
    Grabbing an image from a web page 153
    Downloading a file..154
    Reviewing your downloads...154
Master the Internet App 154
    Setting a home page 154
    Changing the way the web looks 155
    Setting privacy and security options 156

Chapter 12: Your Digital Social Life 157

In Your Facebook..157
    Setting up your Facebook account 158
    Getting the Facebook app..158
    Running Facebook on your phone....................................158
    Setting your status...160
    Uploading a picture to Facebook.....................................161
    Configuring the Facebook app 163
Tweet Suite...163
    Setting up Twitter 164
    Tweeting...165
Even More Social Networking...166

Chapter 13: I See What You're Doing There 167

Samsung Video Calling...167
Hangout with Google..169
    Using Hangouts 169
    Typing at your friends...170
    Using Hangouts as your phone's SMS app 172
    Talking and video chat..172
Connect with Skype..174
    Getting Skype..174
    Chatting with another Skype user 175
    Seeing on Skype (video call)..176

Part IV: Incredible Tasks and Amazing Feats 179

Chapter 14: There's a Map for That 181

Behold the Map 182
Using the Maps app 182
Adding layers 183
How to Find Yourself 185
Finding out where you are 185
Helping others find your location 186
How to Find Other Things 187
Looking for a specific address 187
Finding a business, restaurant, or point of interest 187
Searching for favorite or recent places 189
Locating one of your contacts 189
How to Get There 189
Asking for directions 190
Navigating to your destination 191

Chapter 15: Everyone Say "Cheese" 195

Smile for the Camera App 195
Capturing the moment 196
Deleting immediately after you shoot 197
Doing a self-portrait 198
Shooting a panoramic image 198
Taking a screen shot 199
Camera Settings and Options 200
Finding the settings 200
Setting the flash 201
Changing image resolution 202
Setting video quality 203
Activating location information 204
Choosing the storage device 204
Where Your Photos Lurk 205
Visiting the Gallery app 205
Navigating to an image's location 206
Sharing from the Gallery 207
Image Management 207
Cropping an image 207
Rotating pictures 209
Deleting photos and videos 209

Chapter 16: Listen to the Music 211

Your Top 40 211
Browsing your music library 211
Playing a tune 213
The Hits Just Keep On Coming 216
Borrowing music from your computer 216
Getting music from the Google Play Store 218
Music Organization 219
Reviewing your playlists 220
Building playlists 220
Deleting music 221
Galaxy Note Radio 221

Chapter 17: What Else Does It Do? 223

It's a Clock 223
It's a Calculator 225
It's a Calendar 226
Checking your schedule 227
Reviewing events 228
Creating a new event 229
It's an eBook Reader 231
It's a Game Machine 234
It's Google Now 235
It's a Scribble Pad 236
Using the Action Memo app 236
Capturing and scribbling 238
It's a Tape Recorder 239
It's a Video Player 240

Chapter 18: The Apps Chapter 241

The Google Play Store 241
Visiting the Play Store 242
Obtaining an app 244
Manage Your Apps 246
Reviewing your apps 246
Sharing an app 248
Updating an app 248
Removing an app 249
Controlling your apps 249
Applications Screen Organization 252
Changing the Applications screen view 252
Rearranging apps on the Applications screen 253
Working with Applications screen folders 253

Part V: Nuts and Bolts *255*

Chapter 19: Wireless Wizardry .... .257
    It's a Wireless Life...257
        Understanding the mobile data network 258
        Understanding Wi-Fi 259
        Activating Wi-Fi 259
        Connecting to a Wi-Fi network 260
        Connecting via WPS 261
    A Connection to Share 262
        Creating a mobile hotspot 262
        Tethering the Internet connection 264
    The Bluetooth Way...264
        Understanding Bluetooth..265
        Activating Bluetooth...265
        Pairing with a Bluetooth device...............................266
        Printing to a Bluetooth printer..................................268
    Android Beam It to Me..269
        Turning on NFC 269
        Using Android Beam 269
        Using Jim Beam 269

Chapter 20: Sync, Share, and Store .... .271
    The USB Connection 271
        Connecting the USB cable..272
        Configuring the USB connection 272
        Connecting to a Mac 273
        Disconnecting the phone from the computer 274
    Synchronize Your Stuff 274
        Transferring files..274
        Connecting with Samsung Kies 276
        Sharing files with the cloud 277
    Galaxy Note Storage Mysteries 278
        Reviewing storage stats 278
        Managing files...279
        Dealing with MicroSD storage 280

Chapter 21: Take It Elsewhere .... .281
    Where the Phone Roams 281
    Airplane Mode...282
    International Calling...284
        Dialing an international number 284
        Making international calls with Skype 286
        Taking your Galaxy Note abroad 286

Chapter 22: Customize Your Phone 289
  It's Your Home Screen 289
    Editing the Home screen.. 290
    Changing wallpaper 291
    Adding apps to the Home screen... 292
    Putting an app on the Favorites tray................................... 293
    Slapping down widgets 293
    Building app folders 294
    Rearranging and removing icons and widgets............................ 296
    Adding and removing Home screen panels............................... 297
  Galactic Screen Security 298
    Finding the screen locks 298
    Removing a lock 299
    Applying a password 300
    Setting a PIN 300
    Creating an unlock pattern 300
    Unlocking the phone with your signature 302
    Adding owner info text... 303
  Some Fine-Tuning 304
    Setting sound and vibration options 304
    Changing display settings.. 305

Chapter 23: Keep It Running 307
  Battery Care and Feeding.. 307
    Monitoring the battery.. 308
    Determining what is drawing power 309
    Using Power Saving mode.. 310
    Extending battery life 311
  Regular Maintenance... 312
    Keeping it clean.. 312
    Backing up your phone 312
    Updating the system.. 313
  Help and Troubleshooting.. 314
    Getting help 314
    Fixing random and annoying problems 314
    Getting support 316
  Galaxy Note Q&A 317
    "The touchscreen doesn't work!" 317
    "I lost the S Pen!".. 318
    "The screen is too dark!" 318
    "The screen turns off during a call".................................... 318
    "The battery doesn't charge!" 318
    "The phone gets so hot that it turns itself off!"........................ 318
    "The phone won't do Landscape mode!".................................. 319

Part VI: The Part of Tens 321

Chapter 24: Ten Tips, Tricks, and Shortcuts 323
Spruce Up the Lock Screen 324
Use Galaxy Note Motion Features 325
Personalize the Sound 326
Change Screen Fonts 327
Add Spice to Dictation 328
Choose Default Apps 328
Avoid Data Overages 329
Watch the Phone Dream 331
Find Your Lost Cell Phone 332
Visit Task Manager 332

Chapter 25: Ten Things to Remember 335
Return to a Recent App...335
Lock the Phone on a Call 336
Use Landscape Orientation 336
Follow the Keyboard Suggestions 336
Things That Consume Lots of Battery Juice 337
Check for Roaming 337
Use the + Symbol When Dialing Internationally 338
Get a Docking Stand 338
Snap a Pic of That Contact 338
Use the Search Command 339

Index 341

Introduction

I was thrilled when I first learned about the release of the Galaxy Note 3. I figured that I could write a book about the new device and, because it's much larger than a typical cell phone, write a bigger book — one that's about one-and-a-half times larger than the typical *For Dummies* book.

Alas, I was informed that the book, the one you hold in your hands, would be a normal-size *For Dummies* title. Still, I've managed to cram enough information in here to make using the Galaxy Note 3 an enjoyable and tolerable experience. New devices can be intimidating. I know! So I've written this book to help you get the most from the first-ever hybrid phone/tablet computer.

About This Book

The most important thing to know about this book is that you're not required to read it from cover to cover. I beg you. That's because this book is a reference. It's designed to be used as you need it. Look up a topic in the table of contents or the index. Find something about your phone that vexes you, or something you're curious about. Look up the answer and get on with your life.

Every chapter in this book is written as its own, self-contained unit, covering a specific topic about using your phone. The chapters are further divided into sections representing a task you perform with the phone or explaining how to get something done. Sample sections in this book include

- Starting an app
- Doing some S Pen tricks
- Activating voice input
- Making a conference call
- Attaching media to a text message
- Uploading a picture to Facebook
- Talking and video chat
- Helping others find your location
- Shooting a panoramic image

✔ Browsing your music library

✔ Printing to a Bluetooth printer

✔ Unlocking the phone with your signature

Every section explains a topic as though it's the first one you've read in this book. Nothing is assumed, and everything is cross-referenced. Technical terms and topics, when they come up, are neatly shoved to the side, where they're easily avoided. The idea here isn't to learn anything. This book's philosophy is to help you look it up, figure it out, and get back to your life.

How to Use This Book

This book follows a few conventions for using your phone, so pay attention!

The main way to interact with your phone is by using its *touchscreen,* which is the glassy part of the phone as it's facing you. Buttons also adorn the phone, all of which are explained in Part I of this book.

You can touch the screen in various ways, which are described in Chapter 3.

Chapter 4 discusses text input — typing — which involves using something called the *onscreen keyboard.* Also covered is using the Galaxy Note S Pen for drawing and text input, plus a few special tricks. And, when you tire of typing or drawing, you can always input text on your phone by dictating it.

This book directs you to do things on your phone by following numbered steps. Every step involves a specific activity, such as touching something on the screen; for example:

3. Choose Downloads.

This step directs you to touch the text or item labeled Downloads on the screen. You might also be told to do this:

3. Touch Downloads.

 Various phone options can be turned off or on, as indicated by a gray box with a green check mark in it, as shown in the margin. By touching the box on the screen, you add or remove the green check mark. When the green check mark appears, the option is on; otherwise, it's off.

Oh, and sometimes the check mark is blue, just to keep you on your toes.

Some settings feature a master control, which looks like an On-Off switch, as shown in the margin. Slide the button to the right to activate the switch, turning on a phone feature and changing the switch color to green. Slide the button to the left to disable the feature, changing the switch color to gray.

Foolish Assumptions

Even though this book was written to provide the gentle handholding required by anyone who is just starting out, or who is easily intimidated, I have made a few assumptions.

Number one: I'm assuming that you're still reading the Introduction. That's great. It's much better than getting a foot massage right now or checking the latest Lotto numbers.

My biggest assumptions: You have a Galaxy Note 3 phone. I refer to it as the *Galaxy Note* throughout the book, but it's still the Galaxy Note 3 phone. This text doesn't rely on your use of any particular cellular provider, and I heavily avoid making any Verizon jokes.

More assumptions:

I also assume that you have either a computer or access to a computer. The computer can be a PC (or Windows computer) or a Macintosh. Oh, I suppose it could be a Linux computer instead. In any event, I refer to a computer as *a computer* throughout this book. When directions are specific to a PC or Mac, the book says so.

Programs that run on your Android phone are called *apps*, which is short for *applications*. A single program is an *app*.

Finally, this book assumes that you have a Google account. If you don't, Chapter 2 explains how to configure one. Do so. Having a Google account opens up a slew of useful features, information, and programs that make using your phone more productive.

How This Book Is Organized

This book has been sliced into six parts, each of which describes a certain aspect of the typical Android phone or how it's used.

Part I: What Is This Thing?

This part of the book serves as an introduction to your phone. Chapters cover setup and orientation and familiarize you with how the phone works. Part I is a good place to start — plus, you discover things in this part that aren't obvious from guessing how the phone works.

Part II: Phone Duties

Nothing is more basic for a phone to do than make calls, which is the topic of the chapters in this part of the book. As you may have suspected, your Galaxy Note 3 can make calls, receive calls, and serve as an answering service for calls you miss.

Part III: Keep in Touch

The modern cell phone is about more than simply telephone communications. Part III of this book explores other ways you can use your phone to stay in touch with people, browse the Internet, check your e-mail, do your social networking, exchange text messages, chat by video, and more.

Part IV: Incredible Tasks and Amazing Feats

This part of the book explores the nonphone things your phone can do. For example, your phone can find locations on a map, give you verbal driving directions, take pictures, shoot videos, play music, play games, and do all sorts of other wonderful things that no one would ever think a phone can do. The chapters in this part of the book get you up to speed on those activities.

Part V: Nuts and Bolts

The chapters in this part of the book discuss a spate of interesting topics, from connecting the phone to a computer, using Wi-Fi and Bluetooth networking, and taking the phone overseas and making international calls to customizing and personalizing your phone and the necessary chores of maintenance and troubleshooting.

Part VI: The Part of Tens

Finally, this book ends with the traditional *For Dummies* The Part of Tens, where every chapter lists ten items or topics. For your Galaxy Note, the chapters include tips, tricks, shortcuts, and things to remember.

Icons Used in This Book

This icon flags useful, helpful tips or shortcuts.

This icon marks a friendly reminder to do something.

This icon marks a friendly reminder *not* to do something.

This icon alerts you to overly nerdy information and technical discussions of the topic at hand. Reading the information is optional, though it may win you a pie slice in *Trivial Pursuit*.

Where to Go from Here

Thank you for reading the introduction. Few people do, and it would save a lot of time and bother if they did. Consider yourself fortunate, though you probably already knew that.

Your task now: Start reading the rest of this book — but not the whole thing, and especially not in order. Observe the table of contents, and find something that interests you. Or look up your puzzle in the index. When these suggestions don't cut it, just start reading Chapter 1.

My e-mail address is dgookin@wambooli.com. Yes, that's my real address. I reply to all e-mail I receive, and you get a quick reply if you keep your question short and specific to this book. Although I enjoy saying Hi, I cannot answer technical support questions, resolve billing issues, or help you troubleshoot your phone. Thanks for understanding.

You can also visit my website: www.wambooli.com. This book has its own page on that site, which you can check for updates, new information, and all sorts of fun stuff. Visit often:

```
www.wambooli.com/help/galaxynote3
```

The publisher also offers its own help site, which contains official updates, a cheat sheet, and bonus information. Visit the publisher's official support pages at:

```
www.dummies.com/cheatsheet/samsunggalaxynote3
```

```
www.dummies.com/extras/samsunggalaxynote3
```

Enjoy this book and your Galaxy Note!

Part I

What *Is* This Thing?

getting started
with
Samsung
Galaxy Note 3

web
extras

Visit www.dummies.com for great *For Dummies* content online.

In this part...

- Get started with the Galaxy Note phone
- Work through setup on the Galaxy Note phone
- See how to use your Galaxy Note phone
- Discover parts of the Galaxy Note phone

1

A Note for You

In This Chapter

▶ Liberating the phone from its box

▶ Installing things inside the phone

▶ Charging the battery

▶ Familiarizing yourself with the Galaxy Note

▶ Using optional accessories

▶ Taking the phone with you

▶ Keeping the phone in one place

*T*he Galaxy Note phone is the Reese's Peanut Butter Cup of mobile gizmos: From the chocolate side comes the modern tablet, a large, slate-like device that does many of the same things a computer can do. On the peanut butter side is the cell phone, the 21st century's primary communications device, which suffers from a diminutive screen. Put the two together and you can have something curiously delicious, like a Galaxy Note phone.

This chapter introduces you to the Samsung Galaxy Note. The chapter helps you to get things set up, to identify important parts and pieces, and to provide a gentle, soothing introduction. I believe you'll find that this chapter is far more detailed and entertaining than the tepid *Quick Start* pamphlet. Your phone deserves better than that.

Out of the Box

The first step toward getting the most from the Galaxy Note is to remove it from the confines of its box. Not only does the phone work better outside the box, but its removal is also necessary to complete some initial setup and configuration.

Alas, you probably aren't the first to liberate the phone from its cardboard cradle. Initial setup was most likely done by the friendly folks at the Phone Store. They've probably installed something called a SIM card, configured the Galaxy Note to work with their cellular network, and walked you through the initial account setup and configuration. If so, great — that's less for you to do.

Whether the phone has been set up or not, I encourage you to rifle through the box to locate and identify these items:

- ✔ The phone itself, which may have already been assembled by a Phone Store employee. If not, you'll find the rear cover and battery inside the box, ready to be installed.

- ✔ The all-too-brief pamphlets, warnings, warranties, and perhaps other miscellaneous and potentially useful pieces of paper

- ✔ Earphones for listening to music and making phone calls

- ✔ The charger/data cable, also known as a USB cable

- ✔ The charger head, which is the wall adapter for the charger/data cable

The phone ships with a clingy, static, plastic cover on its screen, back, and sides. Peel away the plastic as if your phone were a banana, although the process would be more delightful if a fruity snack were available upon completion.

The most important doodad is the phone — your Galaxy Note — which might require some assembly, as described in the next section.

- ✔ The S Pen is found inserted into the phone, so don't panic when you can't locate it loose inside the box. See Chapter 3 for information on accessing the S Pen.

- ✔ One accessory I recommend getting right away is a MicroSD card. See the later section "Adding and removing a MicroSD card" for details.

- ✔ Keep the instructions and other information for as long as you own the phone. The phone's box makes an excellent storage place for that stuff — as well as for anything else you don't plan to use right away.

- ✔ If anything is missing or appears to be damaged, immediately contact the folks who sold you the phone.

- ✔ The Galaxy Note 3's charging cable is a USB 3.0 cable. If possible, connect it to a USB 3.0 port on a PC. It still works on other USB ports, but works faster on a USB 3.0 port. These ports, as well as USB cable connectors, are colored blue.

Phone Assembly

The Galaxy Note comes disassembled inside the box. The phone, back cover, and battery require assembly. The Phone Store employee puts everything together for you to configure the phone to work with the company's cellular network.

It rarely happens, but you may be required to perform the initial assembly yourself. Or, more frequently, you need to access the phone's innards to add or replace the MicroSD card or battery. If so, this section contains helpful information, such as taking-apart and putting-back-together details.

Removing the rear cover

Before you can go phone spelunking, you must remove the Galaxy Note's rear cover. Heed these directions:

1. **Ensure that the phone is turned off.**

   See Chapter 2 for details.

2. **Flip the phone over and locate the thumbnail notch at the bottom center of the back cover.**

   Figure 1-1 illustrates where to find the thumbnail hole. Older Galaxy Note phones featured a thumb notch on the upper side of the back cover.

3. **Insert your thumbnail into the notch, and carefully pry the back cover from the phone.**

   The popping noise you hear whilst removing the back cover is normal.

4. **Set aside the cover.**

The Galaxy Note has three items you can access after the back cover is removed (refer to Figure 1-1): the battery, SIM card, and MicroSD card. The following three sections offer specific information on each of these items.

To reassemble the phone, see the later section "Reattaching the phone's rear cover."

Installing and removing the battery

The battery is the largest item you can add or remove inside the phone. It's necessary to remove the battery to access the SIM card slot. It's not really necessary to take out the battery to access the MicroSD card, although it's easier to do so by first removing the battery.

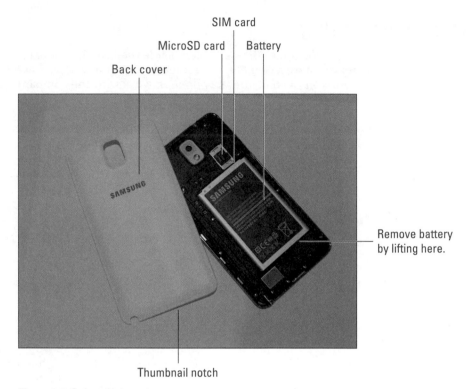

SIM card

MicroSD card   Battery

Back cover

Remove battery by lifting here.

Thumbnail notch

Figure 1-1: Galaxy Note guts.

To remove the battery, insert your thumbnail in the notch in the lower-right (refer to Figure 1-1). Lift the battery out of the phone.

To insert the battery, orient it so that the contacts are up, toward the top of the phone. The text on the back of the battery should be oriented right side up, as shown earlier, in Figure 1-1. Insert the battery top side first, and then insert it the rest of the way, as though you're closing the lid on a tiny box. When the battery is properly installed, it's flush with the back of the phone.

Obviously, if the battery is still in its tiny, plastic bag, you should first remove the bag before inserting the battery into the phone.

If you're setting up your Galaxy Note for the first time, the next task after inserting the battery is to charge it — see the later section "Charge the Battery." Well, put the back cover on first, and then charge the phone.

- ✔ If you're replacing the battery, store the original inside a nonmetallic box in a dark, dry location.

- ✔ If you need to dispose of the battery, do so properly; batteries are classified as hazardous waste and should not merely be placed in the trash.

✔ Replacement batteries are commonly available, some of which may allow you to use your phone for longer periods between charges. Always ensure that you replace the battery with one that's compatible with your specific Galaxy Note model. Using any old battery as a replacement is a hazard and can damage your phone, you, or innocent bystanders.

Installing the SIM card

Your cellular provider uses the *SIM card* to identify your Galaxy Note with its cellular network. If the cheerful human at the Phone Store hasn't installed the SIM card into your Galaxy Note, you need to do it. Obey these steps:

1. **If necessary, remove the phone's back cover.**

   The SIM card is inserted into a slot directly underneath the MicroSD card slot.

2. **Pop the SIM card free from its holder.**

   Press the SIM card until it pops out of the credit-card-size frame.

3. **Insert the SIM card into the SIM card slot.**

   The SIM card fits in only one way: notched end in first, printed side up. Push in the card all the way.

4. **Replace the battery and the phone's back cover.**

   You're done.

If you have trouble inserting the SIM card and a MicroSD card is already installed, you may have to remove the MicroSD card first. See the next section.

✔ You rarely, if ever, need to remove the SIM card.

✔ A typical way to use a SIM is to replace a broken phone with a new one: You plug the SIM from the old phone into the new phone, and instantly the phone is recognized as your own. Of course, the two phones need to use similar cellular networks for the transplant operation to be successful.

✔ SIM stands for Subscriber Identity Module. SIM cards are required for GSM cellular networks and 4G LTE networks.

Adding and removing a MicroSD card

The Galaxy Note doesn't come with a MicroSD card, which is disappointing. The MicroSD card bolsters the phone's storage, adding what's called *removable* storage. As with any portable electronic gizmo, the more storage, the better.

Obtain a MicroSD card for your Galaxy Note. The cards come in capacities of 8GB, 16GB, and 32GB. The higher the capacity, the more expensive the card, so buy the largest capacity you can afford.

To install the MicroSD card inside your Galaxy Note, obey these steps:

1. **Remove the phone's back cover and battery.**

   Specific directions are offered earlier in this chapter.

2. **Locate the slot into which you stick the MicroSD card.**

   Use Figure 1-1 as your guide.

3. **Insert the MicroSD card into its slot.**

   The card goes in only one way. The arrow on the card indicates which edge goes in first; the printed side of the card is facing you as you insert the card.

4. **Reinstall the battery (if necessary), and reassemble the Galaxy Note.**

The MicroSD card must be formatted for use with your phone. Directions are found in Chapter 20.

To remove the card, follow these steps:

1. **Turn off the phone.**

2. **Remove the back cover and the battery.**

3. **Nudge the MicroSD card a tad.**

4. **Use your fingernail to help grab the card and pull it out the rest of the way.**

The card has been liberated.

✔ The MicroSD card might also be referred to as an SD card or media card. It's a standard form of removable media for portable devices, used in mobile phones, cameras, and music players.

✔ MicroSD cards are teensy! Keep them in a safe place where you won't lose them.

✔ You can buy a MicroSD card adapter, which allows its data to be read by computers, via either the standard Secure Digital (SD) memory slot or the USB port.

✔ If you're upgrading to the Galaxy Note from another Android phone, simply remove the MicroSD card from the old phone and install it on the Galaxy Note. By doing so, you instantly transfer your pictures, music, and videos.

Reattaching the phone's rear cover

When you're done rooting around inside your phone, or when it tells you that it's shivering and needs to warm up, you should replace its back cover. The operation works like this:

1. **Line up the top of the back cover with the bottom of the Galaxy Note.**

2. **Working around the back of the phone, gently press the cover into place.**

   The cover snaps as it settles into position.

When the back cover is on properly, it should have no gaps or raised edges. Keep pressing the back cover until you no longer hear any snaps.

Charge the Battery

One of your first duties after assembling your Galaxy Note is to charge its battery. You don't need to turn on the phone to charge its battery — just follow these cinchy steps:

1. **If necessary, assemble the charging cord.**

   Connect the charger head (the plug-thing) to the USB cable that comes with the phone. They fit together in only one way.

2. **Plug the charger head and cable into a wall socket.**

3. **Connect the USB cable to the phone.**

   The charger cord plugs into the multipurpose jack, found at the phone's bottom side. Ensure that you properly orient the connector before jamming it into the phone.

As the phone charges, the touchscreen displays a large, animated battery icon. It's your clue that the gizmo is connected to a power source and charging. The touchscreen turns off after a few seconds.

✔ The Galaxy Note may come with a partially charged battery, often containing enough juice to run setup and get you started. Still, I recommend fully charging the phone before you use it.

✔ You can use the phone while it's charging. Granted, you have to turn the thing on first. That procedure is covered in Chapter 2.

 ✔ You can charge the phone in your car, using what was once called a cigarette lighter. Simply ensure that the cell phone charger in your car features the proper connector for your phone or that it's specifically designed for use with your cell phone brand.

✔ The phone also charges itself when it's plugged into a computer by way of a USB cable. The computer must be on for charging to work.

✔ The Galaxy Note charges more quickly when it's plugged into the wall as opposed to a computer's USB port or a car adapter.

Explore the Galaxy Note

The Galaxy Note is a phone like no other. To help you get better acquainted, peruse this section and familiarize yourself with the names of the specific doodads and pieces.

Identifying important things

The typical Galaxy Note 3 phone is handsomely illustrated in Figure 1-2. The items referenced in the figure are the same terms used elsewhere in this book and in whatever pitiful Galaxy Note documentation exists.

Here are the highlights:

Power/Lock button: The Power Lock button could be called the phone's on/off switch, but it's not. That's because the button does more than just turn the phone on or off. Chapter 2 covers the details.

Volume button: The Galaxy Note's volume control is two buttons in one. Press the top end of the button to set the volume higher; pressing the bottom end sets the volume lower. This button can also be used to control the zoom function when using the phone as a camera. See Chapter 15.

Touchscreen display: The main part of the phone is its *touchscreen* display. It's a see-touch thing: You look at it and also touch it with your fingers to control the phone. That's where it gets the name *touch*screen.

Front camera: The phone's front-facing camera is found above the touchscreen (refer to Figure 1-2). It's used for taking self-portraits as well as for video chat.

Headphone jack: On the top of the phone is a hole by which you can connect standard headphones.

Speaker: The primary phone speaker is located top center on the phone. A second speaker is found at the bottom of the phone.

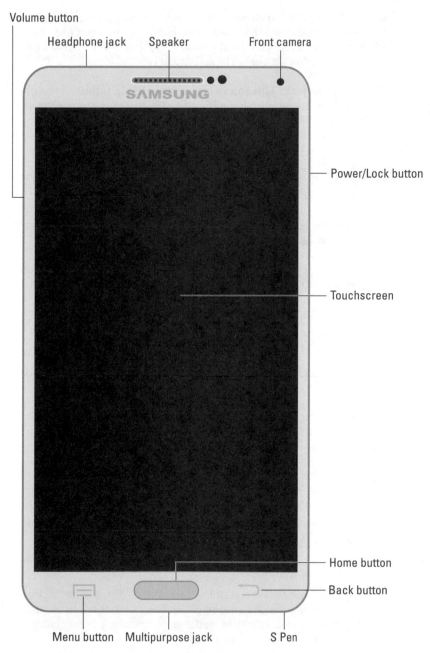

Volume button

Headphone jack   Speaker   Front camera

Power/Lock button

Touchscreen

Home button

Back button

Menu button   Multipurpose jack   S Pen

Figure 1-2: Your phone's face and rump.

Menu, Home, Back buttons: These navigation buttons are used in the Android operating system itself. The Home button is a physical button you press; the Menu and Back buttons are touch-activated. See Chapter 3 for more information on using these buttons.

Multipurpose jack: This important connector is found at the phone's bottom edge, right in the center. It's where the USB/power connector attaches to the phone. The USB cable is used to charge the phone as well as to communicate with a computer. Charging the phone is covered in this chapter; see Chapter 20 for information on sharing files with a computer.

S Pen: This digital stylus is what makes the Galaxy Note special. See Chapter 3 for information about accessing and using the S Pen.

Not shown in Figure 1-2 are a few additional goodies that adorn the sides or rear of the phone. These items include the following:

Microphone: The microphone looks like a tiny hole on the phone's bottom edge. A second, noise-canceling microphone is found on the bottom right side of the phone (near the S Pen).

Rear camera: The phone's main camera is found on the phone's back. It's accompanied by an LED flash.

Other goobers: Various other interesting items adorn your phone. Don't mess with them! Avoid the temptation to stick things into holes on the phone.

Take a moment to locate all the items mentioned in this section, as well as shown in Figure 1-2, on your own Galaxy Note phone. It's important that you know where they are and what they're called.

- The multipurpose jack is customized for the Galaxy Note phone. It's not the same, standard micro-USB connector used on other Android phones. Ditto for the Galaxy Note's USB cable. See Chapter 20 for more information on using the cable.

- The main microphone, on the bottom of the phone, picks up your voice loud and clear. There's no need to hold the phone at an angle for the microphone to work.

- The speaker at the top of the phone (refer to Figure 1-2) is used primarily when making phone calls. The bottom speaker (not shown in Figure 1-2) is used when watching videos or playing games or when a phone call is placed "on speaker."

- The phone's physical buttons — Power/Lock, Volume, and Home — are referred to as *keys* in Google's Android documentation. This book uses the term *button,* although you may find the word *key* used here and in other documentation.

Using earphones

You don't need to use earphones to get the most from your Galaxy Note, but it helps! Though most cell phones don't come with earphones, the Galaxy Note does. Or at least mine did. Sorry if that's not the case for you, but you can always buy earphones, and I recommend that you do.

The earphones that came with (or should have come with) the Galaxy Note are the common earbud style. The earbuds are set into your ears. The sharp, pointy end of the earphones, which you don't want to stick into your ear, plugs into the top of the phone.

Fancy earbuds come with a doodle button somewhere on their wires. The button can be used to mute the Galaxy Note when you're on a call or to start or stop the playback of music when the phone is in its music-playing mode.

You can also use the doodle button to answer the phone when it rings.

A teensy hole on the doodle serves as the phone's microphone. It lets you wear the earphones and talk on the phone while keeping your hands free. If you gesture while you speak, you'll find this feature invaluable.

- ✔ If your Galaxy Note didn't come with earphones, or (more frequently) if they broke, purchase a new set. Ensure that the headset features a microphone; you need to talk *and* listen on a phone.
- ✔ The earbuds are labeled R for right and L for left.
- ✔ See Chapter 16 for more information on using your Galaxy Note as a portable music player.
- ✔ Fully insert the earphone connector into the phone. The person you're talking with can't hear you well when the earphones are plugged in only partway.
- ✔ You can also use a Bluetooth headset with your phone, to listen to a call or some music. See Chapter 19 for more information on Bluetooth.

- ✔ Fold the earphones when you don't need them, rather than wrap them in a loop: Hold the earbuds and connector in one hand, and then pull the wire straight out with the other hand. Fold the wire in half, and then in half again. You can then put the earphones in your pocket or on a tabletop. By folding the wires, you avoid creating one of those Christmas-tree-light wire balls that would otherwise happen.

Adding other accessories

It's difficult to leave the Phone Store without having the nice people there try to sell you many thousands of dollars' worth of phone accessories. Of all the temptations available, the following items may offer you the most happiness:

Multimedia dock: The multimedia dock works like a base station for the Galaxy Note, by propping it up at the perfect angle for viewing videos or using it as a desktop alarm clock. As a bonus, the phone charges while it's nestled in the multimedia dock.

Car mount: This gizmo lets you suction-cup the phone to your car's windshield (or any other flat surface). After the phone is secured, you can use it — hands-free — while driving. See Chapter 14 for more information on using the Galaxy Note's amazing navigation abilities.

Phone jacket: The Phone Store doubtless has an ample repository of various phone cases. Choose something stylish and protective.

A Home for Your Phone

Thanks to its mobile nature, your Galaxy Note phone can go anywhere. You can find your phone across town or overseas or even in the couch cushions or under a stack of books on the nightstand. Because the phone will no doubt become a necessary part of your life in the near future, finding a better location than the couch cushions is probably a good idea.

Toting your Galaxy Note

It's true that many a wild-eyed stare greets the Galaxy Note because of its dominating size and hybrid tablet-phone nature. Still, the thing fits perfectly in your front pocket, clips easily on a belt, or sits snugly in even the teensiest of party purses. To help it survive in these harsh conditions, the Galaxy Note features a proximity sensor.

The *proximity sensor* disables the touchscreen whenever the phone is in a confined space — or even pressed firmly against your cheek. You risk no danger that your phone might accidentally activate its touchscreen and suddenly dial Tibet.

✔ Though it's okay to let go of the phone when you're making a call, be careful not to touch the phone's Power/Lock button or the Home button (refer to Figure 1-2). Touching either button may temporarily enable the touchscreen, which can hang up a call, mute the phone, or do any of a number of other undesirable things.

✔ Don't forget that the phone is in your pocket, especially in your coat or jacket. You might accidentally sit on the phone, or it can fly out when you take off your coat. The worst fate for any cell phone is to take a trip to the laundry. I'm sure that the Galaxy Note has nightmares about it.

Storing the phone

I recommend that you find a permanent place for your phone when you're not taking it with you. Make the spot consistent: on top of your desk or workstation, on the kitchen counter, on the nightstand — you get the idea. Phones are as prone to being misplaced as your car keys and glasses. Consistency is the key to finding your phone.

Then again, your phone rings, so when you lose it, you can always have someone else call your cell phone to help you locate it.

- ✔ I keep my phone on my desk, next to my computer. Conveniently, I have the charger plugged into the computer so that the phone remains plugged in, connected, and charging when I'm not using it.

- ✔ Phones on coffee tables get buried under magazines and are often squished when rude people put their feet on the furniture.

- ✔ Avoid putting your phone in direct sunlight; heat is a bad thing for any electronic gizmo.

- ✔ Do not put your phone in the laundry (see the preceding section). See Chapter 23 for information on properly cleaning the phone.

On, Off, and Configuration

In This Chapter

▶ Turning on the phone

▶ Setting up your Galaxy Note

▶ Adding a Google account

▶ Setting up other online accounts

▶ Locking the Galaxy Note

▶ Turning off your phone

*T*he Galaxy Note phone lacks an On-Off switch. Unlike the common table lamp, your phone has no switch to flip to turn on the thing. Likewise, it has no switch for turning off the phone. Instead, the job is handled by something called the Power/Lock button, which serves several functions beyond the on-off thing.

See? What could be the most basic of operations turns out to be an ordeal that requires an entire chapter of explanation for turning on the phone, unlocking it, locking it, and turning it off. One button does all that. And if you haven't yet experienced the thrill of turning on your phone for the first time, that duty is covered here as well.

Swipe screen to unlock
AIRVOICE WIRELESS

Hello!

Go back in time 40 years and ask someone whether they know how to turn on their telephone. They would probably reply that the phone is "on" all the time or that you have to lift the handset to make a call or answer. O, life was so simple then, but using a telephone was far more dull.

Saying "Hello" to your Galaxy Note involves more than lifting it to your nose. It's a process called *power up,* and this section explains how it works.

Turning on your phone for the first time

The very first time you turn on your Galaxy Note is a special occasion. It's when setup and configuration happens — a necessary process for an advanced device. The good news is that you need to endure this ordeal only once. In fact, if the phone has already been set up and configured by the friendly Phone Store employees, skip to the next section, "Turning on the Galaxy Note."

The specifics of the setup and configuration differ depending on the phone's manufacturer as well as on the cellular provider. Odds are pretty good that the people at the Phone Store helped you through the initial setup process. If not, follow these general steps:

1. **Press and hold the Power/Lock button.**

   You may have to press it longer than you think. When the phone vibrates, or when you see the logo, release the button.

   It's okay to turn on the phone while it's plugged in and charging.

2. **Answer the questions that are presented.**

   The setup process walks you through a series of steps. You're asked to select options for some, if not all, of the following items:

   - Select your language
   - Activate the phone on the cellular network
   - Choose a Wi-Fi network (can be done later)
   - Set the time zone
   - Sign in to your Google account
   - Add other online accounts
   - Set location information

   When in doubt, just accept the standard options as presented to you during the setup process.

   To fill in text fields, use the onscreen keyboard. See Chapter 4 for typing tips and such.

   You can't screw up anything at this point; any selection you make can be changed later. Other sections in this chapter, as well as throughout this book, offer information and advice.

   Having a Google account is important to the setup process. See the later section "Account Setup."

3. **After each choice, touch the Next button or icon.**

The Next icon may resemble a large, right-pointing triangle, as shown in the margin.

4. **Touch the Finish button.**

The Finish button appears on the last screen of the setup procedure.

The good news is that you're done. The better news is that you need to complete this setup only once. From this point on, starting your phone works as described in the next few sections.

After the initial setup is complete, you're taken to the Home screen. See Chapter 3 for details on how it works.

✔ Some AT&T phones require you to use the AT&T Ready2Go app to complete your phone's setup process. See the later section "Setting up with AT&T Ready2Go."

✔ Additional information on connecting your phone to a Wi-Fi network is found in Chapter 19.

✔ Location items relate to the Galaxy Note's use of the GPS, or Global Positioning System. I recommend keeping all location items activated to get the most from your phone.

✔ If you don't yet have a Google account, see the later section "Obtaining a Google account."

✔ See the later sidebar "Who is this Android person?" for more information about the Android operating system.

Turning on the Galaxy Note

To turn on the Galaxy Note, press the Power/Lock button for a second or two. The phone vibrates slightly as it starts. The Samsung logo displays on the touchscreen, and the Samsung theme song plays. It takes a few additional moments for the phone to complete the start-up process.

Eventually, you see the phone's unlock screen. The standard *Swipe* lock is illustrated in Figure 2-1. Unlock the phone by touching the screen and dragging your finger in any direction, as illustrated in the figure.

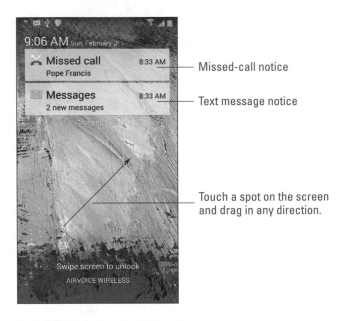

Missed-call notice

Text message notice

Touch a spot on the screen
and drag in any direction.

Figure 2-1: Unlocking the Galaxy Note.

You can drag your finger across the screen anywhere to unlock the phone.
You don't necessarily need to touch it in the exact spot and move in the same
direction as indicated in Figure 2-1.

If you've configured extra security for your Galaxy Note, you might see one
of several other types of lock screens, as illustrated in Figure 2-2. These
lock screens appear instead of the standard Swipe locking screen (refer to
Figure 2-1).

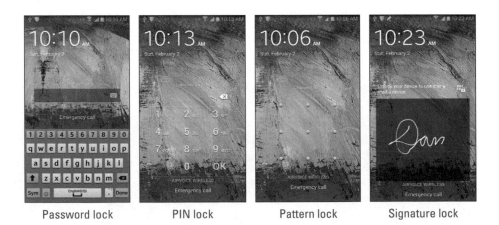

Password lock   PIN lock   Pattern lock   Signature lock

Figure 2-2: Alternative screen locks.

To work the various alternative locks, you must trace a pattern on the screen, type a PIN, type a password, or scrawl your signature (refer to Figure 2-2). See Chapter 22 for details on configuring these alternative screen locks.

After the phone unlocks, you can begin using it.

✔ The phone may provide animation during the unlocking process to assist you. Pay attention to it if you find yourself confused.

✔ You probably won't turn on your phone much in the future. Instead, you'll simply unlock it. See the next section.

✔ In Figure 2-1, the lock screen indicates that one call has been missed and two text messages await review.

✔ It's not necessary to unlock the phone for an incoming call. For information on receiving phone calls, see Chapter 5.

✔ Even if the phone has a security pattern, PIN, or password lock screen, you can still make emergency calls: Touch the *Emergency Call* text on the screen.

Unlocking the phone

Most of the time, you don't turn off your phone. Instead, you lock it. The Galaxy Note locks on its own after a given period of inactivity, or you lock it by pressing the Power/Lock button (covered later in this chapter).

When the phone is locked, it's still on and it can receive calls, e-mail, and other notifications, but the touchscreen is turned off. You unlock the phone by pressing the Power/Lock button. A simple, short press does the trick. Then work the locks as shown in Figures 2-1 and 2-2 and described in the preceding section.

✔ The phone can also be unlocked by pressing the Home key or removing the S Pen.

✔ Touching the touchscreen when the screen is off doesn't unlock the phone.

✔ An incoming call doesn't unlock the phone, but information about the call is displayed on the touchscreen. See Chapter 5 for information on answering the phone.

✔ The Galaxy Note continues to play music while it's locked. See Chapter 16 for more information on using the Galaxy Note as a portable music player.

✔ See Chapter 24 for information on placing app shortcuts on the lock screen. That way, you can unlock the phone by choosing an app to run.

Who is this Android person?

Just like a computer, your phone has an operating system. It's the main program in charge of all the software, or apps, as well as the device's hardware. Unlike on a computer, however, Android is a mobile device operating system, designed primarily for use in cell phones and tablets.

Android is based on the Linux operating system, which is also a computer operating system, though it's much more stable and bug-free than Windows, so it's not as popular. Google owns, maintains, and develops Android, which is why your online Google information is synced with the phone.

The Android mascot, shown here, often appears on Android apps or hardware. He has no official name, though most folks call him Andy.

Account Setup

Your Galaxy Note is home to your various online incarnations. That includes your e-mail accounts, online services, social networking, subscriptions, plus other digital personas. I recommended adding those accounts to your phone as you continue the setup-and-configuration process.

Obtaining a Google account

It's possible to use your Galaxy Note without a Google account, but you'd miss out on a buncha features. By signing in to a Google account, you coordinate whatever information you have on the Internet with your new phone. This information includes your e-mail messages and contacts on Gmail, appointments on Google Calendar, and information and data from other Google Internet applications.

Follow these steps to obtain a Google account if you don't already have one:

1. **Open the computer's web browser program.**

   These steps work best when using a computer with a full-size keyboard and a nice, roomy display.

2. **Visit the main Google page at** www.google.com.

   Type www.google.com into the web browser's address box.

3. **Click the Sign In link or button.**

   Another page opens, where you can log in to your Google account, but you don't have a Google account, so:

4. **Click the link to create a new account.**

   The link is typically found beneath the text boxes where you would log in to your Google account. As I write this chapter, the link is titled Create an Account.

5. **Continue heeding the onscreen directions until you've created your own Google account.**

Eventually, your account is set up and configured.

If you're using your own computer, I recommend that you log off and then log back on to Google, just to ensure that you did everything properly. Also create a bookmark for your account's Google page: Pressing Ctrl+D or Command+D does the job in just about any web browser.

✔ A Google account is free. Google makes zillions of dollars by selling Internet advertising, so it doesn't charge you for your Google account or any of the fine services it offers.

✔ The Google account gives you access to a wide array of free services and online programs. They include Gmail for electronic messaging, Calendar for scheduling and appointments, and an account on YouTube, along with Google Finance, blogs, Google+, Hangouts, and other features that are also instantly shared with your phone.

Setting up with AT&T Ready2Go

When you have a Galaxy Note on the AT&T cellular network, the configuration and setup are handled by the AT&T Ready2Go app. You may have already completed this step before leaving the Phone Store. If not, you can do so now.

The AT&T Ready2Go app works with your Galaxy Note and a computer connected to the Internet to help configure your phone. You fill in your account information, contacts, and other configuration options on a web page using the computer. Then the AT&T mothership sends that information to your Galaxy Note, completing the setup process in one quick action.

✔ The easiest way to run the AT&T Ready2Go app is to look for the Ready2Go notification icon. Pull down the notifications panel and choose AT&T Ready2Go to run the app. Refer to Chapter 3 for more information on accessing notifications.

✔ The primary thing you're doing with the AT&T Ready2Go app is setting up your phone with a Google account. That account — specifically, your Google Gmail account — is the key to connecting the Galaxy Note with a host of services that Google offers for free on the Internet, as well as on your phone. Everything is nicely connected and synchronized — but only after you add your Google account.

Adding other accounts

You don't have to add all your online accounts during the phone's initial setup-and-configuration process. If you've skipped those steps, or when you have more accounts to add, you can easily do so. With your Galaxy Note turned on and unlocked, follow these steps:

1. **Touch the Home button to return to the Home screen.**

   The *Home* screen is the main screen on your phone. You can always get there by pressing the Home button, found at the bottom of the touchscreen.

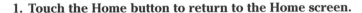

2. **Press the Menu button.**

   The Menu button is found at the bottom of the touchscreen, to the left of the Home button.

3. **Choose the Settings command.**

   The Settings command runs the Settings app. It helps you access internal options and controls for configuring the Galaxy Note. This command is a popular place to visit while you read this book.

4. **Touch the General tab.**

   The Settings app features four tabs across the top of the screen: Connections, Device, Controls, and General. Each tab lists various categories for phone adjustments.

5. **Choose the Accounts item.**

   The Accounts screen lists all accounts configured for use by the Galaxy Note. The list may be empty, or it may contain several accounts.

6. **Touch the Add Account button.**

   A list of account types appears. The list varies, depending on which apps are installed on your phone.

7. **Choose an account to add.**

   For example, you may see Dropbox or Twitter.

8. **Work through the steps on the screen to sign in to the account.**

   Typically, you type your username and password. The phone contacts the Internet and synchronizes your account information.

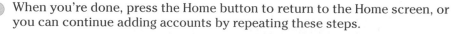

When you're done, press the Home button to return to the Home screen, or you can continue adding accounts by repeating these steps.

✔ See Chapter 10 for specific details on adding e-mail accounts to your Android phone.

✔ Chapter 12 covers social networking on your phone. Refer there for specific information on adding Facebook, Twitter, and other accounts.

Goodbye!

You can dismiss your Galaxy Note in one of several ways. The most popular way is to lock the phone. Another way is to turn off the phone. The most difficult way to dismiss the phone involves a vat of mayonnaise and a howitzer, but this book just doesn't have room enough to properly describe that method.

Locking the phone

To lock your Galaxy Note, press and release the Power/Lock button. No matter what you're doing, the phone's touchscreen display turns off. The phone itself isn't off, but the touchscreen display goes dark and ignores your touches.

✔ Your Galaxy Note will probably spend most of its time locked.

✔ Locking the phone doesn't disconnect a phone call. In fact, it's safer to talk on the phone when it's locked, because you eliminate the risk of accidentally touching anything on the screen.

✔ The Galaxy Note features a *proximity sensor,* which automatically locks the phone whenever its face is close to another object.

✔ Locking doesn't turn off the phone; you can still receive calls while the phone is locked. The phone continues to play music while it's locked, and any timers or alarms you've set will sound. See Chapter 17 for information on setting timers and alarms; Chapter 16 covers playing music.

Controlling the automatic screen lock

The Galaxy Note is configured to automatically lock itself after a given period of inactivity. You can control the time-out value to intervals between 15 seconds and 10 minutes. To confirm or change the time-out, obey these steps:

1. **At the Home screen, press the Menu button and choose the Settings command.**

2. **In the Settings app, touch the Device tab.**

3. **Choose Display.**

4. **Choose Screen Timeout.**

5. **Choose a time-out value from the list that's provided.**

 The standard value is 1 minute.

 6. **Press the Home button to return to the Home screen.**

When you don't touch the screen, or when you aren't using the phone, the lock timer starts ticking. About ten seconds before the time-out value you've set (refer to Step 5), the touchscreen dims. Then the phone goes to sleep. If you touch the screen before then, the lock timer is reset.

 You can thwart the automatic screen time-out by using your face and the Galaxy Note's Smart Stay feature: In the Settings app, choose the Controls tab and then the Smart Screen item. Ensure that a check mark appears by the Smart Stay item. The phone will attempt not to self-lock as long as it sees your adorable face — or even when your face isn't that adorable.

 When the Smart Stay feature is active, the Smart Stay status icon appears atop the touchscreen. See Chapter 3 for more information on status icons and the status bar.

Turning off the phone

To turn off your Galaxy Note, follow these steps:

1. **Press and hold the Power Lock button until the Device Options menu appears.**

 The Device Options menu is shown in Figure 2-3.

2. **Choose the Power Off item.**

 If you change your mind and don't want to turn off the phone, press the Back button to cancel. The button is found at the bottom of the phone, to the right of the Home button.

Figure 2-3: The Device Options menu.

3. **Touch the OK button to confirm.**

You see some animation as the phone shuts itself off. Eventually, the touchscreen goes dark.

When the phone is turned off, it doesn't receive calls or trigger notifications or alarms. Incoming calls go to voice mail; see Chapter 7 for more information on voice mail.

✏ The phone can be charged while it's off. It doesn't charge any faster than when the phone is turned on.

✏ See Chapter 21 for information on the Airplane Mode option (refer to Figure 2-3).

✏ Volume controls at the bottom of the Device Options menu are covered in Chapter 3.

✏ The Restart command is used to turn off the phone and then turn it back on again. This procedure can be used to help fix minor quirks. See Chapter 23 for more information.

3

Rule the Galaxy Note

In This Chapter

▶ Touching the touchscreen

▶ Understanding the navigation buttons

▶ Changing the phone's volume

▶ Exploring the Home screen

▶ Checking notifications

▶ Accessing Quick Actions

▶ Running apps

▶ Working with multiple apps

▶ Playing with the S Pen

*S*imple technology has few, if any, knobs or buttons. Then, as a device grows more complex, more knobs and buttons are added. At one time, having an abundance of switches was considered very high-tech. Then, as the equipment is perfected, it loses its knobs, buttons, and switches. The end result may look smooth and modern, but it presents new users with an awful puzzle: How do you work the thing?

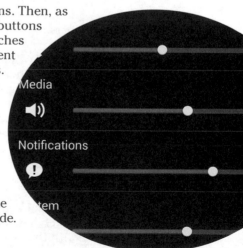

The days of having too many buttons on a phone are in the past. Today's most modern smartphone, the Galaxy Note, has a small smattering of buttons. To control the device, you must master the touchscreen and understand the methods and madness of the Android operating system. Use this chapter as your guide.

Basic Operations

You probably messed around with your phone well before your eyes hit this page. That's fine: The urge to play with new technology can sometimes be unbearable. If not, peruse this section and you'll get the hang of things in no time.

Manipulating the touchscreen

The touchscreen works in combination with one or two of your fingers, or with one of your fingers and the tip of your nose. Oh, why not be adventurous?

No matter how you touch it (and I do recommend fingers), you can use several touchscreen manipulation techniques:

Touch: In this simple operation, you touch the screen. Generally, you're touching an object such as an icon or a control. You might also see the term *press* or *tap*.

Long-press: Touch and hold part of the screen. Some operations, such as moving an icon on the Home screen, begin with the long-press. In fact, this icon-moving operation is called the *long-press drag*.

Double-tap: Touch the screen in the same location twice. A double-tap can be used to zoom in on an image or a map or to zoom out. Because of the double-tap's dual nature, I recommend using the pinch and spread operations instead.

Swipe: When you swipe, you start with your finger in one spot and then drag it to another spot. A swipe can move up, down, left, or right, and it can be fast or slow. It can also be called *flick* or *slide*.

Pinch: A pinch involves two fingers, which start out separated and then are brought together. The pinch is used to zoom out on an image or a map.

Spread: In the opposite of a pinch, you start with your fingers together and then spread them. The spread is used to zoom in.

Rotate: Use two fingers to twist around a central point on the touchscreen, which has the effect of rotating an object on the screen. If you have trouble with this operation, imagine that you're turning the dial on a safe.

You cannot use the touchscreen while wearing gloves, unless they're gloves specially designed for using an electronic touchscreen, such as the gloves that Batman wears.

Button enlightenment

The Menu and Back buttons are touch buttons. As such, they don't really show up on the front of the phone — unless you touch them. After you touch one of the buttons, both buttons light up. They stay lit for a few moments and then go dark. You can adjust the length of time that the buttons stay lit by following these steps:

1. At the Home screen, press the Menu button.

2. In the Settings app, touch the Device tab.

3. Choose the Display item.

4. Choose Touch Key Light Duration.

5. Choose an option.

The Always On option keeps the buttons lit all the time, making them easy to see. This setting doesn't seem to noticeably drain the battery.

When you lock the phone, the touch key lights turn off, no matter which setting you've chosen.

Exploring the navigation icons

Below the touchscreen on your Android phone dwell three buttons: Menu, Home, and Back. These are the navigation icons, which serve common functions no matter what you do on your Android phone.

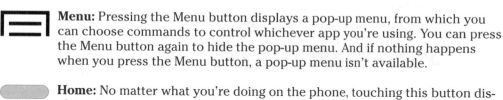

Menu: Pressing the Menu button displays a pop-up menu, from which you can choose commands to control whichever app you're using. You can press the Menu button again to hide the pop-up menu. And if nothing happens when you press the Menu button, a pop-up menu isn't available.

Home: No matter what you're doing on the phone, touching this button displays the Home screen. When you're already viewing the Home screen, touching the Home icon returns you to the main or center Home screen.

Back: The Back button serves several purposes, all of which fit neatly under the concept of *back*. Touch the button once to return to a previous page, dismiss an onscreen menu, close a window, hide the onscreen keyboard, and so on.

These buttons serve other purposes when you long-press them:

S Finder: Long-press the Menu button to start the S Finder search app.

Recent: Long-press the Home button to see a list of recently opened or currently running apps. See the later section "Switching apps" for details.

Multi Window tab: Long-press the Back button to show or hide the Multi Window tab when that feature is activated. See the later section "Playing with Multi Window."

- ✔ Menu and Back are touch buttons. The Home button is a physical button.

- ✔ Even though you may not see the Menu and Back buttons, they're still there. See the nearby sidebar, "Button enlightenment."

- ✔ The Menu icon is essentially the same thing as the Overflow icon. See the section "Using common icons," elsewhere in this chapter.

Setting the volume

The Volume button is found on the side of your Galaxy Note. Press the top part of the button to raise the volume. Press the bottom part to lower the volume.

As you press the Volume button, a graphic appears on the touchscreen to illustrate the relative volume level, as shown in Figure 3-1. You can also use the graphic to set the volume, as shown in the figure.

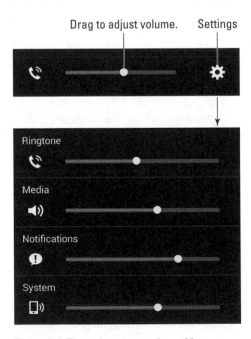

Figure 3-1: The volume-control graphic.

The volume control works for whatever noise the phone is making when you use it: When you're on a call, the volume control sets the level of the call. When you're listening to music or watching a video, the volume control sets the media volume.

✔ When the volume is set all the way down, the phone is placed into Vibration mode.

✔ The Volume button works even when the phone is locked. That means you don't need to unlock the phone to adjust the volume while you listen to music.

✔ The volume can be preset for the phone or its media, alarms, and notifications. See Chapter 22 for more information.

"Silence your phone!"

You hear it all the time: "Please silence your cell phones." The quick way to obey this command on your Galaxy Note is to keep pressing the bottom of the Volume button until the phone vibrates.

The phone can also be silenced from the Device Options menu. Obey these steps:

1. Press and hold the Power/Lock button.

The Device Options menu appears. Volume settings are represented by the three icons shown at the bottom of the menu.

2. Choose the Mute or Vibrate option.

The phone is silenced.

To make the phone noisy again, simply touch the top part of the Volume button.

✔ When the phone is silenced, the Mute icon appears on the status bar.

✔ When the phone is set to vibrate, the Vibrate icon appears on the status bar.

✔ Also see the later section "Using Quick Actions," for more sound-setting options.

✔ It's possible to silence the phone and not place it in Vibration mode. Details are offered in Chapter 22.

Enjoying the accelerometer

An *accelerometer* is the gizmo that determines the Galaxy Note's orientation. Most often, the accelerometer comes into play when you move the phone from an upright position to a horizontal one, as illustrated in Figure 3-2.

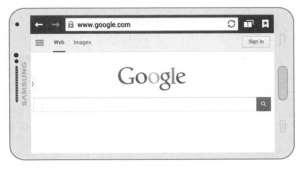

Vertical orientation   Horizontal orientation

Figure 3-2: Vertical and horizontal orientations.

In Figure 3-2, the Internet app (web browser) is used to view a website in both vertical and horizontal locations. Often, websites are easier to view on a phone in horizontal orientation.

- The Home screen does not change its orientation.

- If the screen doesn't rotate, the Screen Rotation feature may be disabled on your Galaxy Note. See the later section "Using Quick Actions" for information on displaying Quick Actions and accessing that feature.

- Another way to employ the Galaxy Note's accelerometer is to activate the Motion feature. See Chapter 24.

- See Chapter 11 for more information on using the Galaxy Note to surf the web.

- A few apps, mostly games, are fixed to one orientation or another. They don't orient themselves when you rotate the phone.

- A fun app for demonstrating the phone's accelerometer is the game Labyrinth. It can be purchased at the Google Play Store, or you can obtain the free version, Labyrinth Lite. See Chapter 18 for more information on the Google Play Store.

Home Screen Chores

The center of activity on your Galaxy Note is the location called the *Home screen*. It's the first thing you see after unlocking your phone, it's where you're returned to when you quit an app, and it appears when you press the Home button. Knowing how to work the Home screen is the key to getting the most from your phone.

Examining the Home screen

The Galaxy Note Home screen is shown in Figure 3-3. It has several points of interest you need to know about.

Here's the list, along with the names of those items, as used throughout this book:

Status bar: The top of the Home screen is a thin, informative strip that I call the *status bar*. It contains notification icons and status icons, plus the current time.

Figure 3-3: The Home screen.

Notifications: These icons come and go, depending on what happens in your digital life. For example, a new notification icon appears whenever you receive a new e-mail message or have a pending appointment. The section "Reviewing notifications," later in this chapter, describes how to deal with notifications.

Phone status: Icons on the right end of the status bar represent the phone's current condition, such as the type of network it's connected to, signal strength, and battery status, as well as whether the speaker has been muted or a Wi-Fi network is connected, for example.

Widgets: These teensy programs can display information, let you control the phone, manipulate a phone feature, access a program, or do something purely amusing.

Multi Window tab: This item appears when the Multi Window feature is active. Touching the tab displays the Multi Window tray. See the later section "Playing with Multi Window" for details.

App icons: The meat of the meal on the Home screen plate is the app icon. Touching this icon runs its program, or *app*.

Panel index: These dots clue you in to which Home screen panel you're viewing. Touch a dot to zoom to that panel, or swipe the dots to whip-pan all the panels.

Dock: The bottom of every Home screen panel contains the same five icons. You can change the first four icons, but the Apps icon remains steady.

Phone: You use the Phone app to make calls. It's kind of a big deal.

Applications: Touch the Apps icon to display the Applications screen, which shows all apps installed on your phone.

Specific directions for using these individual Home screen gizmos are found throughout this chapter.

✔ You may see numbers affixed to some Home screen icons. These numbers indicate pending actions, such as unread e-mail messages, indicated by the icon shown in the margin.

✔ Those icons with numbers on them make excellent candidates for the Dock. See Chapter 22 for information on placing icons on the Dock.

✔ The Home screen is entirely customizable. You can add and remove icons from the Home screen, add widgets and shortcuts, and even change wallpaper images. In fact, feel free to remove all the icons and widgets that were preinstalled by Samsung or your cellular provider. That information is found in Chapter 22.

> ✓ Touching part of the Home screen that doesn't feature an icon or a control does nothing — unless you're using the *live wallpaper* feature. In that case, touching the screen changes the wallpaper in some way, depending on the wallpaper that's selected. You can read more about live wallpaper in — you guessed it — Chapter 22.

Accessing the Home screen panels

The Home screen is many times wider than the one you see on the front of your Galaxy Note. The Home screen has left and right wings, as shown in Figure 3-4. In fact, it can have up to seven total Home screen panels.

Main Home screen panel

Figure 3-4: Home screen panels.

To switch from one panel to the next, swipe the screen left or right. The panel index (refer to Figure 3-3) tells you which panel you're viewing. You can touch any bar in the panel index to instantly zoom to that panel, swipe the index to quickly scan all panels, or press the Home button to zoom to the center panel.

The number of Home screen panels, as well as their arrangement, can be changed. You can have anywhere from one to seven Home screen panels on the Galaxy Note. Chapter 22 describes how to add, remove, and rearrange the panels.

Reviewing notifications

Notifications are represented by wee, small icons at the top of the Home screen, as illustrated earlier, in Figure 3-3. To see what the notifications say, you pull down the notifications panel by dragging your finger from the top of the screen downward. The notifications panel is illustrated in Figure 3-5.

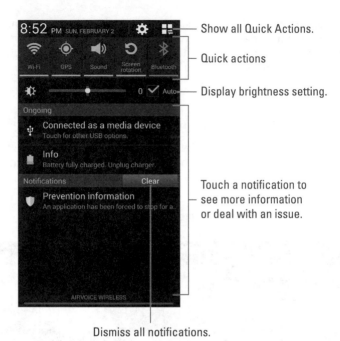

Show all Quick Actions.

Quick actions

Display brightness setting.

Touch a notification to see more information or deal with an issue.

Dismiss all notifications.

Figure 3-5: Reviewing notifications.

Touch a notification to deal with it. What happens next depends on the notification, but most often the app that generated the notification appears, such as Gmail when you touch a new message notification. You might also be given the opportunity to deal with whatever caused the notification, such as a calendar appointment.

Dismiss an individual notification by sliding it to the right or left. To dismiss all notifications, touch the Clear button, illustrated earlier, in Figure 3-5.

Touching a notification opens the app that generated the alert. For example, touching a Gmail notification displays a new message in the inbox.

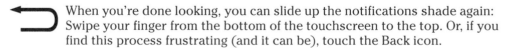

When you're done looking, you can slide up the notifications shade again: Swipe your finger from the bottom of the touchscreen to the top. Or, if you find this process frustrating (and it can be), touch the Back icon.

- A notification icon doesn't disappear after you look at it — and those icons can stack up!

- You can access notifications just about any time you're using the Galaxy Note. You don't necessarily need to be viewing the Home screen to pull down notifications.

✔ When more notifications are present than can be shown on the status bar, you see the More Notifications icon displayed, as shown in the margin. The number on the icon indicates how many additional notifications are available.

✔ Dismissing notifications doesn't prevent them from appearing again later. For example, notifications to update your programs continue to appear, as do calendar reminders.

✔ Some programs, such as Facebook and Twitter, don't display notifications unless you're logged in. See Chapter 12.

Using Quick Actions

Adorning the top of the notifications list are some buttons, as shown in Figure 3-5. These buttons, known as *Quick Actions,* turn on or off certain common phone features. Touch a button to turn a feature on or off, or to adjust more detailed settings.

You can swipe the Quick Actions at the top of the notifications panel left or right to see more. To witness the entire gamut of Quick Actions, touch the Quick Actions icon (refer to Figure 3-5). The screen fills with all available options, as shown in Figure 3-6.

Figure 3-6: All 'dem Quick Actions.

Touch the Edit button on the Quick Actions screen (refer to Figure 3-6) to view the editing screen. You can then drag buttons on or off the notification panel's Quick Actions list, swapping out other buttons you may use more frequently.

The App Galaxy

The Galaxy Note is a handsome phone, but you didn't get one just to admire its beauty. Nope, the true power of your "phablet" lies in the apps, or programs, you use. They truly make the phone useful.

Starting an app

It's cinchy to run an app on the Home screen: Touch its icon. The app starts.

- ✓ Not all of the phone's apps appear on the Home screen. To muster all of them, summon the Applications screen. See the later section "Browsing the Applications screen."
- ✓ App is short for *app*lication.

Quitting an app

Unlike when you use a computer, you don't need to quit apps on your Galaxy Note. To leave an app, touch the Home button to return to the Home screen. That's the most common method, although you can also try touching the Back icon to back out of an app.

- ✓ Some apps feature the Quit command or Exit command, but for the most part you don't quit an app on your phone, not like you quit an app on a computer.

- ✓ If necessary, the Android operating system shuts down apps you haven't used in a while. You can directly stop apps run amok, which is described in Chapter 18.

Working a widget

A *widget* is like an app, but one you don't have to open to see what's going on. For example, in Figure 3-3 (earlier in this chapter), you see widgets. They resemble teensy programs that "float" on the Home screen. To use a widget, simply touch it. What happens after that depends on the widget.

For example, touching the Google Search widget displays the onscreen keyboard and lets you type, or dictate, something to search for on the Internet. A weather widget displays information about the current weather. Social networking widgets may display status updates or tweets, for example.

See Chapter 22 for information on adding and removing Home screen widgets.

Browsing the Applications screen

To behold all apps installed on your Galaxy Note, touch the Apps icon, nestled in the lower-right corner of the Home screen. You see the Applications screen, similar to the one shown in Figure 3-7.

Figure 3-7: The Applications screen.

As with the Home screen, the Applications screen can sport multiple panels. Swipe the screen left or right to hunt down additional apps. The panel index, illustrated in Figure 3-7, shows you how many panels are available and which one you're viewing.

In addition to the panels, the Applications screen sports folders. Figure 3-7 highlights three folders. To view apps within a folder, touch the folder.

To start an app, touch its icon. The app appears full-screen and does whatever magical thing the app does.

✔ The Applications screen is entirely customizable. In Figure 3-7, you see Customizable Grid view. To change the view, touch the Menu button and choose the View Type command. See Chapter 18 for details on arranging apps on the Applications screen.

✔ Widgets are also presented on the Applications screen: Choose the Widgets tab atop the screen to view installed widgets.

✔ For apps you use all the time, consider creating shortcuts on the Home screen. Chapter 22 describes how.

Switching apps

The apps you run on your phone don't quit when you dismiss them from the screen. For the most part, they stay running. To switch between running apps, or any app you've recently opened, long-press the Home button. When you do, you see a list of the most recently accessed programs, as shown in Figure 3-8.

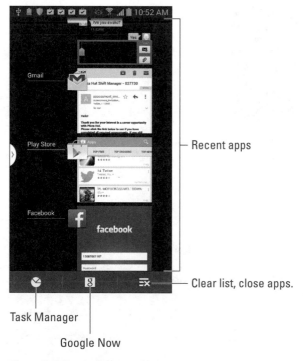

Figure 3-8: Recently opened apps.

Scroll the list of recent apps up and down to peruse the entire list. Choose a recent app from the list to open that app again, or to return to the app if it's already open and running. If you can't find the app you're looking for, start it as you normally would, from either the Home screen or the Applications screen.

 To exit the list of recently used apps, press the Back button.

> ✔ You can summon the list of recent apps at any time you're using the phone.
>
> ✔ See Chapter 24 for information on using the Task Manager.

Playing with Multi Window

The Samsung Galaxy Note phone features a unique multitasking tool called *Multi Window:* It allows you to view two apps at a time.

Before you can use Multi Window, ensure that it's activated: Pull down the notifications panel and choose the Multi Window Quick Action. (You may have to scroll the Quick Actions left or right to find that button.) After it's activated, you see the Multi Window tab on the left side of the Home screen, as illustrated earlier, in Figure 3-3.

To use Multi Window, touch the tab. You see the various apps sitting in the Multi Window tray. Drag an app icon from the tray out onto the screen to start that app. To start a second app, drag another icon from the tray onto the screen.

With Multi Window active, the Home screen is split horizontally or vertically, depending on the phone's orientation. Each side of the split contains a running app, as shown in Figure 3-9, which illustrates the My Music and Gallery apps.

To adjust the window size, drag the separator left, right, up, or down, depending on the phone's orientation. The two windows need not be equal in size.

Tap the separator's button to view the window controls, as illustrated in Figure 3-10. Use the controls to manage the windows and enjoy various Multi Window features.

Multi Window tray

Multi Window tab   App window

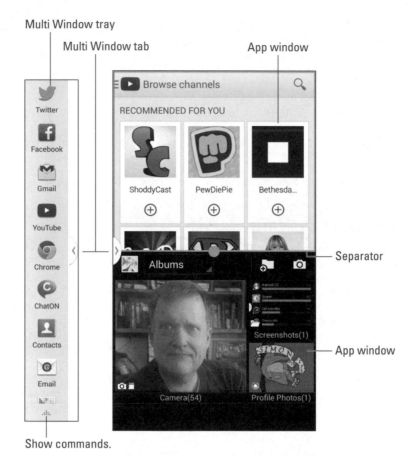

Separator

App window

Show commands.

Figure 3-9: Multi Window in action.

To exit Multi Window, close one window; or expand a window until it's full-screen size. You can also exit Multi Window mode by pressing the Home button.

- ✔ Only certain apps can run in Multi Window. The variety is seen by scrolling the Multi Window tray up and down.

- ✔ Touch the Edit button at the bottom of the Multi Window tray to add or remove apps.

- ✔ You can keep Multi Window active yet hide the tab by long-pressing the Back button. To make the tab reappear, long-press the Back button again.

- ✔ If you prefer the Multi Window tab on the right side of the screen, drag it there by long-pressing your finger on the touchscreen.

- ✔ Your phone always runs multiple apps at one time. The only benefit to Multi Window is that you can view two apps at the same time.

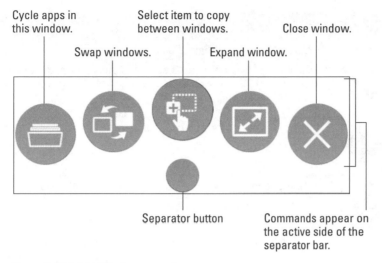

Cycle apps in this window.

Swap windows.

Select item to copy between windows.

Expand window.

Close window.

Separator button

Commands appear on the active side of the separator bar.

Figure 3-10: Multi Window controls.

Using common icons

In additional to the navigation icons, various other icons are commonly used in Android apps. Table 3-1 lists the most popular icons and their functions.

Table 3-1		Common Icons
Icon	*Name*	*What It Does*
◣	Action Bar	Displays a pop-up menu. This teensy icon appears in the lower-right corner of a button.
✚	Add	Adds or creates a new item. The plus symbol (+) may be used in combination with other symbols, depending on the app.
✕	Close	Closes a window or clears text from an input field.
🗑	Delete	Removes one or more items from a list or deletes a message.

(continued)

Table 3-1 *(continued)*

Icon	Name	What It Does
	Done	Dismisses an action bar, such as the text-editing action bar.
	Edit	Lets you edit an item, add text, or fill in fields.
	Microphone	Lets you use your voice to dictate text.
	Overflow	Displays an app's menu or list of commands. This icon is often redundant to the Menu button.
	Refresh	Fetches new information or reloads.
	Search	Search the phone or the Internet for a tidbit of information.
	Settings	Adjusts the options for an app.
	Share	Shares information stored on the phone via e-mail, social networking, or other Internet services.
	Star	Flags a favorite item, such as a contact or web page.

Various sections throughout this book give examples of using the icons. Their images appear in the book's margins where relevant.

In addition to the Settings icon, shown in Tablet 3-1, the Gear icon might be used to summon app settings. This icon looks similar to the one shown in the margin.

The Magical S Pen

The Galaxy Note comes with a handy stylus called the *S Pen*. It's probably the reason you chose the Galaxy Note over those other silly phones that lack a handy digital pen. Your phone's S Pen opens a constellation of opportunities for input and manipulation. Yes, it can do more than just draw mustaches on pictures.

 ✔ See Chapter 4 for information on writing text with the S Pen.

 ✔ Drawing mustaches on pictures is covered in Chapter 17.

Understanding the S Pen

To use the S Pen, slide it out of the phone's case: Grab the cap and yank the thing out. If the phone is locked, pulling out the S Pen unlocks it. You still have to work the PIN, pattern, password, or (especially) signature screen locks, but when the phone has only the swipe lock, it's unlocked right away and ready for action.

Take a moment to locate the S Pen button. It's found near the tip of the S Pen, as illustrated in Figure 3-11. Use that button to help the S Pen perform some of its fancier tricks, but be aware that the button is found on only one side of the S Pen — so there's a right and a wrong way to hold the thing.

It's here.

Figure 3-11: Locating the S Pen button.

You can use the S Pen at any time as a handy substitute for your finger. All touchscreen manipulations you can do with a single finger can be performed by using the S Pen; see the earlier section "Manipulating the touchscreen" for the list of actions.

One S Pen feature you may notice right away is the Air Command control. Keep reading in the next section for more info.

 ✔ Always replace the S Pen when you're done. Stick it back into the slot. You do not want to lose the S Pen! Because:

 ✔ If you lose the S Pen, you can obtain a replacement from Samsung. It's not cheap. Well, not as cheap as I had imagined.

Using Air Command

Most of the fancy things you can do with the S Pen are easily accessed by using the Air Command dingus, shown in Figure 3-12.

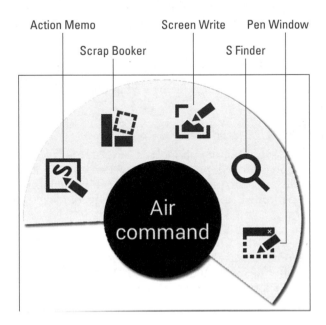

Figure 3-12: The Air Command dingus.

Air Command appears whenever you remove the S Pen from its launching tube. You can also make it appear by pointing the S Pen at the touchscreen (you don't need to touch the screen), and then clicking the S Pen button.

Here are brief descriptions of the Air Command options:

Action Memo: Choosing this item opens the Action Memo window, in which you can jot notes. The notes are accessed from the Action Memo app, found in the Samsung folder on the Applications screen.

Scrap Booker: This feature allows you to copy chunks of the screen into the Scrapbook app. The chunks are graphical images, not the information you've circled by using the S Pen.

Screen Write: The Screen Write command takes a picture of the screen — a _screen shot_ — and then lets you draw in it by using the S Pen. The saved images can be accessed from the Gallery app. See Chapter 15.

S Finder: Use this item to search your tablet — or the Internet — for specific tidbits of information.

Pen Window: After choosing this item, draw a rectangle on the screen, and then choose a mini-app to appear in the rectangle. Only a handful of apps are accessible through the Pen Window.

If you don't see the Air Command gizmus, ensure that it's activated on your Galaxy Note: Open the Settings app, found on the Applications screen. Touch the Controls tab and ensure that the Air Command item's master control switch is in the On (green) position. If it isn't, slide the master control icon to the left.

Doing some S Pen tricks

No other phone user is to laugh at you when you use the S Pen as a substitute for your finger. No, those guys will seethe with jealousy when you demonstrate to them some of these fancy S Pen tricks:

Screen capture and scribble: To take a snapshot of the screen, press and hold the S Pen button and long-press the S Pen to the touchscreen. After about two seconds, you hear a shutter click sound. The screen shot is saved. Further, you can edit the screen shot before saving it. This trick works just like the Screen Write command, covered in the preceding section.

Selective screen capture: Press and hold the S Pen button, and then draw around a chunk of information on the screen. That chunk — the exact size you drew around — is presented on a special screen. Choose an app from the bottom of the screen and the chunk is sent to that app for further manipulation.

Quick-launch the Action Memo app: When you're in dire need of accessing the Action Memo app and using the Air Command control is too bothersome, press the S Pen button and double-tap the screen. *Voilà!*

Text Creation and Editing

In This Chapter

▶ Understanding the onscreen keyboard

▶ Typing special characters

▶ Using predictive text

▶ Swiping for typing

▶ Writing with the S Pen

▶ Dictating text

▶ Editing text on the screen

▶ Selecting, cutting, copying, and pasting text

on't bother looking for it. The Galaxy Note doesn't have a keyboard, at least not the kind of keyboard you're used to. Your typing duties on the phone involve using something called the *onscreen keyboard*. You can also choose to scribble text by using the S Pen or even articulate your thoughts via Google Voice Typing. Don't worry about making mistakes, because text on the Galaxy Note can also be edited, providing you pore over the secrets divulged in this chapter.

Behold the Onscreen Keyboard

Whenever text input is required, your Galaxy Note displays the onscreen keyboard. Don't let it freak you out!

The onscreen keyboard appears on the bottom part of the touchscreen. The keyboard shows up anytime your phone demands text as input, such as when you type an e-mail, write something pithy on the web, or compose a drunken, midnight Facebook status update.

Figure 4-1 illustrates the standard Galaxy Note onscreen keyboard, also known as the Samsung keyboard. The onscreen keyboard you see on your phone may look subtly different because certain keys change their function depending on what you're typing.

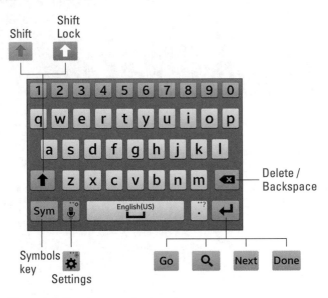

Figure 4-1: The onscreen keyboard.

In Figure 4-1, the onscreen keyboard is shown in Alphabetic mode. You see keys from A through Z in lowercase. You also see the Shift key for producing capital letters, and the Delete key, which works to backspace and erase.

The Enter key changes its look depending on what you're typing. Five variations are shown in Figure 4-1. Here's what each one does:

Enter/Return: Just like the Enter or Return key on a computer keyboard, this key ends a paragraph of text. It's used mostly when filling in long stretches of text, when multiline input is needed, or when you're well-versed in English and can comprehend the concept of a paragraph.

Go: This action key directs an app to proceed with a search, accept input, or perform another action.

Search: You see the Search key appear whenever you're searching for something. Touching the key starts the search.

Next: This key appears whenever you're typing information into multiple fields. Touching this key switches focus to the next field, such as from the Username field to the Password field.

Done: This key appears whenever you've finished typing text in the final field of a screen that has several fields. Sometimes it dismisses the onscreen keyboard, sometimes not.

The large key at the bottom center of the onscreen keyboard is the Space key. The keys to the left and right may change, depending on the context of what you're typing. For example, a www or .com key may appear, in order to assist in typing a web page address or e-mail address. Other keys may change as well, although the basic alphabetic keys remain the same.

- ✒ To display the onscreen keyboard, touch any text field or spot on the screen where typing is permitted.

- ✒ To dismiss the onscreen keyboard, touch the Back button.

- ✒ The keyboard reorients itself when you rotate the phone. The onscreen keyboard's horizontal orientation is wide, so you might find it easier to use.

Everybody Was Touchscreen Typing

The onscreen keyboard appears whenever you need to type text. It happens more often than you think — when you compose e-mail, write a text message, type a web page address, or fill in a form, for example. This section offers tips and suggestions to make your phone typing task tolerable.

Typing one character at a time

The onscreen keyboard is pretty easy to figure out: Touch a letter to produce the character. It works just like a computer keyboard in that respect. As you type, the key you touch is magnified and you hear a faint click. Text appears in a text box or elsewhere on the screen where typing is required. A blinking, vertical cursor tracks the position where the next text is inserted, just like on a computer screen.

- ✒ Above all, it helps to *type slowly* until you get used to the onscreen keyboard.

- ✒ When you make a mistake, touch the Delete key to back up and erase.

- ✒ When you type a password, the character you type appears briefly — but, for security reasons, it's then replaced by a black dot.

- ✒ Tap the Shift key to access uppercase letters. After you type the letter, the Shift key returns to normal operation; you do not need to press and hold (long-press) the Shift key.

- ✒ To type in all caps, tap the Shift key twice. Tap the Shift key again to turn off Shift Lock.

- ✒ People generally accept the concept that composing text on a phone isn't perfect. Don't sweat it if you make a few mistakes as you type text messages or e-mail, though you should expect some curious replies about unintended typos.

- ✒ See the later section "Text Editing", for more details on editing your text.

Accessing special characters

The Galaxy Note's onscreen keyboard has many special symbols available, which you access by touching the Symbol key, labeled Sym back in Figure 4-1. Touching this key gives you access to two additional keyboard layouts, shown in Figure 4-2.

Show alpha keyboard.

Show symbols keyboard 2.

Symbols keyboard 1

Show symbols keyboard 1.

Symbols keyboard 2

Figure 4-2: Onscreen keyboard symbols.

Touch the 1/2 (or first-of-two-pages) key to see the second page, illustrated in Figure 4-2. Touch the 2/2 (second-of-two-pages) key to return to the first page.

To return to the standard alphabetic keyboard, touch the ABC key.

Another trick to access special characters is to long-press a letter key. Doing so displays a pop-up palette of similar and accented characters, such as the ones shown for the A key in Figure 4-3.

Drag your finger over
a character to select it.

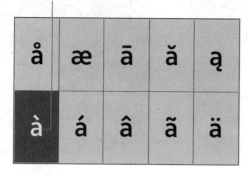

 — Press and hold.

Figure 4-3: A pop-up character palette.

Choose a character from the pop-up palette by dragging your finger to the key you want. Lift your finger to type the given character. (If you accidentally type a special character, just touch the Delete key to erase it.)

- Not every character sports a special pop-up palette.
- Special characters are available in uppercase as well; press the Shift key before you long-press on the onscreen keyboard.

Typing quickly by using predictive text

The Galaxy Note believes itself to be smart enough to guess the next word you type. The feature is called *predictive text.* It works to not only guess the next word but also complete partial works as you're typing.

For example, you may type **abo** and see a list of words starting with *abo* appear: *above, about, abode,* and so on. Touch a word to choose it, or tap the Space key to choose the highlighted word.

In Figure 4-4, I typed the word *I*. The keyboard then suggested the words *am*, *have*, and *will*, with *have* highlighted. Touch any word to insert it into the text, or tap the Space key to insert the word *have*. Touching the chevron displays additional choices.

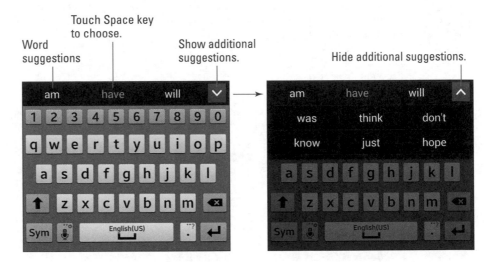

Figure 4-4: Predictive text in action.

When the desired word doesn't appear, continue typing: The predictive-text feature continues making suggestions based on what you've typed. Touch the right word when it appears.

To ensure that the predictive-text feature has been activated on your phone, follow these steps:

1. **At the Home screen, touch the Apps icon.**

2. **Open the Settings app.**

3. **Choose the Controls tab.**

4. **Touch the Language and Input item.**

5. **Touch the Settings icon by the text *Samsung Keyboard*.**

   The Samsung Keyboard Settings screen appears.

6. **Ensure that the master control by the Predictive Text item is in the On (green) position.**

   If not, slide the master control icon to the right.

You can touch the Predictive Text entry (not the master control icon) to view additional options and settings.

Activating Keyboard Swipe

To gain typing speed, consider using the Keyboard Swipe feature. It allows you to type words by dragging your finger over the onscreen keyboard, like mad scribbling but with a positive result.

To ensure that this feature is enabled, follow Steps 1 through 5 from the proceeding section. On the Samsung Keyboard Settings screen, in the Keyboard Swipe section, choose the item Continuous Input. Or, if the dot (radio button) next to Continuous Input is green, you're good to go.

You use gesture typing by dragging your fingers over letters on the keyboard. Figure 4-5 illustrates how the word *hello* would be typed in this manner.

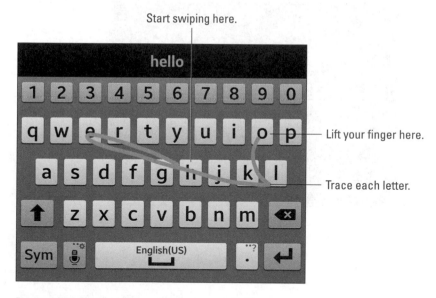

Figure 4-5: Using the keyboard swipe to type *hello.*

The Keyboard Swipe feature may not be active when you type a password or for specific apps on the phone. When it doesn't work, use the onscreen keyboard one letter at a time.

Writing text with the S Pen

The S Pen lets you do more than look erudite while you use your phablet. That's because you can create text using the S Pen just as you would write text on good old-fashioned paper. S Pen input on your Galaxy Note, however is quite hi-tech — if you know the secret.

 To switch to the S Pen input pad, long-press the Settings button on the onscreen keyboard. That key's icon can change, but its location is constant; refer to Figure 4-1. Choose the S Pen input pad item, as shown in the margin.

The S Pen input pad is illustrated in Figure 4-6. To use it, scribble: Write text as you would on a pad of paper. To type even faster when predictive text is active, you can tap word suggestions as they appear.

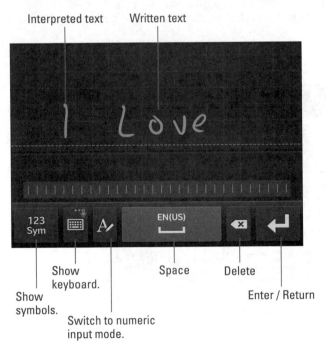

Figure 4-6: Writing text with the S Pen.

Use the Space, Delete, and Enter/Return buttons to help with punctuation. Symbols are found by tapping the Show Symbols button.

To write numbers, tap the A icon (refer to Figure 4-6). Tap the 1 icon, which replaces the A icon, to write letters.

When you're done using the S Pen — for example, when your hand is cramped so badly that it feels like it was run over by a tank — tap the Show Keyboard button. Input mode returns to using the Samsung keyboard for the ol' hunt-and-peck.

Voice Typing and Dictation

The Galaxy Note has the amazing ability to interpret your utterances as text. The Dictation feature can be used instead of typing to give control to your phone or to vent your frustrations.

Activating voice input

The Galaxy Note's voice input feature is officially known as Google Voice Typing. To ensure that this feature is active, obey these steps:

1. **At the Home screen, touch the Apps icon.**

2. **Open the Settings app.**

3. **Choose Language and Input, found on the Controls tab.**

   Touch the Controls tab first, and then choose the Language and Input item.

4. **Ensure that the item Google Voice Typing has a check mark.**

   If not, touch that item to activate Google Voice Typing.

Your primary clue that voice input is active is the Microphone icon, found on the keyboard. If you can see that icon, you're good.

Talking to your phone

The Dictation feature is available whenever you see the Microphone icon, similar to the one shown in the margin. To begin voice input, touch the icon. The Voice Input screen appears, as shown in Figure 4-7. When you see the text *Speak Now,* speak directly at the phone.

Dictation active   Dictation paused

Figure 4-7: The voice input thing.

As you speak, the Microphone button on the screen flashes. The flashing doesn't mean that the phone is embarrassed by what you're saying. No, the flashing merely indicates that the phone is listening, detecting the volume of your voice.

The text you utter appears as you speak. To pause, touch the _Tap to Pause_ text on the screen. To use the keyboard, touch the Keyboard icon just to the left of the Microphone icon, shown in Figure 4-7.

- ✔ The Dictation feature works only when voice input is allowed. Not every app allows voice input.

- ✔ Voice input may not function when no cellular data or Wi Fi connection is available.

- ✔ You have to "speak" punctuation to include it in your text. For example, you say, "I'm sorry comma James period" to have the phone produce the text _I'm sorry, James._

- ✔ You cannot use dictation to edit text. Text editing still takes place on the touchscreen, as described in the later section "Text Editing."

- ✔ Common punctuation marks that you can dictate include the comma, period, exclamation point, question mark, and colon.

- ✔ Pause your speech before and after speaking punctuation.

- ✔ There's no way to dictate a capital letter, although you can say "period" to capitalize the first letter of the next word. (It's easier to edit your text and remove excess periods than to edit your text to capitalize.)

- ✔ The better your diction, the better the results.

Uttering b**** words

The Galaxy Note features a voice censor. It replaces those naughty words you might utter, by placing the word's first letter on the screen, followed by the appropriate number of asterisks.

For example, if *belch* were a blue word and you utter "Belch" when dictating text, the Galaxy Note Dictation feature would place b**** on the screen rather than the word *belch*.

Yeah, I know: Silly. I mean, S****.

The phone knows a lot of blue terms, including the infamous "Seven Words You Can Never Say on Television" (from the George Carlin monologue), but apparently the terms *crap* and *damn* are fine. Don't ask me how much time I spent researching this topic.

See Chapter 24 for information on disabling the voice censor — if you dare.

Text Editing

I doubt that anyone will use the Galaxy Note to compose a novel. Sure, maybe someone will try, but that's not what text editing on a phone is all about. No, it's more about fixing typos (if you bother) and juggling blocks of text. It's a feat that few perform on their cell phones, mostly because they haven't read this section on how it all works.

Moving the cursor

The first part of the editing chore is to move the cursor to the right spot. The *cursor* is that blinking, vertical line where text appears. Then you can type, edit, or paste — or simply marvel that you were able to move the cursor hither and thither.

To move the cursor, simply touch the spot on the text. The cursor relocates to that spot — but maybe not exactly.

 To help apply precision, a cursor tab appears below the text, as shown in the margin. You can move this tab with your finger to move the cursor around in the text in a more specific manner.

After you move the cursor, you can continue to type, press the Delete key to back up and erase, or paste in text copied from elsewhere.

✔ You may see the pop-up Paste button appear above the cursor tab. That's the Paste command, used to paste previously cut or copied text. See the later section "Cutting, copying, and pasting text."

✔ Some words in your text appear with a faint, gray underline. When you move the cursor into one of those words, you may see a pop-up list of suggested alternatives. Choose a word to replace the underlined word, or touch the Delete command to remove the word.

✔ Underlined words appear most often when you use dictation. See the earlier section "Talking to your phone."

Selecting text

Selecting text on a phone works similarly to selecting text in a word processor, with the emphasis on the word *similarly*. As in a word processor, selected text appears highlighted on the touchscreen. You can then delete, cut, or copy the block of selected text.

Start selecting by long-pressing the text or double-tapping a word. Upon success, you see a chunk of text selected, as shown in Figure 4-8.

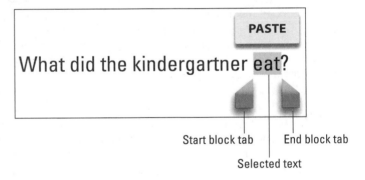

Figure 4-8: Text is selected.

Drag the start and end markers around the touchscreen to define the selected text.

When text is selected, a toolbar appears on the screen, similar to the ones shown in Figure 4-9. You use either toolbar to deal with the selected text: The top toolbar is the stock Android toolbar; the bottom one is Samsung's toolbar.

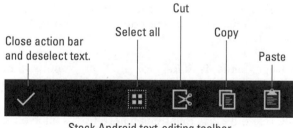

Close action bar and deselect text.　Select all　Cut　Copy　Paste

Stock Android text-editing toolbar

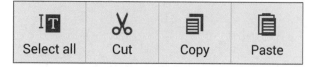

I T
Select all　Cut　Copy　Paste

Samsung text-editing toolbar

Figure 4-9: Text-editing toolbars.

After you select the text, you can delete it by touching the Delete key on the onscreen keyboard. You can replace the text by typing something new. Or you can cut or copy the text. See the next section, "Cutting, copying, and pasting text."

To cancel text selection, touch the Cancel button on the toolbar, or just touch anywhere on the touchscreen outside the selected block.

  ✔ Text selection on a web page works similarly to selecting text elsewhere. The primary difference is that the toolbar lacks a command to cut the text.

  ✔ The official name of the stock Android text-editing toolbar is the Contextual Action Bar. Just thought you'd like to know.

Cutting, copying, and pasting text

Selected text is primed for cutting or copying, which works just like it does in your favorite word processor. After you select the text, choose the proper command from the toolbar atop the touchscreen (refer to Figure 4-9).

For example, to copy the text, choose the Copy command; to cut text, choose Cut; and so on.

Just like on your computer, cut or copied text on your phone is stored in a clipboard. To paste any previously cut or copied text, move the cursor to the spot where you want the text pasted.

✔ A quick way to paste text is to look for the Paste command button above the cursor tab. To see that button, touch anywhere in the text. Touch the Paste command button to paste the text.

✔ You can paste text only into locations where text is allowed. Odds are good that if you see the onscreen keyboard, you can paste text.

Part II
Phone Duties

In this part...

- ✔ Understand how to make phone calls
- ✔ Work with special phone tricks
- ✔ Explore voice mail and Google Voice

Phone 101

In This Chapter

▶ Calling someone

▶ Connecting with a contact

▶ Calling favorite people

▶ Getting a call

▶ Dismissing a call with a text message

▶ Finding missed calls

▶ Perusing the call log

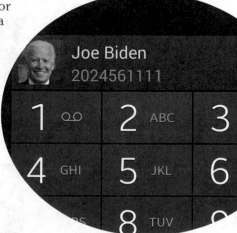

Credit the Bell Telephone Company for its brilliant design: I've never seen a manual (or a book) on how to use the old landline telephone. When it rang, you picked up the handset and started talking. To make a call, you picked up the handset and dialed or punched in a number. It had neither an Enter key nor a Phone button. You heard either a dial tone or a busy signal, or you started talking. Life was simple.

Here in the 21st century, with a device as diverse as the Galaxy Note, making phone calls isn't quite so simple. Gone is the dial. Gone are the buttons. Present are a slew of options and settings that can potentially drive you nuts. To help you fight any frustration, this chapter covers the basic tasks of placing and answering phone calls. Yes, it now takes a whole chapter to do that.

I Just Called to Say . . .

The Phone Company had plenty of sayings, back when there was such a thing as *long distance*. You were urged to place long-distance calls because the Phone Company made a ton of money from them. So slogans were created, such as "Reach out and touch someone" and "It's the next best thing to being there."

Long-distance calling is but a faint memory these days, yet the basic reason for making a phone call remains. The methods have changed, however, which is why I wrote this section.

Making a phone call

Phone dialing duties on your Galaxy Note are handled by the Phone app, found on the Home screen. To place a call, heed these steps:

1. **Touch the Phone app on the Home screen.**

   The Phone app's Keypad tab is illustrated in Figure 5-1. Touch the Keypad tab on your phone so that you can see the keypad, as illustrated in the figure.

2. **Type the number to call.**

   Use the keys on the keypad to type the number. If you make a mistake, touch the Delete button found in the lower-right corner, as shown in Figure 5-1, to back up and erase.

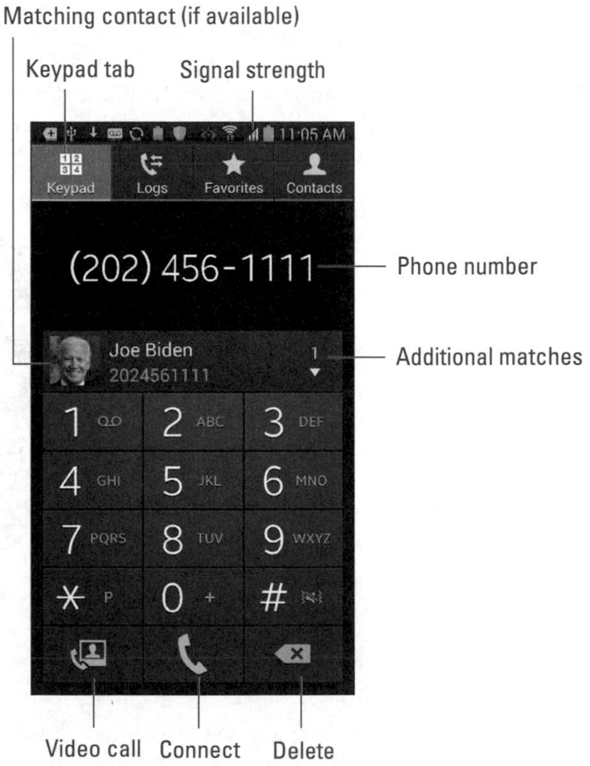

Figure 5-1: Dialing a phone number.

As you type the number, the phone displays contacts whose name or phone number matches what you type. For faster dialing, choose one of those contacts to complete the number.

3. **Touch the green Phone icon to place the call.**

As the phone attempts to make the connection, two things happen:

- *First, the Call in Progress notification icon appears on the status bar.* The icon is a big clue that the phone is making a call or is actively connected.

- *Second, the screen changes to show the number you dialed, similar to the one shown in Figure 5-2.* When the recipient is in the phone's address book, the contact's name, photo, and social networking status (if available) may also appear.

Even though the touchscreen is pretty, at this point you need to listen to the phone: Put it up to your ear and listen. If a headset is attached to the phone, you can listen using that device instead.

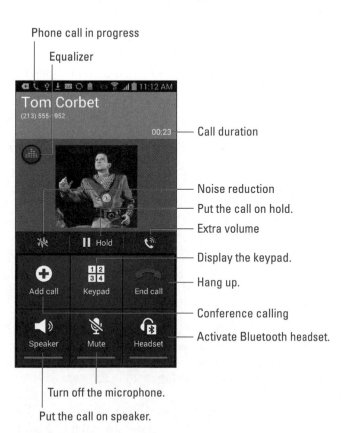

Figure 5-2: A successful call.

4. **When the person answers the phone, talk.**

What you say is up to you, though it's good not to open your conversation with something like, "Remember how that tall tree was leaning toward your house?"

Use the phone's Volume buttons (on the side of the device) to adjust the speaker volume during the call.

5. **To end the call, touch the red End Call button.**

The phone disconnects. You hear a soft *beep*, which is the phone's signal that the call has ended. The Call in Progress notification goes away.

You can do other things while you're making a call: Just press the Home button to run an app, read e-mail, check an appointment, or do whatever. Activities such as these don't disconnect you, though your cellular carrier may not allow you to do other things with the phone while you're on a call.

To return to a call after doing something else, swipe down the notifications at the top of the screen and touch the notification for the current call. You return to the Connected screen, similar to the one shown earlier, in Figure 5-2. Continue yapping. (See Chapter 3 for information on reviewing notifications.)

  ✔ The phone doesn't make the call until you touch the green button.

  ✔ See Chapter 13 for information on the Video Call icon.

  ✔ When you're using earphones, you can press the phone's Power/Lock button during the call to turn off the display and lock the touchscreen. I recommend turning off the display so that you don't accidentally touch the Mute button or End Call button during the call.

  ✔ You can connect or remove the earphones at any time during a call. The call is neither disconnected nor interrupted when you do so.

  ✔ When using a Bluetooth headset, activate the headset *before* you make the call. Touch the Headset button to switch from the phone's speaker and microphone to the Bluetooth headset.

  ✔ You can't accidentally mute or end a call when the phone is placed against your face: A sensor in the phone detects when it's close to something, and the touchscreen is automatically disabled.

  ✔ Don't worry about the phone being too far away from your mouth; it picks up your voice just fine.

  ✔ To mute a call, touch the Mute button, shown in Figure 5-2. The Mute icon, similar to the one shown in the margin, appears as the phone's status (atop the touchscreen).

  ✔ Touch the Speaker button to be able to hold the phone at a distance to listen and talk, which allows you to let others listen and share in the conversation. The Speaker icon appears as the phone's status when the speaker is active.

- Don't hold the phone to your ear when the speaker is active.

- If you're wading through one of those nasty voice-mail systems, touch the Keypad button, shown in Figure 5-2, so that you can "Press 1 for English" when necessary.

- See Chapter 6 for information on using the Add Call and Hold buttons.

- Long-press the asterisk (*) key (refer to Figure 5-1) to insert a pause into the number. The pause appears as a comma, and it inserts a 2-second wait when dialing.

- If you need to dial an international number, press and hold the zero (0) key until the plus-sign (+) character appears. Then input the rest of the international number. Refer to Chapter 21 for more information on making international calls.

- You hear an audio alert whenever the call is dropped or the other party hangs up. The disconnection can be confirmed by looking at the phone, which shows that the call has ended.

- You cannot place a phone call when the phone has no service; check the signal strength, as shown earlier, in Figure 5-1. Also see the nearby sidebar, "Signal strength and network nonsense."

- You cannot place a phone call when the phone is in Airplane mode. See Chapter 21 for information.

Signal strength and network nonsense

One of the phone's most important status icons is the Signal Strength icon. It appears in the upper-right corner of the screen, next to the Time and Battery Strength status icons.

The Signal Strength icon features the familiar bars, rising from left to right. The more bars, the better the signal. An extremely low signal is indicated by zero bars. When there's no signal, you may see a red circle with a line through it (the international No symbol) over the bars.

When your phone is out of its service area but still receiving a signal, you see the Roaming icon, which typically includes an *R* near or over the bars. See Chapter 21 for more information on roaming.

Your phone may also show the Network icon. This icon represents to which type of digital cellular network the phone is connected. Here are some of the different network types:

1X, **E**, **EDGE**, or **GSM**: The original (slow) mobile networks. You may still see icons for these networks when faster networks aren't available.

3G: The third-generation network, which is presently the second-fastest network.

4G, **4G LTE**, **H+**, or **HSPA**: The fastest current-generation cellular data network.

Also see Chapter 19 for more information on the network connection and how it plays a role in your phone's Internet access.

Dialing a contact

The easiest way to call someone you know is to use your Galaxy Note's address book, summon her contact information, and dial her instantly. By keeping names, addresses, and phone numbers in a digital address book, you save wear and tear on your brain, freeing up gray matter for storing the latest celebrity gossip and social trends. Everybody wins!

To dial a contact stored in your phone's address book, touch the Contacts tab atop the Phone app (refer to Figure 5-1) or simply start the Contacts app. Choose the contact you want to dial, and then touch the person's phone number. The contact is instantly dialed, and the call proceeds as described earlier in this chapter.

  ✔ The fastest way to dial a contact is to open the contacts list and swipe the contact's entry to the right.

  ✔ Refer to Chapter 8 for information on using the Galaxy Note's address book.

Calling a favorite

A special contact category in the Galaxy Note's address book is named Favorites. These are folks you call frequently or whose information you need to have handy. To call a favorite, touch the Favorites tab in the Phone app. Touch a favorite contact to display contact information and make the call.

  ✔ As with the phone's contacts list, you can quickly dial a favorite by swiping that entry in the Favorites list to the right.

  ✔ The Favorites tab in the Phone app lists not only contacts who are flagged, or *starred,* as favorites, but also people you frequently contact.

  ✔ Also see the later section "The Call Log," for information on perusing recent calls.

  ✔ Chapter 8 divulges the secret for creating favorite contacts.

Ring, Ring, Ring

It's for you! Cell phones are truly personal. If your Galaxy Note rings, you can pretty much be assured that whoever is calling wants to talk with you. Okay, maybe the person also wants to talk with the "adult in the house," but most of the time, an incoming call is an event. Someone cares enough to call.

Receiving a call

Several things can happen when you receive a phone call on your Galaxy Note:

- ✔ The phone rings or makes a noise signaling you to an incoming call.
- ✔ The phone vibrates.
- ✔ The touchscreen reveals information about the call, as shown in Figure 5-3.
- ✔ The panicked babysitter, eyes wide and out of breath, whispers that the killer is inside the house.

Incoming number

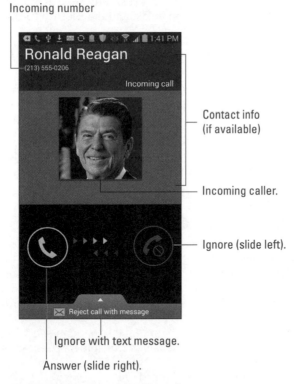

Figure 5-3: There's an incoming call.

Thankfully, the last item in the list happens only in horror movies. The other three possibilities, or a combination thereof, are your signals that you have an incoming call. A simple look at the touchscreen tells you more information, as illustrated in Figure 5-3.

To answer the incoming call, slide the green Answer button to the right (refer to Figure 5-3). Then place the phone — or a headset, if one is attached — to your ear. Say "Hello" or, if you're in a grouchy mood, say "What?" loudly.

To dispense with the incoming call, slide the red Ignore button to the left. The phone stops ringing, and the call is banished into voice mail. You can also touch the Volume button to silence the phone, although this action doesn't immediately banish the incoming call to voice mail.

- ✔ When you're already on the phone and another call comes in, you can touch the green Answer button to accept the call and place the current call on hold. See Chapter 6 for additional information on juggling multiple calls.

- ✔ The contact's picture, such as former President Reagan's photo in Figure 5-3, appears only when you've assigned a picture to that contact. Otherwise, a generic icon shows up.

- ✔ See Chapter 22 for information on making the phone vibrate on an incoming call.

- ✔ If you're using a Bluetooth headset, you touch the control on the headset to answer your phone. See Chapter 19 for more information on using Bluetooth gizmos.

- ✔ The sound you hear when the phone rings is known as the *ringtone*. You can configure your phone to play a number of ringtones, depending on who is calling, or you can set a universal ringtone. Ringtones are covered in Chapter 6.

Rejecting a call with a text message

I'm quite fond of the text-message rejection method. Rather than simply dismiss a call, you can use the tab at the bottom of the Incoming Call screen (refer to Figure 5-3) to display a list of text message replies, as shown in Figure 5-4. Choose one to send that text message to the caller, which I find far more polite than dismissing the call outright.

After you touch the Send button, the incoming call is dismissed. In a few cellular seconds, the person who called receives the selected text message.

The messages shown in Figure 5-4 are ones I created myself. To change the standard dull messages provided on the Galaxy Note, heed these steps:

Existing excuses

Add a new message.

Send the message.

Figure 5-4: Text-message rejection selection.

1. **At the Home screen, press the Menu button.**

2. **Choose Settings to open the Settings app.**

3. **Choose the Device tab atop the Settings app screen.**

4. **Choose the Call item.**

5. **Choose Set Call Rejection Messages.**

   You see the Reject Messages screen. It lists current messages and lets you create new, better ones.

6. **To create a new message, touch the Create button or choose an existing message to edit or replace it.**

   The device has slots for only six messages, so the Create button isn't available when you have six messages.

   Messages are edited like any other text in the Galaxy Note. Refer to Chapter 4 for text editing information.

7. **Touch the Save button to save the message-rejection text.**

Your new messages appear the next time you slide up the Reject Call with Message tab.

- ✔ You can have a maximum of six text-message-rejection replies.
- ✔ To delete a message, visit the Reject Messages screen (follow Steps 1 through 5 in this section), and long-press the entry you want to remove. Choose the Delete command. Touch the OK button to confirm.
- ✔ Not every phone is a cell phone. Sending a text message to Aunt Linda's landline phone just won't work.
- ✔ See Chapter 9 for more information on text messages.

Dealing with a missed call

When you see the notification icon for a missed call looming at the top of the screen, it means that someone called and you didn't pick up. Fortunately, the Galaxy Note remembers all the details for you.

To deal with a missed call, obey these steps:

1. **Pull down the notifications panel.**

   You see the Missed Call notification with details regarding the incoming number and call time. Beneath that information you see two buttons: Call Back and Text Message.

2. **Touch the Call Back button to return the call; touch Text Message to send the other party a text.**

   Or you can choose the notification to view the call log, covered in the next section.

The phone doesn't consider a call you've dismissed as being missed. To review all your calls — incoming, outgoing, dismissed, and missed — see the next section.

The Call Log

In addition to being a phone and a tablet (or *phablet*), the Galaxy Note is a computer. As such, it keeps track of all your phone calls: incoming, outgoing, missed, and rejected. It's something I refer to as the *call log*, although in the Phone app the information is found under the Logs tab, similar to the one in Figure 5-5.

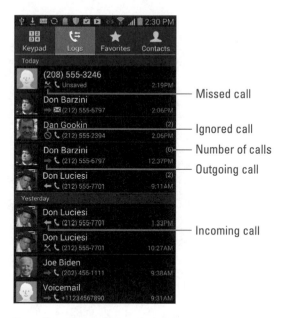

Figure 5-5: The phone's call log.

The Logs tab displays a list of calls similar to the one shown in Figure 5-5. Choose an item to see more details, such as the last several calls made, received, or missed for that number or contact. To dial that contact, touch the green Phone icon.

✔ The call log keeps track of your phone calls for days — even weeks.

✔ Using the call log is a quick way to add a recent caller as a contact: Simply choose an item from the list, and touch the Create Contact button from the Details screen. See Chapter 8 for more information about creating contacts.

✔ Remove an item from the call log by long-pressing its entry. Choose the Delete command, and then touch the Delete button to confirm.

✔ To clear the entire call log, press the Menu button and choose Delete. Place check marks by the entries you desire to remove, or place one check mark by the Select All item to remove everything. Touch the Delete button and then the OK button to confirm.

Super Phone

In This Chapter

▶ Setting up speed dial

▶ Handling multiple incoming calls

▶ Setting up a conference call

▶ Configuring call forwarding options

▶ Banishing a contact to the reject list

▶ Changing the ringtone

▶ Assigning ringtones to your contacts

*Y*our Galaxy Note is blessed with abilities far beyond those of a mere mortal phone. These features would have been scoffed at in the 1940s, ridiculed in the 1950s, met with blank stares in the 1960s, yearned for in the 1970s, and, finally, achieved in the 1980s, but at exorbitant monthly fees.

Today the fees are gone, but the features remain: speed dial, call waiting, call forwarding, three-way calling, and more. These bonus features are ready and eager for you to use them. This chapter discusses these super phone powers.

Super Dialing Tricks

Any mere mortal can use the Phone app on a Galaxy Note phone to key in a number. To take your dialing skills up a notch, consider some of the special dialing tricks carefully explained in this section.

Configuring speed dial

How fast can you dial a phone? Don't even try to attempt a new speed record. That's because the Galaxy Note comes with a Speed Dial feature that will put any of your attempts to shame.

Configure Speed Dial by following these steps:

1. **Open the Phone app.**

2. **If necessary, touch the Keypad tab to see the phone-dialing screen.**

3. **Press the Menu button.**

4. **Choose Speed Dial Setting.**

   The Speed Dial Setting screen appears, similar to the one you see in Figure 6-1. You can assign up to eight speed dial settings on the Galaxy Note; speed dial setting number one is already configured for voice mail, as shown in the figure.

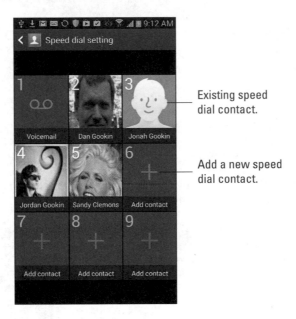

Existing speed dial contact.

Add a new speed dial contact.

Figure 6-1: Speed Dial setup.

5. **Touch a blank number.**

   Blank numbers have plus icons on them (refer to Figure 6-1).

6. **Choose a contact to speed-dial.**

7. **Repeat Steps 5 and 6 to add more speed dial contacts.**

When you're done adding numbers, press the Back button to exit the Speed Dial Setting screen.

Using speed dial is simple: Long-press a number on the keypad to dial a contact. When you release your finger, the speed dial number is dialed.

To review your speed dial settings, follow Steps 1 through 4 in this section.

Adding pauses when dialing a number

Unlike on the ancient telephone, dialing a number on your Galaxy Note isn't an interactive process: You type the number and then touch the green Phone icon to dial. The number is spewed into the phone system like water from a fire hose. When you need to pause the number as it's dialed, you must know the secret.

To insert a pause or wait prompt into a phone number, follow these steps:

1. **Type the number to dial.**

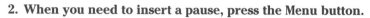

2. **When you need to insert a pause, press the Menu button.**

   Up pops a menu with two options for inserting pauses into a number. How those options appear when chosen is shown in Figure 6-2.

Figure 6-2: Inserting a pause into a phone number.

3. **Choose Add 2-Sec Pause to insert a 2-second pause, or choose Add Wait to create a prompt into the phone number that's dialed.**

The Add 2-Sec Pause command inserts the comma (,) character into the number. When the phone dials the comma, it waits for two seconds and then dials the rest of the number.

The Add Wait command inserts the semicolon (;) character into the number. When the phone dials the semicolon, an onscreen prompt is displayed.

4. **Continue composing the number.**

When you're done, dial the number. When the comma character is encountered, the phone pauses two seconds and then dials the rest of the number. When the semicolon character is encountered, the phone prompts you to continue. Touch the OK button to dial the rest of the number.

The , and ; characters can also be inserted into phone numbers assigned to your contacts. See Chapter 8 for information on contacts and the phone's address book.

Captain Conference Call

Psychologists, and others who wear white lab coats, have determined that human beings can hold only one conversation at a time. Your Galaxy Note isn't under such limitations — it can handle as many as two calls with three different people. (For you folks in white lab coats, that's two other people and yourself, which totals three people.) The secret to performing this feat is divulged in this section.

Putting someone on hold

It's easy to place a call on hold, thanks to the Hold icon found on the In-Call screen and shown in the margin. Touch the Hold button and the person on the other line is "on hold."

To take a call out of hold, touch the Unhold icon, as shown in the margin. On some cellular carriers, the Hold icon may not change to the Unhold icon. In that case, to take a call out of hold, touch the Hold icon again.

You can always touch the Mute icon as opposed to placing a call on hold. That way, you can sneeze, scream at the wall, or flush the toilet and the other person will never know.

Receiving a call when you're on the phone

You're on the phone, chatting it up. Suddenly, someone else calls you. What happens next?

Your Galaxy Note alerts you to the new call. The phone may vibrate or make a sound. Look at the front of the phone to see what's up and you'll see the standard Incoming Call screen (refer to Figure 5-3, in Chapter 5).

You have three options:

Answer the call. Slide the green Answer button to answer the incoming call. The call you're already on is placed on hold.

Send the call directly to voice mail. Slide the red Ignore button. The incoming call is sent directly to voice mail.

Do nothing. The call eventually goes to voice mail.

When you choose to answer the call and the call you're on is placed on hold, you're actually on two calls at that time — but speaking with only one person. Keep reading in the next section.

Juggling two calls

After you answer a second call, as described in the preceding section, your phone is working with two calls at a time. In this particular situation, you can speak with only one person at a time; juggling two calls isn't the same as participating in a conference call.

On some phones, depending on your carrier, after receiving a call while you're on the phone, you may see the Accept Call After prompt. You have two choices:

Put the existing call on hold. Choose the option to answer the incoming call and then return to the original call after you hang up on the new guy.

End the existing call. Choose this option to say goodbye to the current call and start a new conversation.

If you choose to accept the incoming call, or when the Accept Call After prompt doesn't appear, the original call is placed on hold. The touchscreen displays information about both calls, as illustrated in Figure 6-3.

You can do a few things while the phone is handling two calls:

 Swap calls: To switch callers, touch the Swap icon on the touchscreen. Every time you touch this icon, the conversation moves to the other caller. The current person is then put on hold, as shown in Figure 6-3. (The current caller is on top.)

 Merge calls: To combine both calls so that everyone is talking with each other (three people), touch the Merge icon. This icon may not be available if the Merge feature becomes suppressed by your cellular provider.

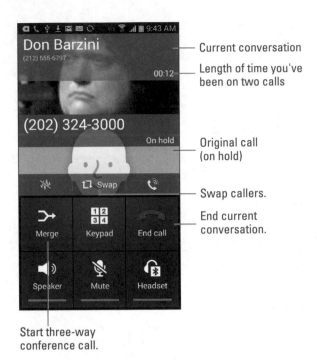

Current conversation

Length of time you've been on two calls

Original call (on hold)

Swap callers.

End current conversation.

Start three-way conference call.

Figure 6-3: Two calls at once.

End: To end a call, touch the End Call button, just as you normally do. The current caller is disconnected, and you're left talking with the person who was on hold.

After one call ends, the conversation returns to the other caller. You can then proceed to talk — discuss the weather, the local sports team, whatever — until you hang up or another call interrupts you.

- The number of different calls your phone can handle depends on your carrier. For most subscribers in the United States, your phone can handle only two calls at a time. In that case, a third person who calls you either hears a busy signal or is sent directly to voice mail.

- If the person on hold hangs up, you may hear a sound or feel the phone vibrate when the call is dropped.

- When you touch the End Call icon using a Galaxy Note phone on the Verizon network, both calls may appear to have been disconnected. That's not the case: In a few moments, the call you didn't disconnect "rings" as though the person is calling you back. No one is calling you back, though: The phone is simply returning you to that ongoing conversation.

Making a conference call

Unlike someone interrupting a conversation with an incoming call, a *conference call* is one that you set out to make intentionally: You place one call and then add a second call. Touch the Merge button in the Phone app, and then everyone is talking. Here's how it works:

1. **Phone the first person.**

Add call

2. **After your phone connects and you complete a few pleasantries, touch the Add Call button.**

   The first person is put on hold.

3. **Dial the second person.**

   You can use the keypad or choose the second person from the phone's address book or from a recent call found in the call log.

   After you connect with the second person, the Galaxy Note touchscreen looks like it does when you're on two calls, as shown earlier, in Figure 6-3.

4. **Touch the Merge button.**

   The two calls are now joined: The touchscreen says *Conference Call,* as shown in Figure 6-4. Everyone you've dialed can talk to, and hear, everyone else.

5. **Touch the End Call button to end the conference call.**

   All calls are disconnected.

Place all calls on hold.

Add another call.

Figure 6-4: Multiple-call mania!

When several people are in a room and want to participate in a call, you can always put the phone in Speaker mode: Touch the Speaker button.

Apparently, you can add a *fourth* conversation to the mix, as shown by the enabled Add Call button, in Figure 6-4. I've not tried this option to see whether it works.

Calls Sent Elsewhere

Banishing an unwanted call is relatively easy on your Galaxy Note. You can forbid the phone from ringing by touching the Volume button. Or you can send the call scurrying off into voice mail by swiping the red Ignore button, as described in Chapter 5.

Other options exist for the special handling of incoming calls. They're the amazing forwarding options, described in this section.

Forwarding phone calls

Call forwarding is the process by which you reroute an incoming call. For example, you can send to your office all calls you receive while you're on vacation. Then you have the luxury of having your cell phone and still making calls but freely ignoring anyone who calls you.

The options for call forwarding on your Galaxy Note are set by using either the Android operating system itself or the controls set up by your cellular provider.

Call forwarding may affect your phone's voice mail service. See Chapter 7 for details.

Forward calls using Android settings

To review the various call forwarding options available on the phone, heed these steps:

1. **At the Home screen, press the Menu button.**

2. **Choose Settings to launch the Settings app.**

3. **On the Device tab in the Settings app, choose the Call item.**

4. **Choose Additional Settings.**

5. **Choose Call Forwarding and then Voice Call.**

If this option isn't available, you must use your carrier's forwarding settings, as described in the next section. Otherwise, you can select one of these four forwarding options:

Always Forward: All incoming calls are sent to the number you specify; your phone doesn't even ring. This option overrides all other forwarding options.

Forward When Busy: Calls are forwarded when you're on the phone and choose not to answer. This option is normally used to send a missed call to voice mail, although you can forward to any number.

Forward When Unanswered: Calls are forwarded when you choose not to answer the phone. Normally, the call is forwarded to your voice mail.

Forward When Unreachable: Calls are forwarded when the phone is turned off or out of range or in Airplane mode. As with the two preceding settings, this option normally forwards calls to voice mail.

6. **Choose an option.**

7. **Set the forwarding number.**

   Or you can edit the number that already appears. For example, you can type your home number for the Forward When Unreached option so that your cell calls are redirected to your home when you're out of range.

8. **Touch the Turn On or Update button to confirm the forwarding number.**

The Call Forwarding status icon appears atop the touchscreen when you've activated a forwarding option.

To disable call forwarding, touch the Turn Off button when you're given the opportunity to type a forwarded phone number. (See Step 7 in the preceding list.)

Call forwarding affects Google Voice voice mail. Unanswered calls that you forward are handled by the forwarding number, not by Google Voice. Further, when you cancel call forwarding, you need to reenable Google Voice on your phone. See Chapter 7 for details.

Forward calls on the Verizon network

When your Galaxy Note is using the Verizon network in the United States, you may have to use special forwarding numbers to forward your calls. You can first try the steps in the preceding section to see whether they work. If they don't, the Verizon forwarding numbers are shown in Table 6-1.

Table 6-1	Verizon Call Forwarding Commands	
To Do This	*Dial This*	*And Then This*
Forward unanswered incoming calls	*71	Forwarding number
Forward all incoming calls	*72	Forwarding number
Cancel call forwarding	*73	None

As an example, to forward all calls to (714) 555-4565, you type ***727145554565** as the phone number. Touch the green Phone icon to forward your calls; you hear only a brief tone after dialing, and then the call ends. After that, any call coming into your phone rings at the other number.

You must disable call forwarding to return to normal cell phone operations: Dial *73.

Rejecting incoming calls

You can configure your phone to forward directly to voice mail any calls received from a specific contact. The phone never even rings. It's a helpful way to deal with a pest! Follow these steps:

1. **Touch the Apps icon on the Home screen.**

   The Applications screen appears.

2. **Open the Contacts app.**

3. **Ensure that the Contacts tab is chosen atop the screen.**

4. **Choose a contact.**

   Swipe through the list of contacts until you find the annoying person that you want to eternally banish to voice mail.

5. **Press the Menu button.**

6. **Choose Add to Reject List.**

   The first time you use this command, you're prompted with a notice. Tap the OK button.

When a contact has been added the reject list, the universal No symbol (or circle-backslash symbol) appears in blue next to the contact's phone number. All calls from the contact are sent directly to voice mail.

To unbanish the contact, repeat these steps but in Step 6, choose the command Remove from Reject List.

Managing the reject list

You don't need to remember exactly which contacts have been added to the reject list. Further, it's possible to manually add numbers, even all numbers from a certain area code or prefix, because the Galaxy Note keeps track of your phone's reject list in one handy spot.

To review or manage the reject list, follow these steps:

1. **At the Home screen, press the Menu button.**
2. **Choose the Settings command to start the Settings app.**
3. **In the Settings app, touch the Device tab and then the Call item.**
4. **On the Call Settings screen, choose Call Rejection.**
5. **Choose Auto Reject List.**

   You see a list of numbers and contacts you've slated for automatic rejection.

To add contacts or phone numbers to the list, touch the Add icon. Type a phone number or choose Match Criteria to use patterns in a number for the swift rejection of entire legions of phone numbers.

To remove an individual from the list, tap the box to the right of the entry to place a green check mark there. Touch the Delete icon to remove that entry from the list. Confirm the deletion to ensure that the number is removed from the reject list.

This feature is one reason you might want to retain contact information for someone with whom you never want to have contact.

Intergalactic Ringtones

A *ringtone* is the sound your Galaxy Note makes when you have an incoming call. You may already know that. What you may not know is that you're not stuck with the preconfigured ringtone. You can even change the ringtone for individual contacts. This section explains how it works.

Choosing the phone's ringtone

To select a new ringtone for your phone, or to simply confirm which ringtone you're using already, follow these steps:

1. **At the Home screen, press the Menu button.**
2. **Choose Settings.**

   The Settings app appears.

3. **Choose the Device tab, and then choose Sound.**

4. **Choose Ringtones.**

   When a ringtone app is installed, you may see a menu that asks you which source to use for the phone's ringtone. Choose Media Storage.

5. **Choose a ringtone from the list that's displayed.**

   Scroll the list. Tap a ringtone to hear a preview. Choose Silent when you don't want the phone to have a ringtone.

6. **Touch OK to accept the new ringtone, or touch Cancel to keep the phone's ringtone as is.**

See the later section "Creating your own ringtones," for information on broadening the ringtone selection.

✔ You can also set the ringtone that's used for notifications: In Step 4 in the preceding list, choose Default Notification Sound rather than Ringtones.

✔ Text messaging ringtones are set from within the Messaging app. See Chapter 9.

✔ The Zedge app has oodles of free ringtones available for preview and download, all shared by Android users around the world. See Chapter 18 for information about the Google Play Store and how to download and install apps such as Zedge on your phone.

Setting a contact's ringtone

Ringtones can be assigned by contact so that when your annoying friend Larry calls, you can have your phone yelp like a whiny puppy. Here's how to set a ringtone for a contact:

1. **Choose the Contacts app from the Applications screen.**

   Touch the Apps icon on the Home screen to see the Applications screen.

2. **From the list, choose the contact to which you want to assign a ringtone.**

3. **Choose the Ringtone item.**

   The current ringtone is shown below the Ringtone heading. The word *Default* appears when a custom ringtone hasn't been chosen.

   If prompted, choose the Media Storage item to use the Android operating system for ringtone selection. If you have a ringtone app installed, you can choose it instead. (See Chapter 24 for information on the Always/Just Once choice.)

4. **Choose a ringtone from the list.**

Whenever the contact calls, the phone uses the ringtone you've specified.

To remove a specific ringtone for a contact, repeat the steps in this section but choose Default Ringtone in Step 4. This choice sets the contact's ringtone to be the same as the phone's ringtone.

Creating your own ringtones

Your ringtone selection on the Galaxy Note isn't limited to the paltry choices offered on the Ringtones list. That's because you find, near the bottom of the list, the Add button. Use that button to bring in your own sounds to the phone's ringtone repertoire.

To begin your ringtone adventure, first collect or create a suitable tune. It can be any audio file on the phone: one you create by using a special app, a file transferred from another device, or a chunk of audio downloaded from the Internet. Various chapters elsewhere in this book describe the details.

After the audio file is on your phone, follow Steps 1 through 4 in the earlier section "Choosing the phone's ringtone." Then continue with these directions:

5. **Touch the Add button at the bottom of the Ringtones list.**

6. **If prompted, choose the Sound Picker app.**

   You can also choose a file management or cloud storage app, such as Dropbox. If so, you use that app to browse for an audio file to use as a ringtone.

7. **Pluck a new ringtone from the Sound Picker app.**

   The app presents sounds by category. Browse your phone's music by choosing the Songs, Albums, or Artists categories. Choose the Folders category to peruse your Galaxy Note's storage system to look for audio files.

8. **Touch an item to preview the ringtone.**

9. **Touch the Done button to set the ringtone.**

   Or you can touch the Back button to select another audio snippet.

The music or audio you choose becomes the phone's ringtone. Or if you followed these steps for setting a contact's ringtone, the new sound is applied to only that contact.

To restore the phone's ringtone, follow the steps outlined in the earlier section "Choosing the phone's ringtone." Choose a new ringtone from the Ringtones list.

- Information on downloading files (such as audio files) from the Internet is found in Chapter 11.

- When you want to explore music on your phone, see Chapter 16.

- Refer to Chapter 18 for information on downloading audio apps from the Google Play Store.

- Chapter 20 covers file transfer from a computer to your Galaxy Note.

Voice Mail and Beyond

In This Chapter

▶ Configuring basic voice mail

▶ Retrieving messages

▶ Getting a Google Voice account

▶ Adding another phone to Google Voice

▶ Using the Google Voice app

*Y*ou know the drill: "At the sound of the tone, please leave your message." Is it even necessary to ask any more? Can't the message simply say "Beep!"? Your astute friends would figure it out. Those not paying attention wouldn't leave a message, which is probably a good thing. Whether they leave a message or not, you can always check the phone to see who has called, as described in Chapter 5. This chapter covers everything else having to do with leaving a message at the tone.

Plain Old, Boring Carrier Voice Mail

The most basic, and most stupid, form of voice mail is the free voice-mail service provided by the cellular provider. It's a standard feature with few frills and nothing that stands out differently, especially for your nifty Android phone.

Destiny Hope
+1-818-555-1123
Received: 4:23PM (12 secs)

Simon. You never call me anymore. You know how muc
you, bye.

 Carrier voice mail picks up missed calls as well as those calls you thrust into voice mail. A notification icon, looking similar to the one shown in the margin, appears whenever someone has left you a new voice mail message. You can use the notification to dial into your carrier's voice mail system and listen to your calls. While you listen, you can use the phone's dialpad to delete messages or repeat messages or use other features you probably don't know about because no one ever pays attention.

Setting up carrier voice mail

If you haven't yet done it, set up voice mail on your phone. I recommend doing so even if you plan to use another voice mail service, such as Google Voice. That's because carrier voice mail remains a valid and worthy fallback for when those other services don't work.

Your Galaxy Note comes preconfigured to use the My Carrier voice mail service, which is tied into your cellular provider. The cellular provider's voice mail number has also been preconfigured for you. You can check these items by opening the Settings app. Obey:

1. **Start the Settings app.**

   It's found on the Applications screen.

2. **Choose Call from the Device tab.**

3. **Choose Voicemail Service.**

   It should list My Carrier as the only option, unless you've configured another service, such as Google Voice (covered later in this chapter).

To complete the carrier voice mail setup, you call into the service and set up your account. Follow these steps:

1. **Open the Phone app, found on the Home screen.**

2. **Ensure that the Keypad tab is selected.**

3. **Long-press the 1 button.**

   The 1 button is the speed dial shortcut to enter the carrier's voice mail system. If this is the first time you've called, you have to work through some initial setup.

4. **Work through the directions.**

   You need to use the onscreen keypad to respond to the cellular provider's vocal prompts. Touch the Speaker button to hear the cheerful robot, and respond by using the keypad.

5. **Set your name, a voice mail password, a greeting, and various other options as guided by your cellular provider's cheerful robot.**

   Just so that you remember the personal identification number (PIN) for your voice mail account, write it down on the following line:

   Your voice mail account PIN: _____

6. **Touch the End Call button when you tire of listening to the cheerful robot.**

I highly recommend that you choose a customized greeting for your voice mailbox. Callers who don't hear your voice sometimes don't leave messages, because they mistakenly believe that they've dialed the wrong number.

Retrieving your messages

When you have voice mail pending, the New Voicemail notification icon appears on the status bar, as shown in the margin. You can either pull down this notification to connect to the voice mail service or dial into the voice mail service by long-pressing the 1 key on the Phone app's keypad.

After the voice mail service answers, you're asked to type your voice mail password. Type your password.

In case you need to remember the prompts, you can write them down here:

Press _____ to listen to the first message.

Press _____ to delete the message.

Press _____ to skip a message.

Press _____ to hear the menu options.

Press _____ to hang up.

The commands differ from carrier to carrier. On AT&T, for example, the * key is the Cancel key, and 7 is the Delete key.

If you don't delete a message, it stays in your voice mail inbox. You're prompted to delete the message the next time you dial into carrier voice mail.

Wonderful Google Voice

Perhaps the best option I've found for working your voice mail is something called *Google Voice.* It's more than just a voice mail system: You can use Google Voice to make phone calls in the United States, place cheap international calls, and perform other amazing feats. In this section, I extol the virtues of using Google Voice as the Galaxy Note's voice mail system.

- ✔ Even when you choose to use Google Voice, I still recommend setting up and configuring the boring carrier voice mail, as covered earlier in this chapter.

- ✔ With Google Voice configured as your phone's voice mail service, your voice mail messages arrive in the form of a Gmail message. The message's text is a transcription of the voice mail message.

- ✔ Better than reading a Gmail message is receiving a Google Voice message by using the Google Voice app. See the later section "Using the Google Voice app."

✔ You may need to reset Google Voice after using call forwarding. See Chapter 6 for more information on call forwarding, and see the next section for information on reestablishing Google Voice as your phone's voice mail service.

Configuring Google Voice

You need to create a Google Voice account on the Internet before you configure your Galaxy Note to use its voice mail service. Start your adventure by visiting the Google Voice home page on the Internet: `http://voice.google.com`. I recommend using a computer to complete these steps:

1. **If necessary, sign in to your Google account on the Google Voice web page.**

   You use the same account name and password that you use to access your Gmail.

2. **Accept the terms of service, if prompted.**

3. **Choose to use your existing mobile number.**

4. **Type your Galaxy Note's phone number, if prompted.**

   Google Voice checks for availability.

5. **Select the option to use Google Voice Lite.**

   Upon success, you see the Verify Your Phone step appear on the computer's screen. Google Voice calls your phone and prompts you to type a 2-digit number that appears on the screen.

6. **Click the Call Me Now button.**

   Google Voice dials your phone to confirm the number.

7. **Answer the incoming call.**

   You might want to display the keypad and use the speaker while you're on this call.

8. **Use the keypad to type the number on the computer screen.**

   On my computer's screen I see the number 10. I type that number on my Galaxy Note to confirm my account.

9. **Use your phone to configure Google Voice.**

   You set your name and a greeting — typical voice mail stuff.

10. **On the computer, type and confirm a PIN number.**

    The PIN is used to access Google Voice via your phone. Again, this process is typical for setting up any voice mail account.

11. **On your phone, dial the phone number displayed on the computer's screen.**

    It's a long, complex, weird-looking number. Type it in exactly. Effectively, you're programming the phone to forward unanswered calls to the Google Voice service.

    A confirmation message appears briefly on the phone, indicating that the action was successful.

12. **On the computer screen, click the Continue button.**

    You're done.

A Google Voice access number appears on the computer screen. Write that number here for future reference:

My Google Voice access number: (_____) _____ - _____

I also recommend creating a contact for your Google Voice access number. Create the new contact per the directions in Chapter 8. And while you're at it, consider bookmarking the Google Voice website on your computer.

Though this step configures a Google Voice account, you still need to program your phone to use Google Voice as its voice mail service. That's best accomplished by installing the Google Voice app. See the later section "Using the Google Voice app."

Google Voice offers a host of features: international dialing, call forwarding, and other stuff I am not aware of and, honestly, am quite afraid of. It's possible, however, merely to use Google Voice as a voice mail service, which is what I recommend.

Adding a second line to Google Voice

When you already have a Google Voice account, you add your Galaxy Note's phone number to the list of phone numbers already registered for Google Voice. Here's how that's done:

1. **Visit the Google Voice web page on the Internet:** voice.google.com.

   This process works best using a computer.

2. **Click the Gear icon in the upper right corner of the Google Voice home page, and choose the Settings command from the menu.**

   The Settings command may change its location in a future update to the Google Voice web page. If so, the purpose of this step is to access the Settings screen, where you register phone numbers for use with Google Voice.

3. **Click the Add Another Phone link.**

4. **Work the steps to verify your phone for use with Google Voice.**

   As this book goes to press, the steps involve typing a name for the phone, such as *My Beloved Galaxy Note 3,* and then typing the phone's number, including the area code.

   Eventually, Google Voice needs to call your cell phone.

5. **Use the dialpad on your phone to type the code number you see on the computer's screen.**

   After confirming the code number, you see your Galaxy Note listed as a registered phone — but you're not done yet.

6. **Click the Activate Voicemail link.**

   You must activate your phone for it to work with Google Voice. This step is the most important one in adding your cell phone number to Google Voice!

7. **On your phone, dial the number you see on your computer screen, or otherwise obey the instructions to forward your busy, unanswered, or unreachable calls to the Google Voice number.**

   Refer to Chapter 6 for more detail on call forwarding options.

8. **On the computer, click the Done button.**

Your Galaxy Note is now registered for use with Google Voice.

Using the Google Voice app

Google Voice transcribes your voice mail messages, turning the audio from the voice mail into a text message you can read. The messages all show up eventually in your Gmail inbox, just as though someone sent you an e-mail rather than left you voice mail. It's a good way to deal with your messages, but not the best way.

The best way to handle Google Voice is to use the Voice app, available from the Google Play Store. Use the Play Store app to search for and install the Google Voice app. (See Chapter 18 for details on the Google Play Store.)

After the Google Voice app is installed, you have to work through the setup, which isn't difficult: The goal is to switch over the phone's voice mail number from the carrier's voice mail system to Google Voice. Eventually, you see the app's main interface, which looks and works similarly to an e-mail program. You can review your messages or touch a message to read or play it, as illustrated in Figure 7-1.

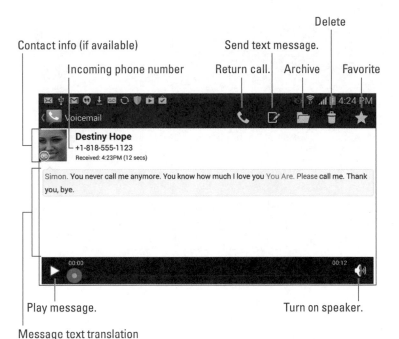

Delete

Contact info (if available)   Send text message.

Incoming phone number   Return call.   Archive   Favorite

Play message.   Turn on speaker.

Message text translation

Figure 7-1: Voice mail with the Google Voice app.

 When new Google Voice messages come in, you see the Google Voice notification icon appear, as shown in the margin. Pull down the notifications, and choose the Voicemail from *Whomever* item to read or listen to the message.

- With Google Voice installed, you see two notices for every voice mail message: one from Google Voice and another for the Gmail message.

- Not every icon shown in Figure 7-1 appears when the phone is in the vertical orientation. Those commands (Delete and Add Star) are available by pressing the Menu button.

- The Google Voice app works only after you acquire a Google Voice account and add your Galaxy Note's phone number to that account. See the earlier section "Configuring Google Voice."

- The text translation feature in Google Voice is at times astonishingly accurate and at other times not so good.

- The text *Transcript Not Available* appears whenever Google Voice is unable to create a text message from your voice mail or the Google Voice service is temporarily unavailable.

Part III
Keep in Touch

Learn how to format messages in the Email app at www.dummies.com/extras/
samsunggalaxynote3.

In this part...

- ✔ Understand how to use the address book
- ✔ Work with text messaging
- ✔ Explore Gmail and e-mail
- ✔ Discover the web on your Galaxy Note 3
- ✔ Get going with social networking
- ✔ Dig into text, voice, and video chat

The People in Your Galaxy

In This Chapter

▶ Examining your phone's contacts

▶ Sorting and searching contacts

▶ Building new contacts

▶ Getting a contact from a map search

▶ Editing contact information

▶ Putting a picture on a contact

▶ Dealing with duplicate contacts

▶ Deleting contacts

I felt embarrassed when a friend of mine (an older friend) gave me a gift. It was an address book. Actually, I believe it's called a *day planner*. Apparently, long ago, people jotted down the names and addresses of the people they knew. They'd add extra tidbits, such as birthdays. My day planner gift even had a spot for writing down an e-mail address. For that, I had to shake my head sadly.

Your Galaxy Note is more than up to the task of storing information about the people you know. It makes sense: The phone not only makes calls to your friends but can also send e-mail, navigate to their homes or offices, and perform plenty of other tricks. Day planner? Bah! You don't need one. Your phone is now your address book.

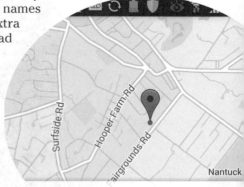

egrounds Restaurant
★★★★
views

The Digital Address Book

The Galaxy Note's address book is accessed via an app named Contacts. That app is tightly linked to the Phone app, which makes sense because you most often use the phone's address book when making a call. That's not all you can do with the Contacts app.

Accessing the address book

To peruse your phone's address book, open the Contacts app. You may find a shortcut for this app on the Home screen; otherwise, look for it on the Applications screen. You can also view your contacts by touching the Contacts tab in the Phone app.

Figure 8-1 shows the Contacts app. Try to locate the items illustrated in the figure on your Galaxy Note's screen in preparation for the quiz at the end of this chapter.

Scroll the list by swiping your finger. You can use the index on the right side of the screen (refer to Figure 8-1) to quickly scroll the list up and down or to hop to a specific letter of the alphabet.

Search contacts.

Switch to Phone app.

Contact groups   All contacts

Favorites

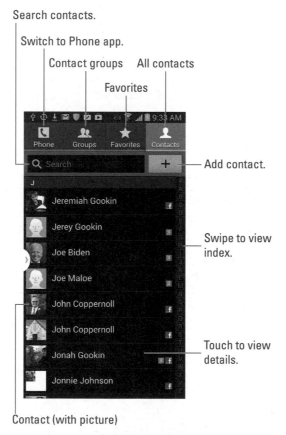

Add contact.

Swipe to view index.

Touch to view details.

Contact (with picture)

Figure 8-1: The Galaxy Note's address book.

To do anything with a contact, you first have to choose it: Touch a contact's name on the screen, and you see more information, similar to what's shown in Figure 8-2.

Return to contacts list.　　Favorite

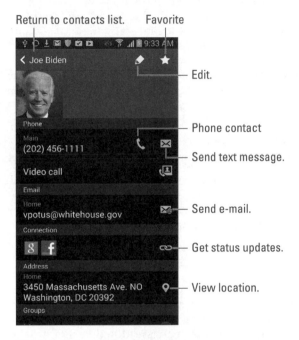

— Edit.

— Phone contact

— Send text message.

— Send e-mail.

— Get status updates.

— View location.

Figure 8-2: More detail about a contact.

The list of activities you can do with the contact depends on the information shown and the apps installed on your phone. Here are some options:

Place a phone call. To call the contact, touch one of the contact's phone entries, such as Home or Mobile. You touch the entry itself or touch the Phone icon by the entry.

Start a video call. Contact the human using both voice and video. See Chapter 13 for details on video calls.

Send a text message. Touch the Text Message icon, shown in Figure 8-2, to send the contact a text message. See Chapter 9 for information about text messaging.

Compose an e-mail message. Touch the Email link to compose an e-mail message to the contact. When the contact has more than one e-mail address, you can choose to which one you want to send the message. Chapter 10 covers using e-mail on your phone.

View social networking info. To see the latest status updates for a contact, touch the person's social networking icon (refer to Figure 8-2). See Chapter 12 for additional information on social networking.

Locate your contact on a map. When the contact has a home or business address, you can touch the little doohickey next to the address, shown in Figure 8-2, to summon the Maps app. Refer to Chapter 14 to see all the fun stuff you can do with Maps.

Oh, and if you find birthday information for a contact, you can view it as well. Singing "Happy Birthday" is something you have to do on your own.

 ✔ When you're done viewing the contact, press the Back button.

 ✔ Information about your contacts is pulled from multiple sources: your Google account, the phone's storage, and your social networking sites.

 ✔ When you see duplicated information for a contact, it's probably because the information comes from two or more of those sources. See the later section "Linking identical contacts" for information on how to combine duplicates in the phone's address book.

Searching contacts

Just suppose that you have too many friends. A game of hide-and-go-seek would take ages, especially in Laurie's house because it's so huge. Your Galaxy Note isn't quite that big, but it can pack in a lot of friends. Rather than scroll your phone's address book with angst-riddled desperation, touch the Search text box, found atop the Contacts app screen (refer to Figure 8-1).

Type a few letters of the contact's name into the Search box. As you type, you see the list of contacts narrow to the few who match the characters you typed. Touch a name from the search list to view the contact's information.

 ✔ To clear a search, touch the X button, found in the Search text box.

 ✔ No, there's no correlation between the number of contacts you have and how popular you are in real life.

Some New Friends

Everyone makes friends in their own way. Sometimes, a shy smile does the trick, but I've found that having someone hand me a crisp $100 bill is quite effective. No matter how you acquire new friends, the Contacts app is well equipped to help you add them.

Adding a contact from the call log

One of the quickest ways to build up your phone's address book is to add people as they phone you. After someone calls, visit the call log to add that person. Obey these steps:

1. **Open the Phone app.**

2. **Touch the Logs tab at the top of the screen.**

3. **Choose the phone number from the list of recent calls.**

   The phone number is shown by itself, minus any contact picture or other information.

4. **Touch the Create Contact button.**

   When the number belongs to an existing contact, touch the Update Existing button and choose the contact from the phone's address book.

5. **Choose your Google account as the location to store the new contact.**

   By choosing your Google account, you ensure that the contact's information is duplicated from your phone to your Google account on the Internet.

   If you prefer another account, such as your Yahoo! account, choose it from the list. The contact information is then coordinated with that specific account.

   The Device choice keeps the contact information only on your phone. It will not be shared with other accounts. I don't recommend choosing this option until you're familiar with using your phone.

6. **Fill in the contact's information.**

   Fill in as many blanks as you know about the caller: name and e-mail address, for example, and other information, if you know it. If you don't know any additional information, that's fine; just filling in the name helps clue you in to who is calling the next time that person calls (using the same number).

   I recommend that you add the area code prefix to the phone number, if it's not automatically added for you. We are in the age of 10-digit phone numbers.

7. **Touch the Save button to create the new contact.**

You can merge duplicate contacts when you accidentally create a new contact where one already exists. See the later section "Linking identical contacts."

You can also create new contacts from an e-mail message, similarly to the way you create contacts by using the call log: In the Email app, touch the picture icon on an incoming message, and then proceed with Steps 4 through 7 in this section. Refer to Chapter 10 for information on using your phone to read e-mail.

Creating a new contact from scratch

Sometimes, it's necessary to create a contact when you meet another human being in the real world or, perhaps, when you're stalking them and already have an abundance of info. In either case, you have a contact to create, and the process commences thusly:

1. **Open the Contacts app.**

   Ensure that the Contacts tab is selected at the top of the screen.

2. **Touch the Add New Contact button.**

   The icon looks like a plus sign, similar to the one shown in the margin.

3. **If prompted, choose an account as the place to store the contact.**

   I recommend choosing Google, although if you use Yahoo! as your main online storage repository and that option is presented as a choice, choose it instead.

4. **Fill in the information on the Create Contact screen as the contact begrudgingly gives you information.**

   Fill in the text fields with the information you know: the name, phone, e-mail address, and so on.

   To add a field, such as a second phone number, touch the green Plus icon on the touchscreen. To remove a field, touch the red Minus icon.

   Touch the gray button to the left of the phone number to specify the type of number, such as Home, Work, or Mobile. The same type of button is found to the left of the Email and Address fields.

   To fill in even more information, touch the Add Another Field button at the bottom of the list.

5. **Touch the Save button to complete the editing and add the new contact.**

You can also create new contacts by using your Gmail account on a computer. This option offers you the luxury of using a full-size keyboard and roomy computer screen.

Importing contacts from your computer

Your computer's e-mail program is doubtless a useful repository of contacts you've built up over the years. You can export these contacts from your computer's e-mail program and then import them into your Galaxy Note. It's not the simplest thing to do, but it's a quick way to build up your phone's address book.

The key is to save or export your computer e-mail program's records in the *vCard* (`.vcf`) file format. These records can then be imported into the phone and read by the Contacts app. The method for exporting contacts varies depending on the e-mail program:

- **In the Windows Live Mail program,** choose Go⇨Contacts, and then choose File⇨Export⇨Business Card (.VCF) to export the contacts.

- **In Windows Mail,** choose File⇨Export⇨Windows Contacts, and then choose vCards (Folder of .VCF Files) from the Export Windows Contacts dialog box. Click the Export button.

- **On the Mac,** open the Address Book program, and choose File⇨Export⇨Export vCard.

After the vCard files are created, connect the phone to your computer and transfer the vCard files from your computer to the phone. Directions for making this type of transfer are found in Chapter 20.

After the vCard files have been copied to the phone, you need to import them into the Contacts app. Follow these steps:

1. **While using the Contacts app, press the Menu button.**

2. **Choose Import/Export.**

3. **Choose the Import from USB Storage command.**

4. **Choose to save the contacts to your Google account.**

    Obey any additional commands that are presented, such as the option to import all the files when multiple vCard files are present.

The imported contacts show up in the contacts list. They're also synchronized to your Gmail account, which instantly creates a backup copy.

If the contacts aren't found, they might have been saved to the MicroSD card instead of the phone's internal (USB) storage. Repeat these steps, but choose Import from SD Card in Step 3.

Mixing in social networking contacts

You can pour your whole gang of friends and followers into your Galaxy Note from your social networking sites. The operation is automatic: Simply add the social networking site's app to the phone's app inventory as described in Chapter 12. At that time, either you're prompted to sync the contacts or they're added instantly to the phone's address book.

To ensure that the accounts are being synchronized, obey these steps:

1. **Start the Contacts app.**

2. **Ensure that the Contacts tab is chosen.**

   You'll find the Contacts tab at the top of the screen.

3. **Press the Menu button.**

4. **Choose Accounts.**

   You see a list of online accounts added to the phone.

5. **Choose an account.**

   For example, touch your Facebook account item.

6. **Ensure that a green check mark is found by the Sync Contacts item.**

   You can synchronize other account options as well, depending on what you see listed.

7. **Touch the Sync Now button.**

8. **Press the Back button once and repeat Steps 5 through 7 to synchronize additional social networking sites.**

See Chapter 12 for more information on social networking with your Galaxy Note.

If you've configured your Galaxy Note using the AT&T Ready2Go app (as discussed in Chapter 2), your social networking accounts have already been added to the phone.

Finding a new contact by location

When you use the Maps app to locate a restaurant or cobbler or an all-night discount liquor outlet, you can quickly create a contact for that business based on its location. Here's how:

1. **Open the Maps app.**

   It's found on the Apps menu.

2. **Search for a location.**

   You can find oodles of information on using the Maps app in Chapter 14.

3. **Touch the location's card that appears on the map.**

   The card is part of the map search results, described in Chapter 14. When you touch the card, additional information is displayed, similar to what's shown in Figure 8-3.

Business location

Pretend that you're calling.

Figure 8-3: A business has been located.

4. **Touch the Phone icon as though you were calling the place.**

   But you're not calling the place: By touching the Phone icon, you start the Phone app, where the location's phone number is displayed.

5. **Touch the Add to Contacts button.**

   The button appears whenever you are about to call a number that isn't in the phone's address book.

6. **Choose Create Contact.**

7. **Fill in information about the business.**

   You don't have to type the phone number, but do type the business name.

8. **Touch the Save button.**

   The new contact is created.

The preferred technique to save a business location in the Maps app is to flag that location as a favorite. See Chapter 14 for details.

Address Book Management

Nothing is more terrifying to cell phone owners than having to change phone numbers. They dread it more than having to move or having to change their Facebook status from In a Relationship to Single. I suppose that the dread comes from having to inform *everyone you know* of your new number and the burden that such a task places on your friends.

Well, fret not, gentle reader. Updates to your contacts happen frequently. Making changes is simple. That's because the Contacts app features ample tools to ease the burden, plus some features that make your address book management duties less of a pain.

Making basic changes

To make minor touch-ups on any contact, start by locating and displaying the contact's information. Touch the Edit icon that looms large at the top of the screen, as shown earlier, in Figure 8-2.

Change or add information by touching a field and editing or replacing the text. Add information by touching the green Plus icon next to an item.

Some information cannot be edited. For example, fields pulled in from social networking sites can be edited only by that account holder on the social networking site.

When you're done editing, touch the Save button.

Adding a contact picture

The simplest way to add a picture to a contact is to have the image already stored in the phone. You can snap a picture and save it, grab a picture from the Internet, or use any image already stored in the phone's Gallery app. The image doesn't even have to be a picture of the contact — any image will do.

After the contact's photo — or any other suitable image — is stored on the phone, follow these steps to update the contact's information:

1. **Locate and display the contact's information.**

2. **Touch the icon where the contact's picture would sit, or touch the existing picture assigned to the contact.**

   The icon shows a generic placeholder when no picture is assigned.

3. **Select how you want to create a new contact image.**

   You have four options:

   Image: Choose a photo you've already taken or one stored in the phone's Gallery.

   Pictures by People: Similar to the Image choice, this item limits the selection to tagged pictures.

   Take Picture: Use the camera right now to snap an image of the contact.

S Note: Use the S Note app to create a contact image.

If you choose the Image option, continue with Step 4. If you choose to take a picture, use the phone's camera to snap the picture. Touch the Save button, and then skip down to Step 6.

4. **Browse the Gallery to look for a suitable image.**

5. **Touch the image you want to use for the contact.**

   The next step is to crop the image so that only the portion relevant to the contact is presented.

6. **If you see the Complete Action Using prompt, choose the Crop Picture item.**

   The Crop Picture item is related to the Gallery, which is the traditional Android photo-management app.

7. **Optionally, crop the image.**

   Drag the blue rectangle to include the portion of the image you want for the contact, as shown in Figure 8-4.

8. **Touch the Done button to crop the image and assign it to the contact.**

   The image now appears whenever the contact is referenced on your phone.

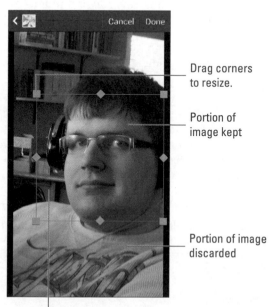

Drag corners to resize.

Portion of image kept

Portion of image discarded

Drag crop rectangle.

Figure 8-4: Cropping a contact's image.

You can add pictures to contacts on your Google account by using any computer. Just visit your Gmail Contacts list to edit a contact. You can then add to that contact any picture stored on your computer. The picture is eventually synced with the same contact on your Galaxy Note.

- ✔ Pictures can also be added by your Gmail friends and contacts when they add their own images to their accounts.

- ✔ You may also see pictures assigned to your contacts based on pictures supplied on Facebook or other social networking sites.

- ✔ Some images in the Gallery may not work for contact icons. For example, images synchronized with your online photo albums may be unavailable.

- ✔ To get rid of the contact's existing picture, edit the contact. Touch the image and choose the Remove command. You cannot remove or change images for contacts linked from social networking sites.

Making a favorite

A *favorite* contact is someone you stay in touch with most often. The person doesn't have to be someone you like — just someone you (perhaps unfortunately) phone often, such as your parole officer.

 To create a favorite, display a contact's information and touch the Star icon. When the star is highlighted, the contact is flagged as one of your favorites.

Favorite contacts appear on their own tab in the Contacts app as well as in the Phone app (refer to Figure 8-1). To quickly access a favorite, choose one from the tab.

- ✔ To remove a favorite, touch the contact's star again. Removing a favorite doesn't delete the contact.

- ✔ A contact has no idea whether he's one of your favorites, so don't believe that you're hurting his feelings by not making him a favorite.

Linking identical contacts

Your Galaxy Note can pull in contacts from multiple sources (such as Facebook, Gmail, and Twitter). Because of this, you may discover duplicate contact entries in the phone's address book. Rather than fuss over which contact to use, you can join them together. Here's how:

1. **Open the Contacts app.**

2. **Select one of the duplicate contacts.**

   For example, if you have two Peter Griffins in your phone's address book, choose one of them — doesn't matter which.

3. **Press the Menu button and choose Link Contact.**

   You see a list of contacts that the phone guesses could be identical. It also shows the entire list of contacts in case the guess is incorrect. Your job is to find the duplicate contact.

4. **Choose the duplicate contact from the list.**

   The contacts are merged, appearing as a single entry in the contacts list.

Joined contacts aren't flagged as such in the address book, but you can easily identify them by the two icons next to the contact's name. For example, back in Figure 8-1, the contact Jonah Gookin has information linked from both Google and Facebook accounts. In Figure 8-2, you see that Vice President Biden is also linked from both Google and Facebook.

Unlinking a contact

Sometimes, the phone may put together two contacts who must be torn asunder. The process is simple, at least according to these steps:

1. **Display the improperly joined contact.**

   As an example, I'm friends on Facebook with other humans named Dan Gookin. My phone mistakenly joined my address book entry with another Dan Gookin.

2. **Touch the Link icon found in the contact's Connection section.**

   The Link icon looks similar to the one shown in the margin.

   You see the list of sources and account names linked into the same contact.

3. **Touch the red Minus button to the left of an account to separate it.**

4. **Touch the OK button to confirm.**

   That contact is separated.

You don't need to actively look for improperly joined contacts as much as you'll just stumble across them. When you do, feel free to unlink them.

Removing a contact

Every so often, consider reviewing your phone's address book. Purge those folks whom you no longer recognize or remember. It's simple:

1. **Display the contact's information in the Contacts app.**

2. **Press the Menu button, and choose the Delete command.**

3. **Touch OK to remove the contact from your phone.**

Because the contacts list is synchronized with your Gmail contacts for your Google account, the contact is also removed there.

✔ You may not be able to delete contacts associated with specific accounts, such as your social networking friends. To remove those contacts, go to the source, such as Facebook or Twitter.

✔ Removing a contact doesn't kill the person in real life.

9

Message for You!

In This Chapter

▶ Composing a text message

▶ Receiving text messages

▶ Forwarding a text message

▶ Texting pictures, videos, and media items

▶ Managing your text messages

▶ Exploring text messaging alternatives

*Y*ou may view your Galaxy Note as a phone. This observation merely betrays your age. For young people, a cell phone is used primarily to send and receive text messages. Yes, *text*. The telegraph may be long dead, but the youth of today rely on short quips of text far more than they rely on voice communications. My own kids talk on their cell phones for maybe 15 minutes a month and send thousands of text messages. Read this chapter and you can join their ranks.

Life in Less Than 160 Characters

I can think of several reasons to use your Galaxy Note's texting abilities. First, texting is short and quick. Second, unlike a phone call, texting is quiet. Third, it's probably the only way you'll get your children or grandchildren to communicate with you.

On the Galaxy Note, the texting adventure takes place in the Messages app. You'll find it on the phone's Home screen, typically assigned to the Favorites tray.

⮕ Don't text while you're driving or while you're in a movie theater or in any other situation where it's dangerous and inappropriate to be paying more attention to your phone than to your surroundings.

✔ Your cellular service plan may charge you per message for every text message you send. Some plans feature a given number of free (included) messages per month. Other plans, favored by teenagers (and their parents), feature unlimited texting.

✔ The process of sending and receiving text messages is commonly called *texting*.

✔ The nerdy term for text messaging is *SMS*, which stands for Short Message Service.

Composing a text message

Text messages are sent primarily to other cell phones. As long as you have a mobile number to send to, or a contact with a mobile phone, you can fire away the text message.

To send a text message, open the Messages app. If the app opens to a specific conversation, press the Back button to return to the main Messages screen. The main screen lists all your text message conversations; touch a conversation to peruse any earlier dialogues.

Sending a new message works differently, depending on whether you want to continue a conversation or start up a new conversation.

To continue a conversation, choose that contact or phone number from the Messages app main screen. Type a new missive in the Enter Message text box. Touch the Send icon (shown in the margin) to whisk off the message. Then wait on tenterhooks until the other party replies.

To begin a new message to a contact or phone number, follow these steps:

1. **Touch the New Message icon on the Messages app main screen.**

   The New Message icon is shown in the margin.

2. **Type the phone number or a contact's name into the Enter Recipient text box.**

   As you type the number, any matching contacts appear in a list; choose a contact to save yourself some typing time.

3. **If you're composing a gang text, type additional numbers or contact names.**

   Normally, you text only one person at a time. When you specify multiple contacts, you create a *gang text*.

4. **Type the message in the Enter Message field.**

   Touch the field to select it. The onscreen keyboard appears. Type your message, but be brief: A text message has a 160-character limit. You can check the character count indicator on the screen to see whether you're nearing the limit, as shown in Figure 9-1.

What you say

Delete conversation.

Contact info   Phone contact

What they say

Attachment

Type message here.

Figure 9-1: Typing a text message.

5. **Touch the Send icon.**

   The message is sent instantly. That speed is no guarantee that the other party replies instantly, if at all. Even the quickest reply I've seen takes several seconds to appear.

6. **Read the reply.**

7. **Repeat Steps 4 through 6 as needed — or eternally, whichever comes first.**

There's no need to continually look at your phone while waiting for a text message. Whenever your contact chooses to reply, you see the message recorded as part of an ongoing conversation. See the next section.

You can also send a text message from the Contacts app: Display information about a contact and touch the Text Messaging icon next to the contact's phone number, as shown in the margin. After you touch that icon, the

Common text message abbreviations

Texting isn't about proper English. Indeed, many of the abbreviations and shortcuts used in texting are slowly becoming part of the English language, such as LOL and BRB.

The weird news is that these acronyms weren't invented by teenagers. Sure, the kids use them, but the acronyms find their roots in the Internet chat rooms of yesteryear. Regardless of a shortcut's source, you might find it handy for typing messages quickly. Or, maybe you can use this reference for deciphering an acronym's meaning. You can type acronyms in either upper- or lowercase letters.

2	To, also
411	Information
BRB	Be right back
BTW	By the way
CYA	See you
FWIW	For what it's worth
FYI	For your information
GB	Goodbye
GJ	Good job
GR8	Great
GTG	Got to go
HOAS	Hold on a second
IC	I see
IDK	I don't know
IMO	In my opinion
JK	Just kidding

K	Okay
L8R	Later
LMAO	Laughing my a** off
LMK	Let me know
LOL	Laugh out loud
NC	No comment
NP	No problem
NRN	No reply needed (necessary)
OMG	Oh my goodness!
PIR	People in room (watching)
POS	Person over shoulder (watching)
QT	Cutie
ROFL	Rolling on the floor, laughing
SOS	Someone over shoulder (watching)
TC	Take care
THX	Thanks
TIA	Thanks in advance
TMI	Too much information
TTFN	Ta-ta for now (goodbye)
TTYL	Talk to you later
TY	Thank you
U2	You too
UR	You're, you are
VM	Voice mail
W8	Wait
XOXO	Hugs and kisses
Y	Why?
YW	You're welcome
ZZZ	Sleeping

Messages app starts and you can compose the message. (Refer to Chapter 24 for information on how to handle the Complete Action Using prompt, should you see one.)

✔ Quickly compose a text message to a contact by swiping that person's entry to the left in the Contacts app.

✔ If you've sent the message to a phone number instead of to a contact, consider adding that number to the phone's address book. One way to do that is to long-press the number and choose the command to create a new contact. See Chapter 8 for information on creating new contacts.

✓ You can send text messages only to cell phones. Aunt Jane cannot receive text messages on her landline that she's had since the 1960s.

✓ A *tenterhook* is a type of hook used to stretch woolen fabric for drying purposes. The phrase *on tenterhooks* refers to the fabric's tension and is a metaphor for anxiety or suspense.

✓ Do not text and drive. Do not text and drive. Do not text and drive.

Receiving a text message

Whenever a new text message arrives, you see the message appear briefly at the top of the phone's touchscreen. Then you see the Messages / New Message notification, similar to the one shown in the margin.

To view the message, pull down the notifications panel, as described in Chapter 3. Touch the messaging notification, and that conversation window immediately opens.

Forwarding a text message

Forwarding a text message isn't the same as forwarding e-mail. In fact, for forwarding information, e-mail has text messaging beaten by well over 160 characters. (Refer to the nearby sidebar, "Whether to send a text message or an e-mail.")

Though you can forward a text message, you cannot forward an entire conversation. Only one text bubble can be forwarded at a time. Here's how it works:

1. **If necessary, open a conversation in the Messages app.**

2. **Long-press the text entry (the cartoon bubble) that you want to forward.**

3. **From the menu that appears, choose the Forward command.**

   From this point on, forwarding the message works the same way as sending a new message from scratch.

4. **Type the recipient's name (if the person is a contact) or phone number.**

   The text you're forwarding appears, already written, in the Enter Message text field.

5. **Touch the Send icon to forward the message.**

You can choose the Copy command in Step 3 to copy the text in the bubble and then paste it elsewhere on the Galaxy Note. See Chapter 4 for details on copying and pasting text.

Whether to send a text message or an e-mail

Sending a text message is similar to sending an e-mail message. Both involve the instant electronic delivery of information to someone else. Both methods of communication have their advantages and disadvantages.

The primary limitation of a text message is that it can be sent only to another cell phone. E-mail is available to anyone who has an e-mail address.

Text messages are pithy; short and to the point. They're informal, more like quick chats. Indeed, the speed of reply is often what makes text messaging useful. Like sending e-mail, however, sending a text message doesn't guarantee a reply.

An e-mail message can be longer than a text message. You can receive e-mail on just about any Internet-connected device. E-mail message attachments (pictures, documents) are handled better, and more consistently, than text message (MMS) media.

Finally, e-mail is considered a wee bit more formal than a text message. Still, if you're after formal, make a phone call or, better, send a letter.

Multimedia Messages

Even though the term *texting* sticks around, a text message can contain media, usually a photo, although short videos and audio can also be attached to a text message. Such a message ceases to be a mere *text* message. No, it becomes a *multimedia* message.

- ✔ Multimedia messages are handled by the Messages app, the same app you use for text messaging on your Galaxy Note.

- ✔ Not every mobile phone can receive multimedia messages. Rather than receive the media item, the recipient may be directed to a web page where the item can be viewed on the Internet.

- ✔ The official name for a multimedia text message is Multimedia Messaging Service, which is abbreviated MMS.

Attaching media to a text message

To show total disregard for its nickname, text messaging lets you send pictures, videos, music, or other types of media with the message. Doing so creates a *multimedia* message. The good news is that attaching media is simple. The better news is that you can use the same Text Messaging app to accomplish this task.

The trick works like this:

1. **Compose a message as you normally do.**

2. **Touch the Attach icon.**

   The icon is shown in the margin. It's located just to the right of the Enter Message text box (refer to Figure 9-1).

3. **Choose an app from the Attach menu.**

   A menu appears, listing apps capable of generating multimedia or other attachments. The variety depends on the apps installed on your phone.

4. **If the Complete Action Using menu appears, choose a specific app to complete the task.**

   Refer to Chapter 24 for information on the Always/Just Once choice. For now, choose Just Once.

5. **Use the app you choose to create or select the media content.**

   For example, choose the Image item to send a photo or video from the Gallery. Choose Take a Picture to use the Camera app to snap a quick photo.

6. **Edit the media or work the onscreen controls to complete the process.**

   You may have to choose which item to send. You may also be informed that the picture or video is too large. If so, obey the directions on the screen to make the attachment more suitable for a multimedia text message.

7. **Touch the Send icon.**

   In just a few short, cellular moments, the receiving party will enjoy your multimedia text message and attachment.

Another way to send a multimedia message is to start at the source, such as the app that creates media, like the Camera app. Use the Share icon in that app to choose the Messages app for sharing (attaching) the media to a message.

   ✔ Multimedia text messages handle attachments of a limited size. If something won't attach, it's too big.

   ✔ See Chapter 15 for information on using the Galaxy Note's camera. When taking pictures or shooting video, refer to that chapter for information on properly setting the image or video size for attachment as a multimedia text message.

Saving media from a text message

Any media you receive in a text message appears in a cartoon bubble. To save the media, such as a photograph, follow these steps:

1. **Long-press the media cartoon bubble in the text message conversation.**

2. **Choose Save Attachment.**

3. **Place a check mark by the media item you want to save.**

   The items are listed by filename, which can be confusing, especially when a single message contains multiple media items.

4. **Touch the Save button.**

   The media is saved to the phone's internal storage or to the MicroSD card (if one is installed).

To view or hear the media, you must summon the appropriate app on your phone. The Gallery app is used to view visual media; use either the Music app or Play Music app to listen to audio.

See Chapter 15 for details on using the Gallery app. Text message attachments are found in the Download album.

Text Message Management

You don't have to manage your messages. I certainly don't. Your Galaxy Note does give you the potential for message management. For example, if you want to destroy evidence of a naughty conversation, or even do something as mild as change the text messaging ringtone, it's possible.

Removing messages

Though I'm a stickler for deleting e-mail after I read it, I don't bother deleting my text message threads. That's probably because I have no pending divorce litigation. Well, even then, I have nothing to hide in my text messaging conversations. If I did, I would follow these steps to delete a conversation:

1. **Open the conversation you want to remove.**

   Choose the conversation from the main screen in your phone's text messaging app.

2. **Touch the Delete icon.**

   The icon is shown in the margin, and also in Figure 9-1.

3. **Touch the OK button to confirm.**

   The conversation is gone.

If these steps don't work, an alternative is to open the Messages app main screen and long-press the conversation you want to zap. Choose the Delete command from the pop-up menu, and then touch the OK button to confirm.

Setting the text message ringtone

There's no reason that your Galaxy Note should sound the same boring notification ringtone for everything, especially when a new text message arrives. Spice things up a bit by following these steps:

1. **Open the Messages app.**
2. **Ensure that you're viewing the main screen, which lists all your conversations.**

   If you're not viewing that screen, press the Back button.
3. **Press the Menu button.**
4. **Choose the Settings command.**
5. **Tap the More tab and choose the Select Ringtone command.**
6. **If prompted, choose an app to select the ringtone.**

   The Media Storage app uses the phone's standard list of ringtones.

   See Chapter 24 for information on dealing with the Always/Just Once decision.
7. **Pluck a ringtone from the list.**
8. **Touch the OK button.**

 While you're viewing the Settings screen (refer to Steps 1 through 4 in the step list), add or remove the green check mark by the Vibrate option, depending on whether you like the phone vibrating on an incoming text message.

Text Messaging Alternatives

Life doesn't turn totally dismal when you find yourself unduly bound by text message limitations on your cell phone contract. Just because you can send and receive only 250 messages a month doesn't mean that you and your friends must stay horribly out of touch or that your thumbs will atrophy from a lack of typing. A smattering of free alternatives to text messaging are available:

Google Hangouts: The most popular choice is to use Google Hangouts. It has the ability to send text messages to cell phones. It's also the preferred text messaging app on many Android phones. Beyond that, it's a good texting program alternative; plus, it has video chat features.

Opt out of text messaging

You don't have to be a part of the text messaging craze. Indeed, it's entirely possible to opt out of text messaging altogether: Simply contact your cellular provider and have them disable text messaging on your phone. You might even be able to opt out by using your account on the cellular provider's website. After making the setting, you'll never again be able to send or receive a text message.

People opt out of text messaging for a number of reasons. A big one is cost, if the kids keep running up the text messaging bill. Disabling the text messaging feature is often easier than continuing to pay all the usage surcharges. Another reason is security: Although cell phone viruses are rare, the scammers love sending malicious text messages. If you opt out, you don't have to worry about any SMS security risks.

Skype: Beyond making cheap international phone calls, you can text-chat by using the Skype app. Just set up a connection with your friends on Skype and you can type until your fingers wear into nubs; text chatting on Skype is free.

Carrier chat: Some cellular providers offer their own texting apps, such as AT&T Messages on the AT&T network. These apps work, but they don't avoid the surcharges you may encounter when you have text messaging limits. The apps are merely the carrier's own alternative to the Galaxy Note's Messages app.

About the only limitation to using alternative apps like Google Hangouts and Skype is that you can chat only with friends who have accounts on those services. Google Hangouts isn't as limiting, because anyone who has a Google (or Gmail) account also has a Google Hangouts account. You can even connect with Google users on a computer for chatting.

See Chapter 13 for more information on Google Hangouts and Skype.

Galactic E-Mail

In This Chapter

▶ Configuring e-mail accounts

▶ Receiving a new message

▶ Creating and sending e-mail

▶ Working with e-mail attachments

▶ Making an e-mail signature

▶ Choosing the default e-mail account

▶ Changing the server delete option

I'm certain the first letter ever sent was met with great anticipation and excitement. Those ancient people not only knew that they were making history but also wanted to know what the letter said. Therefore, it's my guess that the first thing they did when the letter arrived was shout, "Quick! Find someone who knows how to read!"

You probably know how to read. What you may not know is how to handle the basic e-mail chore on your phone. I'll admit that e-mail isn't as popular as it once was. Text messaging is the primary method of textual communications on a cell phone. That doesn't diminish your basic e-mail duties, all of which can be handled adeptly by the Galaxy Note.

E-Mail on the Galaxy Note

Just to keep things interesting, e-mail is handled by two separate apps on your phone: Gmail and Email. You might also use an AOL or Yahoo! e-mail app, but the two stock Android apps are Gmail and Email.

The Gmail app hooks directly into your Google Gmail account. It's a copy of all the Gmail you send, receive, and archive, just as you can access on the Internet by using a web browser.

The Email app is used to connect to non-Gmail electronic mail, such as the standard mail service provided by your Internet service provider (ISP), a web-based e-mail system such as Microsoft Live mail, or your large organization's corporate e-mail.

Regardless of the app, electronic mail on your phone works just like it does on a computer: You can receive mail, create new messages, forward mail, send messages to a group of contacts, work with attachments, and more. As long as your phone has a data connection, e-mail works just peachy.

✔ Peruse the Google Play Store for e-mail apps specific to your favorite online e-mail repository, such as an AOL or Yahoo! e-mail app. Your cellular provider may have preinstalled such apps for you. If not, see Chapter 18 for information about obtaining new and wonderful apps for your Galaxy Note.

✔ The Gmail app is updated frequently. To review any changes since this book went to press, visit my website at

        www.wambooli.com/help/android/gmail

✔ The Email app can be configured to handle multiple e-mail accounts, as discussed later in this section.

✔ Although you can use your phone's web browser to visit the Gmail website, you should use the Gmail app to pick up your Gmail.

✔ If you forget your Gmail password, visit this web address:

        www.google.com/accounts/ForgotPasswd

Setting up an e-mail account

The Email app is used to access web-based e-mail, or *webmail,* such as Yahoo!, Windows Live, and others. It also lets you read e-mail provided by an Internet service provider (ISP), an office, or another large, intimidating organization. To get things set up regardless of the service, follow these steps:

1. **Start the Email app.**

   Look for it on the Applications screen, along with all other apps on your phone.

   If you haven't yet run the Email app, the first screen you see helps configure your e-mail account. Continue with Step 2. Otherwise, you're taken to the Email inbox.

   See the next section for information on adding additional e-mail accounts.

2. **Type the e-mail address you use for the account.**

That .com key on the onscreen keyboard helps you quickly type an e-mail address, although if the address ends in .net or .org, you'll have to type it the old-fashioned way.

3. **Type the account's password.**

4. **Touch the Next button on the screen.**

If you're lucky, everything is connected smoothly and you see the Account Options screen. Move on to Step 5.

If you're unlucky, you have to specify the details, which include the incoming and outgoing server information, often known by the bewildering acronyms POP3 and SMTP. Plod through the fields shown on the screen, filling in the information as provided by your ISP, although you primarily need to specify only the incoming and outgoing server names.

5. **Set the account options.**

Use the Sync Schedule to tell the phone how frequently you want your e-mail checked. I chose 15 minutes, which helps keep me on top of my e-mail. The Peak Schedule item lets you increase the frequency for certain times of the day.

Ensure that you place a check mark by the Sync Email option. That way, your e-mail account is synchronized between the phone and the e-mail server. If you forget this option, e-mail may not show up on the phone. (Check other Sync items, if presented, to keep your phone and the online service up-to-date.)

Also place a check mark by the option Notify Me When Email Arrives so that the phone generates a notification whenever you receive new messages.

6. **Touch the Next button.**

7. **Give the account a name and confirm your own name.**

The account is given your e-mail address as a name. If you want to change the name, type something new into that field. For example, I name my ISP's e-mail account *Main* because it's my main account. For my Yahoo! mail account, I typed *Yahoo* as the name.

The Your Name field lists your name as it's applied to outgoing messages. So if your name is really Edith Arachnidoa and not ea1450, you can make that change now.

8. **Touch the Done button.**

You're done.

The next thing you see is your e-mail account inbox. The phone proceeds to synchronize any pending e-mail you have in your account, updating the screen as you watch. See the section "You've Got Mail" to see what to do next.

Adding more e-mail accounts

The Email app can be configured to collect mail from multiple sources. You can add a Yahoo! Mail account, a Windows Live account, your corporate e-mail account, or what-have-you. Follow through with these steps:

1. **Open the Email app.**

2. **Press the Menu button and choose the Settings command.**

   If you don't see the Settings command, you probably aren't at the top level of the Email app: Touch the app icon in the upper left corner of the screen until you see the Email app's main screen.

3. **Touch the Add Account button atop the screen.**

   The Set Up Email screen appears.

4. **Type your e-mail address and password into the appropriate text fields.**

5. **Leave unchecked the item Send Email from This Account by Default.**

   The Galaxy Note uses only one of your e-mail accounts for sending e-mail. To set that account, see the later section "Setting the default e-mail account."

6. **Touch the Next button.**

   At this point, the process proceeds as described in the preceding section, starting just after Step 4.

Repeat these steps to add additional e-mail accounts. E-mail from the accounts you configure is accessed by using the Email app.

  ✔ New e-mail accounts can also be added from within the Settings app: Chose the Accounts item found under the General tab. Touch the Add Account item and choose Email from the menu.

  ✔ The Accounts item in the Settings app lists all your current Email accounts, as well as social networking and other accounts you've set up on your phone. You can use that screen to peruse and modify the accounts, should anything change.

Setting up a corporate account

The most difficult, yet most useful, type of e-mail account you can add to the Galaxy Note is your organization's corporate account. Specifically, you're adding a Microsoft Exchange Active Sync account. This process can be quite easy, such as when adding a Microsoft Live account, or even easier if you follow my basic advice: Have your corporate IT people do it.

I'm serious. If the folks in IT don't want to do it, they may provide you with a handy Android "cheat sheet" on how to configure the account. The cheat sheet should contain the necessary cryptic information and codes necessary to configure the account on your Galaxy Note. Keep in mind that these extra steps aren't created to annoy you: Corporate e-mail must be more secure than other e-mail, which is why you must endure the superfluous gyrations to get things configured.

You've Got Mail

Your Galaxy Note, like all Android phones, works flawlessly with Gmail. In fact, if Gmail is already set up to be your main e-mail address, you'll enjoy having access to your messages all the time from your phone.

Non-Gmail e-mail, handled by the Email program, must be set up before it can be used, as covered earlier in this chapter. After completing the quick and occasionally painless setup, you can receive e-mail on your phone just as you can on a computer.

Getting a new message

You're alerted to the arrival of a new e-mail message in your phone by a notification icon. The icon differs depending on the e-mail's source.

For a new Gmail message, you see the New Gmail notification, similar to the one shown in the margin, appear at the top of the touchscreen.

For a new e-mail message, you see the New Email notification.

Specific e-mail apps may sport their own icons, such as the Yahoo! Mail icon. Look for that as well, as long as you've added a Yahoo! Mail or similar account.

To review pending e-mail, swipe down the notifications panel. You see either a single notification representing the most recent message or the total number of pending messages listing the various senders and subjects. Touch the notification to visit either the Gmail app or Email app to read the message.

Checking the inbox

To peruse your Gmail, start the Gmail app. You might find its icon on the Home screen. On the Applications screen, you may find its icon nestled in the Google folder. A typical Gmail inbox is shown in Figure 10-1.

Figure 10-1: The Gmail inbox.

To check your Email inbox, open the Email app. You see a single account's inbox, or you can choose to view the universal inbox, shown as Combined view in Figure 10-2.

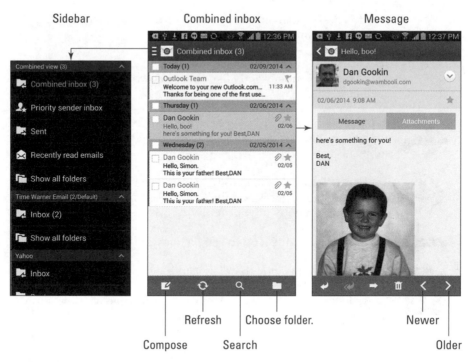

Figure 10-2: Messages in the Email app.

Don't bother looking for your Gmail inbox in the Combined View window (refer to Figure 10-2). Gmail is its own app; your Gmail messages don't show up in the universal inbox.

- Search your Gmail messages by touching the Search icon (refer to Figure 10-1).

- Gmail is organized using *labels*, not folders. To see your Gmail labels, view the sidebar by touching the app icon, as shown in Figure 10-1.

- Multiple e-mail accounts gathered in the Email app are color coded. When you view the combined inbox, you see the color codes to the left of each message. The color is shown by each account in the navigation drawer, which you can see near the bottom of the sidebar in Figure 10-2.

- To view an individual account's inbox, choose the account from the sidebar.

Reading e-mail

As mail comes in, you can read it by choosing a new e-mail notification, as described earlier in this chapter. Reading and working with the message operate much the same whether you're using the Gmail app or Email app.

Touch a message in either the Gmail or Email app to read it. Swipe the message up or down by using your finger.

To work with the message, use the icons that appear onscreen. These icons, which may not look exactly like those shown in the margin, cover common e-mail actions:

Reply: Touch this icon to reply to a message. A new message window appears with the To and Subject fields reflecting the original sender(s) and subject.

Reply All: Touch this icon to respond to everyone who received the original message, including folks on the Cc line. Use this option only when everyone else must get a copy of your reply.

Forward: Touch this icon to send a copy of the message to someone else.

Delete: Touch this icon to delete a message.

These icons appear at the bottom of the message window in the Email app, as shown earlier, in Figure 10-2 (on the far right).

You may not see the Reply All and Forward icons in the Gmail app when the phone is in the vertical orientation. Rotate the phone to see the icons, or touch the Action Overflow icon, shown in the margin, to find the Reply All and Forward commands.

- ✔ Browse messages by swiping the screen left or right. The left and right chevrons in the Email app (shown at the bottom right in Figure 10-2) can be used to peruse newer and older messages.

- ✔ Favorite messages, identified by the icon in the margin, can be viewed or searched separately, making them easier to locate later.

- ✔ If you've properly configured the Email program, you don't need to delete messages you've read. See the section "Configuring the server delete option," later in this chapter.

- ✔ I find it easier to delete (and manage) Gmail using a computer.

Make Your Own E-Mail

Though I use my phone often to check e-mail, I don't often use it to compose new messages. That's because most e-mail messages don't demand an immediate reply. When they do, or when the mood hits me and I feel the thirst that only an immediate e-mail message can quench, I compose a new e-mail message on my Galaxy Note using the methods presented in this section.

Writing a new electronic message

Creating a new e-mail epistle works similarly with both the Gmail and Email apps. The key is to touch the Compose icon: The Compose icon for Gmail is shown in the margin; refer to Figure 10-2 for the location of the Compose icon in the Email app.

The e-mail composition screen is similar in both the Gmail and Email apps, as illustrated in Figure 10-3. The procedure works the same: Fill in the To, Subject, and message content fields. As you type in the To field, matching contacts from the phone's address book appear. Choose one from the list that appears. As with any e-mail message, you can send to multiple recipients.

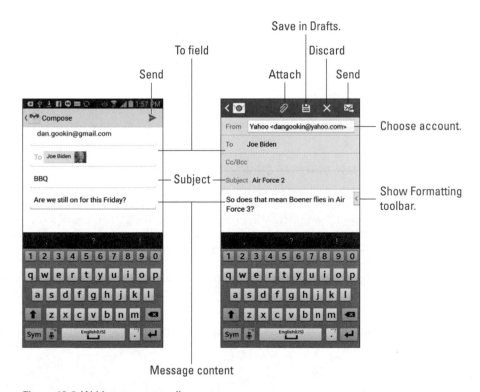

Figure 10-3: Writing a new e-mail message.

Add the CC and BCC fields by pressing the Menu button and choosing the Add Cc/Bcc command.

When you have more than one e-mail account configured for the Email app, you can select which e-mail address to use for sending the message. Touch the From field, shown in Figure 10-3, to choose an account. The account being used appears on the screen, such as Yahoo! (shown in the figure).

To send the message, touch the Send icon, as illustrated for both the Gmail and Email apps in Figure 10-3.

- To save a message without sending, press the Menu button in the Gmail app and choose the Save Draft command. In the Email app, touch the Save in Drafts icon, illustrated earlier, in Figure 10-3.

- Unsent or saved messages can be resurrected by choosing the Drafts folder from the sidebar. (Touch the app icon in the upper left corner of the screen to view the sidebar, shown in Figures 10-1 and 10-2.) Open the message to continue editing; touch the Send icon to whisk it off to the recipient(s).

- To cancel a message in the Gmail app, press the Menu button and choose the Discard command. In the Email app, touch the Discard icon (refer to Figure 10-3). Touch the Discard button to confirm.

- Copies of the messages you send in the Email app are stored in the Sent mailbox. In Gmail, sent messages are saved in your Gmail account.

- You can use the Formatting toolbar in the Email app to change the way the text looks in your message.

Sending e-mail to a contact

A quick and easy way to compose a new message is to open your Galaxy Note's Contacts app. Locate the human to whom you want to send an e-mail, displaying their information on the screen. Touch the Email icon next to their e-mail address, similar to the one shown in the margin. Choose either the Email or Gmail app, and then compose the message.

- If you use Gmail most of the time, choose the Gmail app icon and then touch Always. That way, you won't be bothered by the Complete Action Using prompt while sending e-mail.

- Refer to Chapter 24 for information on dealing with the Complete Action Using prompt.

Message Attachments

The key to understanding e-mail attachments on your Galaxy Note is to look for the paperclip icon. After you find that icon, you can either deal with an attachment for incoming e-mail or add an attachment to outgoing e-mail.

✔ In the Gmail app, image attachments appear in the message. To save an attachment, tap the image (at the bottom of the message) to view it full screen. Choose the Save command.

✔ In the Email app, attachments are highlighted at the top of the message. Touch the Attachments button to view the attachment(s) in a list. Touch the Preview button to behold the attachment, or touch the Save button to save it.

✔ Image attachments saved from your e-mail can be found by opening the Gallery app. Look for your saved attachments in the Download album.

✔ Your Galaxy Note can't open every type of attachment. When you receive an attachment that cannot be opened, reply to the message by asking for another copy of the attachment, but in a common file format.

✔ Common image-file formats include PNG and JPEG for pictures. Common document formats are PDF, DOCX, HTML, and RTF.

✔ Non-images attachments can be viewed by using the Downloads app. See Chapter 11.

✔ The easiest way to send an attachment from your phone is to open the app that created (or that lists) the item you want to send. Touch the Share icon and choose either the Email or Gmail app to compose a new message with the item selected as an attachment.

✔ The Email app features a paperclip icon used to add attachments, which is the traditional method used on computer e-mail programs. Touch that icon, and then choose an app to attach something created by, or stored in, that app.

✔ To add an attachment to a Gmail message, press the Menu button and choose the Attach command. Choose an app, and then use the app to create or select something to attach.

✔ It's possible to attach multiple items to a single e-mail message. Just keep touching the Attachment icon for the message to add additional goodies.

✔ The variety of items you can attach depends on which apps are installed on the phone.

E-Mail Configuration

After the initial setup, you have little left to configure or fine-tune when it comes to collecting and sending e-mail on your Galaxy Note. Those items worthy of your attention are presented for consideration in this section.

Creating a signature

I highly recommend that you create a custom e-mail signature for sending messages from your Galaxy Note. Here's my signature:

```
DAN

This was sent from my Galaxy Note 3.
Typos, no matter how hilarious, are unintentional.
```

To create an e-mail signature in Gmail, obey these directions:

1. **At the Gmail app's main screen, press the Menu button.**

2. **Choose the Settings account.**

3. **Choose your Gmail account from the list.**

    Touch your e-mail address as it's shown on the touchscreen.

4. **Choose Signature.**

5. **Type, scribble, or dictate your signature.**

6. **Touch OK.**

You can obey these same steps to change your signature; the existing signature shows up after Step 4.

To set a signature for the Email app, heed these steps:

1. **At the Email app's main screen, press the Menu button.**

2. **Choose the Settings command.**

3. **Choose the Account Settings item.**

4. **Select a specific account from the list.**

    You create a separate signature for each e-mail account.

5. **Choose Signature.**

6. **Create a new signature or edit the existing signature.**

    Feel free to change your signature from the one preset by Samsung or your cellular provider.

7. **Touch the Done button.**

When you have multiple accounts in the Email app, repeat these steps to configure a signature for each one.

Setting the default e-mail account

The Email app selects one of your e-mail accounts to use as the primary sending account. So, no matter which account you use to compose e-mail, that single "default" account is the one from which e-mail is sent. To change or review that setting, follow these steps:

1. **At the Email app's main screen, press the Menu button.**

2. **Choose Settings.**

3. **Choose Account Settings.**

   You see all your e-mail accounts in a list. The default account, which is used for sending messages, shows a blue check mark. If you're okay with that choice, you're done! Otherwise, continue with Step 4.

4. **Choose the account that you want to make the default.**

5. **On the next screen, place a check mark by the Default Account item.**

For some reason, my phone had trouble sending e-mail from some of my accounts. It took a while to get the setting correct, but eventually I chose the most reliable account as the default.

Configuring the server delete option

Non-Gmail e-mail that you fetch on your phone typically remains on the e-mail server. That's because, unlike a computer's e-mail program, the phone's Email app doesn't delete messages after it picks them up. The advantage is that you can retrieve the same messages later by using a computer. The disadvantage is that you can end up retrieving mail you've already read and replied to.

You can control whether the Email app removes messages after they're picked up. Follow these steps:

1. **Open the Email app and display the main screen, such as the combined inbox.**

2. **Press the Menu button and choose the Settings command.**

3. **Choose Account Settings.**

   All the phone's e-mail accounts are listed.

4. **Choose an e-mail account.**

5. **Touch the More Settings button.**

6. **Choose the Incoming Settings item.**

   If you can't find an Incoming Settings command, you're dealing with a web-based e-mail account, in which case there's no need to worry about the Server Delete option.

7. **Beneath the item Delete Email from Server, choose the option When I Delete from Inbox.**

   The only other option besides When I Delete from Inbox is Never. If you see the Never option, choose the other one.

8. **Touch the Done button.**

After you make or confirm this setting, messages you delete in the Email app are also deleted from the mail server. That means the message won't be picked up again, not by the phone, another mobile device, nor any computer that fetches e-mail from that same account.

- Mail you retrieve using a computer's mail program is deleted from the mail server after it's picked up. That's normal behavior. Your phone cannot pick up mail from the server if a computer has already deleted it.

- Deleting mail on the server isn't a problem for Gmail. No matter how you access your Gmail account, from your phone or from a computer, the inbox lists the same messages.

It's a World Wide Web We Weave

In This Chapter

▶ Looking at a web page on your phone

▶ Browsing around the web

▶ Bookmarking pages

▶ Working with multiple browser windows

▶ Finding stuff on the web

▶ Sharing a link

▶ Saving images and links

▶ Changing the home page

I can be honest: The web was not designed to be viewed on a cell phone. Even when using the Galaxy Note, with its lovely and large screen, the web experience is limiting. It's like viewing the Grand Canyon through a knothole in a fence: The visual experience isn't quite as fulfilling as intended.

You probably know the web well. Browsing the web on your Galaxy Note works similarly to how it works on a computer. This chapter highlights the basics of the web on your phone and describes useful ways to make the visual experience more rewarding — like having a chain link fence around the nudist colony.

✔ The Galaxy Note has apps for Gmail, social networking (Facebook, Twitter, and others), YouTube, and potentially other popular locations or activities on the web. I highly recommend using these applications on the phone over visiting their websites using the phone's Internet app.

✔ If possible, activate the phone's Wi-Fi connection before you venture out on the web. See Chapter 19 for more information on Wi-Fi.

Web Web Web

The web adventure begins with the named Internet app, found on the Favorites tray on the Home screen.

When you first open the Internet app, you're taken to the home page. Figure 11-1 shows the Yahoo! website. The home page you see may be different, and you're free to change it to something else at your whim; see the later section "Setting a home page."

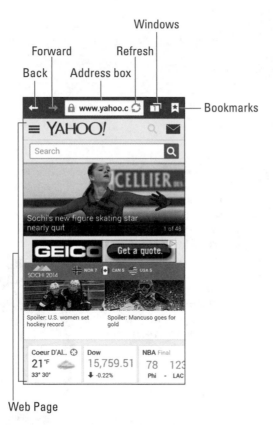

Figure 11-1: The Internet app beholds the Yahoo! home page.

Because your cell phone screen isn't a full desktop screen, not every web page looks good on it. Here are a few tricks you can use:

🖊 Pan the web page by dragging your finger across the touchscreen. You can pan up, down, left, and right.

- ✏ Many websites are smart enough to display mobile versions of their pages. Text is automatically formatted for the phone's screen. Although:

- ✏ If you'd rather see the same version of a web page that you'd view on a computer, press the Menu button and choose the Desktop View command.

- ✏ Pinch the screen to zoom out, or spread two fingers to zoom in. (Not every web page can be resized by zooming in or out.)

- ✏ Tilt the phone to its side to read a web page in Landscape mode. Then you can spread your fingers or double-tap on the touchscreen to make teensy text more readable.

- ✏ In addition to the Internet app, your Galaxy Note comes with the Google Chrome app. It's found in the Google folder on the Applications screen. Both Chrome and the Internet app feature similar commands. If you use Chrome on a desktop, I recommend using Chrome on your Galaxy Note as well.

- ✏ Here's a secret: The Internet app is based on the Chrome app. They both feature the same commands and features, but the Internet app has a different look to it, plus certain customizations made by Samsung. Still, if you want to use the Chrome app, use it instead of the Internet app.

Visiting a web page

To visit a web page, type its address in the Address box (refer to Figure 11-1).

You can also type a search word, if you don't know the page's exact address. Touch the Go key on the onscreen keyboard to search the web or visit a specific web page.

If you don't see the Address box, swipe your finger so that you can see the top of the screen, where the Address box lurks.

You click links on a page by using your finger on the touchscreen: Touch a link to "click" it and visit another page on the web.

- ✏ To reload a web page, touch the Refresh icon found in the Address box. Refreshing updates a website that changes often, and the command can also be used to reload a web page that may not have loaded completely the first time.

- ✏ To stop a web page from loading, touch the Stop (X) button that replaces the Refresh icon in the Address box.

- ✏ You can use the S Pen to click links on a web page. You may find doing so to be far more accurate than trying to stab at links using your plump fingers.

Browsing back and forth

The basic navigation tools you need for browsing the web are found atop the Internet app's window, shown in Figure 11-1.

 To return to a previous web page, touch the Back icon next to the Address bar or press the Back button below the touchscreen.

To go forward, or to return to the page you were on before you used the Back button, touch the Forward icon next to the Address bar.

To review the long-term history of your web browsing adventures, touch the Bookmarks icon. On the Bookmarks screen, touch the History tab. Previous places you've visited are organized chronologically. To view a page you visited weeks or months ago, choose it from the History list.

 To clear the History list, press the Menu button while viewing the list, and choose the Clear History command.

Working with bookmarks

Bookmarks are the electronic breadcrumbs you drop as you wander the web. Need to revisit a website? Look up its bookmark. This advice assumes, of course, that you bother to create (I prefer *drop*) a bookmark when you first visit the site. Here's how it works:

1. **Visit the web page you want to bookmark.**
2. **Press the Menu button.**
3. **Choose the Add Bookmark command.**
4. **If necessary, edit the bookmark title.**

   The bookmark is given the web page name, which might be kind of long. I usually edit the name to something shorter. Shorter names are easier to read on the Bookmarks screen.

5. **Touch the Save button.**

   The bookmark is created and added to the list of bookmarks.

 To use a bookmark, touch the Bookmarks icon atop the Internet app's screen (refer to Figure 11-1). Choose a bookmark thumbnail from the Bookmarks tab list.

- Remove a bookmark by long-pressing its thumbnail on the Bookmarks screen. Choose the Delete command. Touch the OK button to confirm.
- Bookmarks from the Internet app can be placed on the Home screen: Long-press the bookmark thumbnail, and choose the command Add Shortcut to Home.

Managing multiple web page windows

The Internet app sports more than one window, so you can have multiple web pages open at a time. You can summon another window in one of several ways:

- ✔ **To open a link in another window,** long-press the link and choose the Open in New Window command from the menu that appears.

- ✔ **To open a bookmark in a new window,** long-press the bookmark and choose the Open in New Window command.

- ✔ **To open a blank browser window,** press the Menu button and choose New Window.

You switch between windows by touching the Windows icon found atop the Internet app's screen (refer to Figure 11-1). Choose a window from the list, as shown in Figure 11-2. When the list of windows is too tall, swipe it up and down to peruse what's available.

Figure 11-2: Switching web browser windows.

To switch to an open window, choose it from the list. You can close a window by touching the Minus (–) button to the right of the window's name.

✔ New windows open using a page you select. See the section "Setting a home page," later in this chapter, for information.

 ✔ For secure browsing, you can go *incognito*: Press the Menu button and choose the command Incognito Mode. When you go incognito, the Internet app won't track your history, leave cookies, or keep other evidence of which web pages you've visited.

Searching the web

The handiest way to find things on the web is to use the Google Search widget, often found floating on the Home screen and shown in Figure 11-3.

Figure 11-3: Google Search widget.

Choosing the Google Search widget ushers you into the Google Now app, which is a lot more than just searching the web. See Chapter 17 for details.

 ✔ You can always visit Google's main search page by using the Internet app.

 ✔ Or, what-the-hey: Be different and use Bing: www.bing.com.

Finding text on a web page

To locate text on a web page, press the Menu button and choose the Find on Page command. Type the search text into the Find on Page box. As you type, found text is highlighted on the screen. Use the up or down triangles to the right of the search box to page through the document. Touch the Back icon to dismiss the Find on Page contextual action bar after you've finished searching.

Sharing a web page

There it is! It's that web page that you just *have* to talk about to everyone you know. The gauche way to share the page is to copy and paste it. Because you're reading this book, however, you know the better way to share a web page. Heed these steps:

1. **Go to the web page you desire to share.**

   Actually, you're sharing a *link* to the page, but don't let my obsession with specificity deter you.

2. **Press the Menu button and choose the Share Via command.**

   You see a long list of apps displayed on the Share Via menu. The variety and number of apps depend on what's installed on your phone.

3. **Choose a method to share the page.**

   For example, choose Email to send the link by e-mail, or choose Facebook to share the link with your friends.

4. **Do whatever happens next.**

   Whatever happens next depends on how you're sharing the link: Compose the e-mail, write a comment in Facebook, or whatever. Refer to various chapters throughout this book for specific directions.

You cannot share a page you're viewing in an Incognito window.

That Downloading Thrill

One of the most misused words in all technology is *download*. People don't understand what it means. It's definitely not a synonym for *transfer* or *copy*, though that's how I most often hear it used.

For the sake of your Galaxy Note, a *download* is a transfer of information into your phone from another device, a computer, or the Internet. When you send something from the phone, you *upload* it. There. Now the nerd in me feels much better.

You can download information from a web page into your phone. It doesn't work exactly like downloading does on a computer, which is why I wrote this section.

✔ There's no need to download apps to your phone. Apps are obtained from the Google Play Store. See Chapter 18.

✔ While the phone is downloading information, you see the Downloading notification. To review the downloaded item, choose this notification when the download is complete.

Grabbing an image from a web page

The simplest thing to download is an image from a web page. It's cinchy: Long-press the image. You see a pop-up menu appear, from which you choose the Save Image command.

✔ The image is stored on your phone. You can view the image by using the Gallery app; downloaded images are saved in the Download album. Refer to Chapter 15 for information on the Gallery.

✔ The Downloads app can be used to review all items downloaded from the Internet to your phone. See the later section "Reviewing your downloads."

Downloading a file

When a link opens a document on a web page, such as a Microsoft Word document or an Adobe Acrobat (PDF) file, you can download that information to your phone. Simply long-press the link and choose the Save Link command from the menu that appears.

You can view the saved file by using the Downloads app. See the next section.

Reviewing your downloads

To peruse a list of items downloaded from the Internet, or otherwise obtained via the download process on your Galaxy Note, open the Downloads app. You'll find it eagerly awaiting your attention on the Applications screen: Look in the Samsung folder.

The Downloads app lists downloaded items, organized by date. To view a download, touch an item in the list. The appropriate app starts, displaying the downloaded item on the touchscreen.

- ✓ Some of the items you download cannot be viewed. When this happens, you see an appropriately rude error message.

- ✓ You can quickly review any download by choosing the Download notification.

- ✓ Manage the downloads list by long-pressing any entry. When you do, a toolbar appears atop the screen. Use its icons to share or delete the downloaded item. As long as the toolbar is visible, you can touch items on the downloads list to select them.

Master the Internet App

More options and settings and controls exist for the Internet app than for just about every other app on your Galaxy Note. It's complex. Rather than bore you with every dang doodle detail, I thought I'd present only a few of the options worthy of your attention.

Setting a home page

The *home page* is the first page you see when you start the Internet app, and it's the first page that's loaded when you fire up a new window. To set your home page, heed these directions in the Internet app:

1. **Browse to the page that you want to set as the home page.**

2. **Press the Menu button and choose the Settings command.**

    The Internet app's Settings screen appears.

3. **Choose Set Homepage.**

Four options are presented:

Default Page: This page is one that was preset by either Samsung, your cellular provider, or even Google.

Current Page: The page you're viewing, which you conveniently set at Step 1.

Most Visited Sites: This page displays a clutch of six websites you frequent.

Other: This setting lets you type in a web page address, which you don't have to do because you obeyed Step 1.

4. **Choose the Current Page item.**

5. **Touch the Done button.**

The home page is set.

The home page you chose now appears whenever you start the Internet app or open a new window.

If you want your home page to be blank, and not set to any particular web page, choose the Other option in Step 3. In the Set text box, type `about:blank`. That's the word *about,* a colon, and then the word *blank,* with no period at the end and no spaces in the middle. Touch the OK button to set a blank home page. Not only is it the fastest web page to load, it's also the web page with the most accurate information.

Changing the way the web looks

You can do a few things to improve the way the web looks on your phone. First and foremost, don't forget that you can orient the phone horizontally to see the wide view of any web page.

From the Settings screen, you can also adjust the text size used to display a web page. Heed these steps while using the Internet app:

1. **Press the Menu button.**

2. **Choose Settings.**

3. **Choose Screen and Text.**

4. **Adjust the Text Scaling control to set the size of text on the web.**

Use the preview window to gauge when your eyes can happily enjoy web page text.

5. **Press the Back button when you're done.**

I don't make any age-related comments about text size at this time, and especially at this point in my life.

Setting privacy and security options

With regard to security, my advice is always to be smart and think before doing anything questionable or tempting on the web. Use common sense. One of the most effective ways that the Bad Guys win is by using *human engineering* to try to trick you into doing something you normally wouldn't do, such as click a link to see a cute animation or a racy picture of a celebrity or politician. As long as you use your noggin, you should be safe.

As far as the phone's settings go, most of its security options are already enabled for you, including the blocking of pop-up windows (which normally spew ads).

If web page cookies concern you, you can clear them from the Settings window. Obey these steps while using the Internet app:

1. **Press the Menu button and choose the Settings command.**

   The Settings screen appears.

2. **Choose the Delete Personal Data item.**

3. **Place check marks by the items you want to remove.**

   For example, Browsing History removes all record of the websites you've visited. The Cookies and Site Data item removes any personal information you may have input, and Passwords deletes any saved passwords — always a good idea on a smartphone.

4. **Touch the Done button to purge your personal information.**

5. **Back at the Privacy screen, you might consider removing check marks by the options Remember Form Data and Remember Passwords.**

   Touch the box by each item to remove the check mark.

You might be concerned about various warnings regarding location data. What they mean is that the phone can take advantage of your location on Planet Earth (using the phone's GPS, or Global Satellite Positioning system) to help locate businesses and people near you. I see no security problem in leaving this feature on, although you can disable location services as described in Chapter 14.

Your Digital Social Life

In This Chapter

▶ Getting the Facebook app

▶ Sharing your life on Facebook

▶ Sending pictures to Facebook

▶ Tweeting on Twitter

▶ Discovering social networking opportunities

*I*n a world where people proclaim to value their privacy, it seems like every aspect of the human existence finds itself broadcast to the universe via the technology of social networking. It makes sense, too. After all, you and I dwell in a culture where the most desired goal of today's youth is not to be successful or happy. No, the driving force behind our culture is the desire to be famous. Social networking is the path one takes to reach that goal.

Thus endeth my rant.

If you desire to achieve fame via the ersatz-paved trail of social networking, your Galaxy Note is more than up to the task. Even if you're only curious or you want to stare, agape, at the antics of others, social networking is a useful tool. You can keep in touch, tell others what you're doing, and, yes, potentially become famous using your Galaxy Note and the fine suggestions I offer in this chapter.

In Your Facebook

Of all the social networking sites, Facebook is the king. It's *the* online place to go to catch up with friends, send messages, express your thoughts, share pictures and videos, play games, and waste more time than you ever thought you had.

✔ You can access Facebook on the web by using the Internet app, but I highly recommend that you use the Facebook app described in this section.

✔ The Facebook app is frequently updated. Review any new information by visiting my website:

www.wambooli.com/help/android/facebook

Setting up your Facebook account

The best way to use Facebook is to have a Facebook account, and the best way to do that is to sign up at www.facebook.com by using a computer. Register for a new account by setting up your username and password.

Don't forget your Facebook username and password!

Eventually, the Facebook robots send you a confirmation e-mail. You reply to that message, and the online social networking community braces itself for your long-awaited arrival.

After you're all set up, you're ready to access Facebook on your Android phone. To get the most from Facebook, however, you need the Facebook app. Keep reading in the next section.

Getting the Facebook app

Your Galaxy Note most likely doesn't come with the Facebook app. If so, great! If not, you can obtain the Facebook app for free from the Google Play Store. This app is your red carpet to the Facebook social networking kingdom.

To get the Facebook app, go to the Google Play Store and search for the Facebook for Android app. Download that app. If you need specific directions, see Chapter 18, which covers using the Play Store app.

After you install the Facebook app, you may see the Facebook notification icon. Choose that icon and complete the steps required to complete the installation.

Running Facebook on your phone

The first time you behold the Facebook app, you'll probably be asked to sign in. Do so: Type the e-mail address you used to sign up for Facebook, and then type your Facebook password. Touch the Log In button.

If you're asked to sync your contacts, do so. I recommend choosing the option to synchronize all your contacts, which adds all your Facebook friends to the Galaxy Note's Contacts app, the phone's address book. Touch the Sync button in the upper right corner of the screen to begin using Facebook.

Eventually, you see the Facebook News Feed, similar to what's shown in Figure 12-1.

Figure 12-1: The Facebook app.

When you need a respite from Facebook, press the Home button to return to the Home screen.

The Facebook app continues to run until you either sign out or turn off the phone. It may also time-out after a period of inactivity. To sign out of Facebook, choose the Log Out command found at the bottom of the sidebar and shown in Figure 12-1. Touch the Confirm button.

✏ Show the sidebar by touching the Facebook app icon. To hide the sidebar, touch that icon again.

✏ Refer to Chapter 22 for information on placing a Facebook shortcut or widget on the Home screen.

✏ Use the Like, Comment, or Share buttons beneath a News Feed item to like, comment on, or share something. You can see other comments by choosing Comment item.

✏ To update the News Feed, swipe down on the screen.

✏ Notifications for Facebook appear atop the touchscreen. They look similar to the one shown in the margin.

Setting your status

The primary thing you live for on Facebook, besides having more friends than anyone else, is to update your status. It's the best way to share your thoughts with the universe — far cheaper than skywriting and far less offensive than a robocall.

To set your status, follow these steps in the Facebook app:

1. **Touch the Status button at the top of the screen.**

   Refer to Figure 12-1 for the Status button's location. If you don't see it, ensure that you're viewing the News Feed and swipe all the way up to the tippy-top of the feed.

   The Write Post screen is where you type your Facebook musing, similar to what's shown in Figure 12-2.

2. **Type something pithy, newsworthy, or typical of the stuff you read in Facebook.**

   When you can't think of anything to post, take off your shoes, sit down, and take a picture of your feet against something else in the background. That seems to be really popular.

3. **Touch the Post button.**

Status update text

Share status.

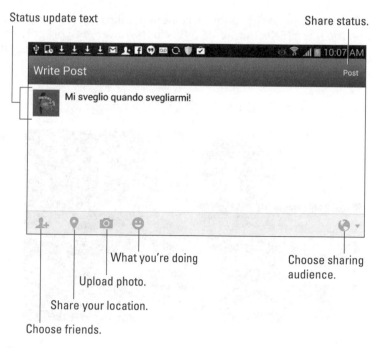

What you're doing

Choose sharing audience.

Upload photo.

Share your location.

Choose friends.

Figure 12-2: Updating your Facebook status.

You can also set your status by using the Facebook widget on the Home page, if it's been installed: Touch the What's on Your Mind text box, type your vital news tidbit, and touch the Share button.

Uploading a picture to Facebook

One of the many things your Galaxy Note can do is take pictures. Combine this feature with the Facebook app and you have an all-in-one gizmo designed for sharing the various intimate and private moments of your life with the ogling throngs of the Internet.

The picture posting process starts by touching the Photo icon in the Facebook app. Refer to Figures 12-1 and 12-2 for popular Photo icon locations on the main screen and the Write Post screen. After touching the Photo icon, you have two choices:

✔ First, you can select an image from pictures shown on the Photo Selection screen. These are images found on the phone. Touch an image, or touch several images to select a bunch, and then proceed with the steps listed later in this section.

✔ Second, you can take a picture by using the phone's camera.

If you elect to use the phone's camera to take a picture, touch the Camera icon on the Photo Selection screen. (It's in the lower left corner.) You then find yourself thrust into Facebook's camera app, shown in Figure 12-3. This is not the same app as the Camera app, covered in Chapter 15.

Switch cameras (front/back)   Flash control

Gallery

Take picture.

Record video.

Figure 12-3: Snapping a pic for Facebook.

Use the onscreen controls to take your picture. Or you can shoot a quick video by touching the Record Video icon, shown in Figure 12-3. When you're done, touch the Gallery icon, also shown in Figure 12-3.

To proceed with uploading the image, follow these steps:

1. **Touch an image in the Photo Selection screen to select it.**

2. **Tap the image to (optionally) add a tag.**

   You can touch someone's face in the picture and then type his name. Choose from a list of your Facebook friends to apply a name tag to the image.

3. **Use the Rotate button to reorient the image, if necessary.**

   The button's icon is shown in the margin. Please don't try to annoy me on Facebook by posting improperly oriented images.

4. **Touch the Compose button.**

   The Compose button is shown in the margin.

5. **Add a message to the image.**

   At this point, posting the image works just like adding a status update, similar to what's shown in Figure 12-2.

6. **Touch the Post button.**

The image is posted as soon as it's transferred over the Internet and digested by Facebook.

The image can be found as part of your status update or News Feed, but it's also saved to Facebook's Mobile Uploads album.

The Facebook app appears on the Share menus that you find in various apps on the Galaxy Note. Choose that item to send to Facebook whatever it is you're looking at. (Other chapters in this book give you more information about the various Share menus and where they appear.)

Configuring the Facebook app

To control the Facebook app's options and configuration, choose the App Settings command found on the sidebar. Don't let the options overwhelm you! Two of them worthy of your attention are Refresh Interval and Notification Ringtone.

Choose Refresh Interval to specify how frequently the app checks for new Facebook activities. You might find the 1-hour value to be too long for your frantic Facebook social life, so choose something quicker. Or, to disable Facebook notifications, choose Never.

You can manually refresh the Facebook app by swiping down the screen.

The Notification Ringtone item on the Facebook app's Settings screen sets which sound plays when Facebook has an update. Choose the Silent option when you don't want the app to make noise upon encountering a Facebook update.

Press the Back button to leave the Settings screen and return to the main Facebook screen.

Tweet Suite

Twitter is a social networking site, similar to Facebook but with increased brevity. On Twitter, you write short spurts of text that express your thoughts or observations, or you share links. Or, you can just use Twitter to follow the thoughts and twitterings, or *tweets,* of other people.

- ✔ A message posted on Twitter is a *tweet.*

- ✔ A tweet can be no more than 140 characters long. That number includes spaces and punctuation.

✔ You can post messages on Twitter and follow others who post messages. It's a good way to get updates and information quickly, from not only individuals but also news outlets and other organizations.

Setting up Twitter

The best way to use Twitter on your Android phone is to already have a Twitter account. Start by going to `http://twitter.com` on a computer and follow the directions there for creating a new account.

After you've established a Twitter account, you need to obtain the Twitter app for your Galaxy Note; it doesn't come preinstalled. Visit Google Play Store and download the Twitter app from Twitter, Inc. Refer to Chapter 18 for details on downloading apps to your phone.

When you start the Twitter app for the first time, touch the Sign In button. Type your Twitter username or e-mail address, and then type your Twitter password. After that, you can use Twitter without having to log in again — until you turn off the phone or exit the Twitter app.

Figure 12-4 illustrates the Twitter app's main screen, which shows the current tweet feed. See the next section for information on *tweeting,* or updating your status using the Twitter app.

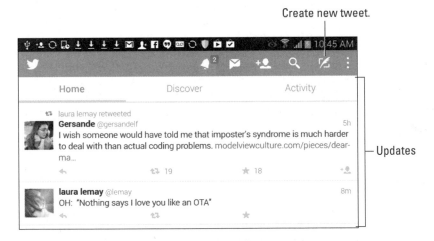

Figure 12-4: The Twitter app.

The Twitter app comes with companion widgets you can affix to the Home screen. Use the widgets to peruse recent tweets or compose a new tweet. Refer to Chapter 22 for information on adding widgets to the Home screen.

Tweeting

The Twitter app provides an excellent interface to the many wonderful and interesting things that Twitter does. Of course, the two most basic tasks are reading and writing tweets.

To read tweets, choose the Home category, as shown in Figure 12-4. Recent tweets are displayed in a list, with the most recent information at the top. Scroll the list by swiping it with your finger.

To tweet, touch the Create New Tweet icon, shown in Figure 12-4. Use the New Tweet screen, shown in Figure 12-5, to compose your tweet.

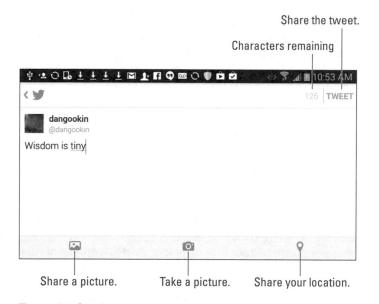

Share the tweet.

Characters remaining

Share a picture.   Take a picture.   Share your location.

Figure 12-5: Creating a tweet.

Touch the Tweet button to share your thoughts with the Twitterverse.

- You have only 140 characters for creating your tweet. That includes spaces.

- The character counter in the Twitter app lets you know how close you're getting to the 140-character limit.

- Twitter itself doesn't display pictures, other than your account picture. When you send a picture to Twitter, you use an image-hosting service and then share the link, or URL, to the image. All that complexity is handled by the Twitter app.

- The Twitter app appears on various Share menus in other apps. You use those Share menus to send to Twitter whatever you're looking at.

Even More Social Networking

The Internet is nuts over social networking. Facebook may be the king, but you'll find lots of landed gentry out for that crown. It almost seems as though a new social networking site pops up every week. Beyond Facebook and Twitter, other social networking sites include, but are not limited to,

- ✔ Google+
- ✔ LinkedIn
- ✔ Meebo
- ✔ Myspace

I recommend first setting up the social networking account on a computer, similar to the way I describe it earlier in this chapter for Facebook and Twitter. After that, obtain an app for the social networking site using the Google Play Store. Set up and configure that app on your Android phone to connect with your existing account.

- ✔ See Chapter 18 for more information on the Google Play Store.

- ✔ Google+ is Google's social networking app, which is related to the Hangouts app. See Chapter 13 for information on using Hangouts.

- ✔ The HootSuite app can be used to share your thoughts on a multitude of social networking platforms. It can be obtained from the Play Store, as described in Chapter 18.

- ✔ As with Facebook and Twitter, you may find your social networking apps appearing on Share menus in various apps. That way, you can easily share your pictures and other types of media with your online social networking pals.

I See What You're Doing There

In This Chapter

▶ Placing a Samsung video call

▶ Setting up Google Hangouts

▶ Text chatting in a hangout

▶ Doing a video chat

▶ Using the Skype app

▶ Typing to your Skype friends

▶ Making a Skype video call

*B*ack in the 1960s, it was called the *picture phone*. Just like the flying car, its introduction to the world was only a few years off. Definitely, you would know that the future had arrived when you would make a video phone call. Well, the future has arrived, but you probably don't have a picture phone in your house. Or do you?

The Galaxy Note comes with a front-facing camera. Bingo. There's your picture phone. Armed with the proper app, you can make video calls. It's ready, and it's happening right now. Unfortunately, you still have to wait a while for that flying car.

Samsung Video Calling

Your Galaxy Note offers a communications tool called Video Call. It's a feature that's interesting and exciting, but one that's available only to folks who also have a Samsung phone with similar technology. So unless the whole famdamily has Galaxy Notes or other Galactic phones, you'll have to use the video calling methods described elsewhere in this chapter.

You can place a Samsung video call in the same way that a traditional phone call is made. The difference is touching the Video Call icon, shown in the margin, to place the call. That icon is found in the Phone app on the keypad screen. It's also found on a contact's information screen in the Contacts app.

The Video Call screen is shown in Figure 13-1. When the other party answers, you see both of you on the screen. Use the onscreen controls, illustrated in the figure, to adjust the phone's features.

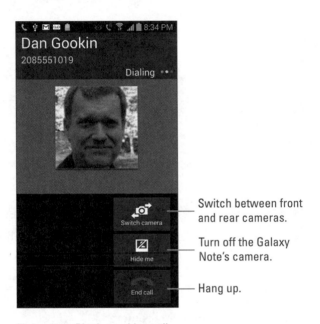

Switch between front and rear cameras.

Turn off the Galaxy Note's camera.

Hang up.

Figure 13-1: Placing a video call.

During the call, use the Mute button to mute the phone's microphone. You can swipe the images of yourself and the other person to swap their positions.

To end the call, touch the End Call icon.

✔ When you place a video call to someone who isn't using a Samsung phone, the phone claims that the connection failed. Touch the OK button and try phoning the traditional way.

✔ This trick works only with Samsung phones — specifically, those that share the same technology as your Galaxy Note.

✔ Video calling is available only over the high-speed 3G and 4G/LTE networks. Yes, it consumes hordes of data. The odds of surcharges increase the more you use the Video Call feature and the longer your calls are.

✔ Press the Menu button during a call to view various in-call options, such as Speaker Off and Switch to Headset, and some curious options, such as Enable Cartoon View.

✔ Call waiting isn't available for video calls. If someone else calls while you're in a video call, they're sent to voice mail.

Hangout with Google

Video chat is different from a Samsung video call. The big difference is that you can chat with anyone who uses the same app, whether they have a Samsung phone or not. Heck, the other person may even have a computer or a tablet. It's all made possible by the Google Hangouts app.

Using Hangouts

The Hangouts app is found in the Google folder on the Applications screen. If the app isn't there, you can always obtain a free copy from the Google Play Store; see Chapter 18.

Hangouts hooks into your Google account. If you have any previous conversations, they're listed on the main part of the screen, as shown in Figure 13-2. On the right side of the screen, you see a specific conversation, although it peeks in only when the phone is held vertically.

The Hangouts app listens for incoming conversation requests, or you can start your own. You're alerted via notification of an impending Hangout request. The notification icon is shown in the margin.

✔ Conversations are archived in the Hangouts app. To peruse a previous text chat, choose it from the list, as shown in Figure 13-2. Part of the previous chat shows up on the right side of the screen.

✔ If you've configured the Hangouts app for text messaging, the text messages appear in the archive with the SMS flag, as shown in Figure 13-2. Also see the later section "Using Hangouts as your phone's SMS app."

✔ Video chats aren't archived, but you can review when the call took place and with whom by choosing a video chat item.

✔ To remove a previous conversation, long-press it. Touch the Trash icon that appears atop the screen. You can also swipe a conversation left or right to remove it.

✔ To use Hangouts, your friends must have Google accounts. They can be using computers or mobile devices — it doesn't matter which — but they must have a camera available to enable video chat.

Text message

Text hangout

Add friends/View contacts.

Previous conversation

Group video call

Figure 13-2: Google Hangouts.

Typing at your friends

Text chatting is one of the oldest forms of communications on the Internet. It's where people type text back and forth at each other, which can be tedious, but it remains popular. To text-chat in the Hangouts app, obey these steps:

1. **Choose a contact listed on the screen, or fetch one by touching the Add icon.**

   When you touch the Add icon, you're starting a new hangout. Choosing a contact already on the screen continues a hangout. Even a previous video hangout can become a text hangout.

   When you choose a hangout with multiple people, all of them receive a copy of the message.

2. **Touch the Action bar by the contact's name and choose Hangouts.**

   The Action bar, illustrated in Figure 13-3, lets you choose between starting a new hangout or sending a text message (SMS). For this exercise, you're starting a hangout.

Current conversation

Action bar   Video chat

Take photo.
Share location.

Type here.

Figure 13-3: Text-chatting.

A clue that you're starting a hangout is the Video Chat icon, shown in Figure 13-3. When the Phone icon appears instead, you're sending a text message.

3. **Type your message, as shown in Figure 13-3.**

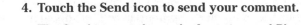

4. **Touch the Send icon to send your comment.**

   The Send icon replaces the Location and Photo icons when you start to type.

You type, your friend types, and so on, until you grow tired or the battery dies.

Adding more people to the hangout is always possible: Press the Menu button and choose New Group Hangout. Choose a friend from those listed to invite them into the hangout.

 You can leave the conversation at any time to do other things with your phone. To return to any ongoing hangout, choose the Hangouts notification, shown in the margin.

Using Hangouts as your phone's SMS app

Google is pushing the Hangouts app as an obvious replacement for the text messaging app on Android phones. If you enjoy using Hangouts, you can switch from the Messages app to Hangouts for text messaging.

To use Hangouts as the Galaxy Note's text messaging app, follow these steps:

1. **Open the Hangouts app.**

2. **Press the Menu button and choose Settings.**

   If you don't see settings, ensure that you're viewing the main Hangouts screen.

3. **Choose SMS.**

4. **On the SMS screen, place a check mark by the Turn On SMS option.**

   The Hangouts app is now the phone's text messaging app.

With SMS activated in the Hangouts app, all incoming text messages are received in that app. You can still use the Messages app to send a text message, but the replies are received in the Hangouts app.

To restore the Messages app as the phone's SMS app, repeat the steps in this section but remove the check mark in Step 4.

Talking and video chat

Take the hangout up a notch by touching the Video icon (refer to Figure 13-3). When you do, your friend receives a pop-up invite, as shown in Figure 13-4. Slide the Video icon to the right to begin talking.

Slide here to accept.

Slide this thing.

Slide here to ignore.

Figure 13-4: Someone wants to video-chat!

Figure 13-5 shows what an ongoing video chat might look like. The person you're talking with appears in the big window; you're in the smaller window. Other video chat participants appear at the bottom of the screen as well, as shown in the figure.

The onscreen controls (shown in Figure 13-5) may vanish after a second; touch the screen to see the controls again.

To end the conversation, touch the Exit Video Chat icon. Well, say goodbye first, and then touch the icon.

✔ When you're nude, or just ugly, decline the video chat invite. Then choose that contact and reply with a text message or voice chat instead. Explain verbally how you look.

✔ Use the Speaker icon to choose how to listen when you video-chat. You can choose to use the phone's speaker, headphones, and so on.

✔ When video-chatting with multiple contacts, choose a contact from the bottom of the screen to see that person in a larger format in the center of the screen.

✔ If you want to make eye contact, look directly into the phone's front-facing camera. It's right above the touchscreen, just to the right of the speaker.

Switch to text chat.

Exit video chat.

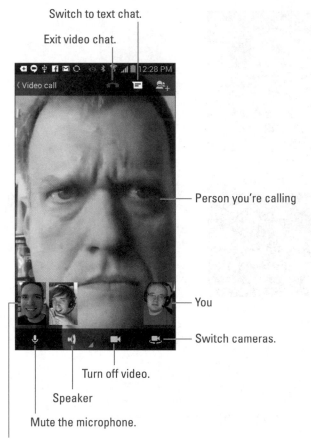

Person you're calling

You

Switch cameras.

Turn off video.

Speaker

Mute the microphone.

Others in the hangout

Figure 13-5: Video chat in the Hangouts app.

Connect with Skype

The popular Skype app is used the world over as a free way to make Internet phone calls and to video-chat. Plus, if you're willing to pony up some money, you can make inexpensive calls to phones around the world.

Getting Skype

Your Galaxy Note doesn't come with the Skype app preinstalled. To get Skype, visit the Google Play Store (described in Chapter 18) and obtain the Skype app. In case you find multiple apps, get the one that's from the Skype company itself.

To use Skype, you need a Skype account. You can sign up while using the app, or you can visit www.skype.com on a computer to complete the process by using a nice, full-size keyboard and wide-screen monitor.

When you start the Skype app for the first time, work through the initial setup screens. You can even take the tour. Be sure to have Skype scour the phone's address book for contacts you can Skype. This process may take a while, but if you're just starting out, it's a great help.

- ✔ Skype is free to use. Text chat is free. Voice and video chat with one other Skype user are also free. When you want to call a real phone, or video-chat with a group, you need to boost your account with Skype Credit.

- ✔ It's doesn't cost extra to a gang-video-chat in the Hangouts app.

- ✔ Don't worry about getting a Skype number, which costs extra. That's used mostly for incoming calls and, well, that's why you have a phone.

- ✔ Also see Chapter 21, which covers making inexpensive international phone calls by using the Skype app.

Chatting with another Skype user

Text chat with Skype works similarly to texting with the Messenger or Hangouts apps. The difference is that the other person must be a Skype user. So in that respect, a Skype text chat works a lot like a Hangouts chat, covered earlier in this chapter.

To chat, follow these steps:

1. **Start the Skype app and sign in.**

   You don't need to sign in when you've previously run the Skype app. Like most apps on your phone, Skype continues to run until you sign out or turn off the phone.

2. **At the main Skype screen, touch the People tab and choose a contact.**

   Or you can choose one of the contact icons shown on the main screen.

3. **Type your text in the text box.**

   The box is found at the bottom of the screen. It says Type a Message Here.

4. **Touch the blue arrow icon to send the message.**

   As long as your Skype friend is online and eager, you'll be chatting in no time.

At the far right end of the text box, you find the Smiley icon. Use this icon to insert a cute graphic into your text.

✔ The Skype Chat notification, shown in the margin, appears whenever someone wants to chat with you. It's handy to see, especially when you may have switched away from the Skype app to use another app. Choose that notification to get into the conversation.

✔ To stop chatting, touch the Back icon. The conversation is retained in the Skype app, even after the other person has disconnected.

✔ For the chat to work, the other user must be logged in on Skype and available to chat.

Seeing on Skype (video call)

Placing a video call with Skype is easy: Start up a text chat as described in the preceding section. After the conversation starts, touch the Video Call icon. The call rings through to the contact, and if they want to video-chat, they pick up in no time and you're talking and looking at each other.

When someone calls you on Skype, you see the Skype incoming-call screen, similar to the one shown in Figure 13-6. Touch the Answer Voice Call icon to answer as a voice-only call; touch the Answer Video Call icon (if it's available) to answer using video. Touch Decline to dismiss the call, especially when it's someone who annoys you.

The incoming-call screen (on the left in Figure 13-6) appears even when the phone is sleeping; the incoming call wakes up the phone, just as a real call would.

When you're in a Skype video conversation, the screen looks like the one shown on the right in Figure 13-6. Touch the screen to see the onscreen controls if they disappear.

Touch the red End Call button to end the call.

✔ Voice and video chat on Skype over the Internet are free. When you use a Wi-Fi connection, you can chat without incurring a loss of your cellular plan's data minutes.

✔ You can chat with any user in your Skype contacts list by using a mobile device, a computer, or any other gizmo on which Skype is installed.

✔ Video chat is available only on cell phones, tablets, and computers that have front-facing cameras. Some cell phone plans may forbid video chat.

✔ Video chat may be available only over Wi-Fi or 4G connections.

✔ If you plan to use Skype a lot, get a good headset.

✔ It's impossible to tell whether someone has dismissed a Skype call or simply hasn't answered. Though Skype has no voice mail so that you can leave a message when someone doesn't answer, you can still send a text message that they can read later.

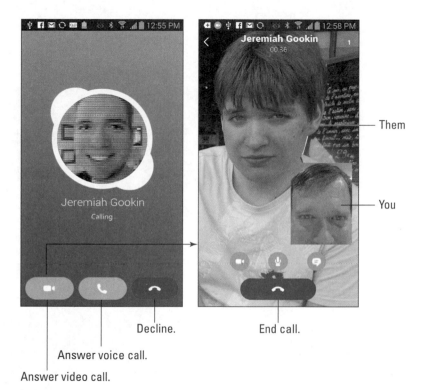

Them

You

Decline.

End call.

Answer voice call.

Answer video call.

Figure 13-6: A Skype call.

Part IV
Incredible Tasks and Amazing Feats

Learn how to peruse various shooting modes in the Camera app at www.dummies.com/extras/samsunggalaxynote3.

In this part...

- ✔ Understand how to use the Maps app
- ✔ Work with the phone's camera
- ✔ Explore music on an Android phone
- ✔ Discover interesting apps
- ✔ Drool over getting even more apps

There's a Map for That

In This Chapter

▶ Exploring your world with Maps

▶ Adding layers to the map

▶ Finding your location

▶ Sharing your location

▶ Searching for places

▶ Finding someone or something

▶ Using the Galaxy Note as a navigator

*A*fter searching for a few minutes, Alan finally found Susan. "Are you all right?" he asked.

"Fine," she said, getting to her feet and dusting herself off. "If Dr. Cornelius ever expects the general public to adopt teleportation, he had better iron out the kinks."

Alan thought for a moment. "Speaking of Cornelius," he began, "where is the beloved professor? For that matter, where is a Mexican restaurant? I need tacos."

Susan deftly pulled out her Galaxy Note 3. In a flash, she summoned the Maps app and quickly located a nearby taco stand.

"Cornelius can wait," muttered Alan. "I need my tacos now!"

"I'm just glad that I've read Chapter 14 in Dan Gookin's book *Samsung Galaxy Note 3 For Dummies,* published by John Wiley & Sons," Susan said. "Otherwise, we'd be wandering aimlessly and yearning for tacos."

Behold the Map

It's one of the most amazing apps on your phone. The Maps app charts the entire country. It plots out freeways, highways, roads, streets, avenues, drives, bike paths, addresses, businesses, and points of interest.

Using the Maps app

Start the Maps app by choosing it from the Applications screen, or you may find a shortcut to the Maps app lurking on the Home screen. If you're starting the app for the first time or if it has been updated recently, you can read its What's New screen; touch the OK button to continue.

The Galaxy Note communicates with the Global Positioning System, or GPS, satellites to hone in on your current location. (See the later sidebar "Activate your locations!") Your location is shown on the map, similar to the one you see in Figure 14-1. The position is accurate to within a given range, as shown by the location-in-a-blue-circle on the map.

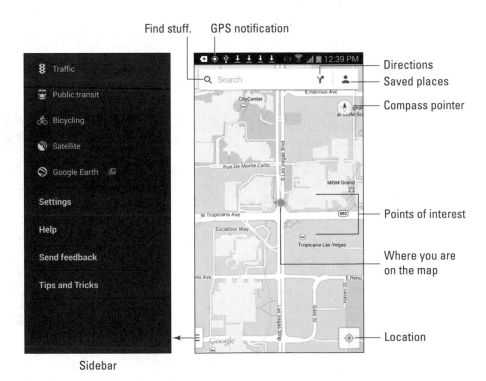

Figure 14-1: Your location on a map.

Here are some fun things you can do when viewing the basic street map:

Zoom in: To make the map larger (to move it closer), double-tap the screen. You can also spread your fingers on the touchscreen to zoom in.

Zoom out: To make the map smaller (to see more), pinch your fingers on the touchscreen.

Pan and scroll: To see what's to the left or right, or at the top or bottom, of the map, drag your finger on the touchscreen; the map scrolls in the direction you drag your finger.

Rotate: Using two fingers, rotate the map clockwise or counterclockwise. Touch the compass pointer (shown earlier, in Figure 14-1) to reorient the map with north at the top of the screen.

Perspective: Touch the screen with two fingers and swipe up or down to view the map in perspective. You can also tap the Location icon to switch to Perspective view. To return to flat-map view, touch the Compass Pointer icon (refer to Figure 14-1).

The closer you zoom in to the map, the more detail you see, such as street names, address block numbers, and businesses and other sites — but no tiny people.

- ✓ The blue triangle (refer to Figure 14-1) shows in which general direction the phone is pointing.

- ✓ When the phone's direction is unavailable, you see a blue dot as your location on the map.

- ✓ To view the sidebar, touch the icon shown in Figure 14-1. Swipe the navigation drawer to the left to return to the Maps app.

- ✓ When all you want is a virtual compass, similar to the one you lost as a kid, you can get a Compass app from the Google Play Store. See Chapter 18 for more information about the Google Play Store.

Adding layers

You add details from the Maps app by applying layers: A *layer* can enhance the map's visual appearance, provide more information, or add other fun features to the basic street map, such as Satellite view, shown in Figure 14-2.

The key to accessing layers is to touch the Sidebar icon in the lower left corner of the screen. The sidebar displays several layers you can add, such as the Satellite layer, shown in Figure 14-2. Another popular layer is Traffic, which lists updated travel conditions.

To remove a layer, choose it again from the navigation drawer; any active layer appears highlighted. When a layer isn't applied, the street view appears.

Your approximate location and direction

Sidebar

Figure 14-2: The Satellite layer.

Activate your locations!

The Maps app works best when you activate all the phone's location technology. Activation may have been done when you first configured the Galaxy Note. Even so, I recommend that you confirm activation of the location settings: At the Home screen, press the Menu button and choose Settings to run the Settings app. Touch the Connections tab and then choose Location Services. Ensure that green check marks appear by all items described in the following list:

Access to My Location: An overall control that permits apps to access the phone's location technology.

Use GPS Satellites: Allows your phone to access the Global Positioning System (GPS) satellites, although it's not that accurate. That's why you need to activate the Wireless Network service to fully use your phone's location abilities.

Use Wireless Networks: Allows software access to your location by using Google technology. Specifically, the phone checks for nearby Wi-Fi networks and uses that data to hone your position.

See Chapter 19 for information on activating the Galaxy Note's Wi-Fi setting.

How to Find Yourself

Allow me to save you tons of time and buckets of money: You don't need a self-help course. You don't need to climb a mountain, visit a head shrink, discover your inner beauty, or fight demons from your childhood. Seriously, you're a good person, so you can understand that my references to "finding yourself" mean that you'll use the Maps app on your Galaxy Note to discover exactly where you are.

Finding out where you are

The Maps app shows your location as a blue dot or compass arrow on the screen. But *where* is that? I mean, if you need to phone a tow truck, you can't just say, "I'm the blue triangle on the orange slab by the green thing."

Well, you *can* say that, but it probably won't do any good.

To find your current street address, or any street address, long-press a location on the Maps screen. Up pops a bubble, similar to the one shown in Figure 14-3, that gives your approximate address.

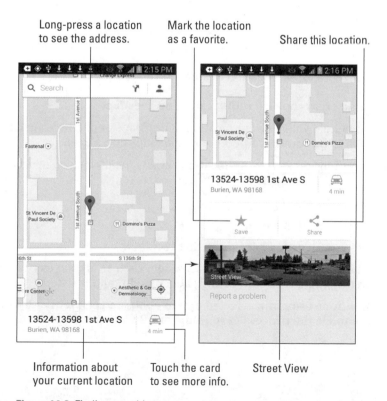

Long-press a location to see the address.

Mark the location as a favorite.

Share this location.

Information about your current location

Touch the card to see more info.

Street View

Figure 14-3: Finding an address.

If you touch the card, you see a screen with more details and additional information, shown on the right in Figure 14-3.

Route

- This trick works only when your phone has Internet access. When Internet access isn't available, the Maps app is unable to communicate with the Google map servers.

- To make the card go away, touch anywhere else on the map.

- The time display under the car icon (see the car in Figure 14-3) indicates how far away the address is from your current location. The car icon may appear as the generic Route icon, shown in the margin.

- When you have *way* too much time on your hands, play with the Street View command. Choosing this option displays the location from a 360-degree perspective. In Street view, you can browse a locale, pan and tilt, or zoom in on details to familiarize yourself with an area, for example — whether you're familiarizing yourself with a location or planning a burglary.

Helping others find your location

You can use the Maps app to send your current location to a friend or even to an enemy — if you like to live dangerously. If your pal has a phone with smarts similar to your Galaxy Note's, he can use the coordinates to get directions to your location. Maybe he'll bring tacos!

To send your current location to someone else, obey these steps:

1. **Long-press your current location on the Map.**

   To behold your current location in the Maps app, touch the Location icon in the lower right corner of the Maps app screen.

   After long-pressing your location (or any location), you see a card displayed, showing the approximate address.

2. **Touch the card.**

3. **Touch the Share icon.**

   Refer to Figure 14-3 for this icon's location.

4. **Choose the app to share the message, such as Messages (for text messaging), Gmail, Email, or whichever useful app is listed.**

5. **Continue using the selected app to choose a recipient and otherwise complete the process of sending your location to that person.**

The recipient can touch the link in the text message, e-mail, or what-have-you to open your location in her phone's Maps app. When the location appears, the recipient can follow my advice in the later section "Asking for directions" to reach your location. Don't loan them this book, either — have them purchase their own copy. And bring tacos. Thanks.

How to Find Other Things

Just as you can search the Internet with Google, you can search the real world using the Maps app. The app may not help you find love, wealth, or fame, but it most certainly can help you locate the best tacos in town. The key is to use the Search text box atop the Maps app screen, as illustrated earlier, in Figure 14-1.

Looking for a specific address

To locate an address, type it into the Search box; for example:

```
1600 Pennsylvania Ave., Washington, D.C. 20006
```

Touch the Search button on the onscreen keyboard to find that specific address. The next step is getting directions, which you can read about in the later section "How to Get There."

- ✔ You don't need to type the entire address. Oftentimes, all you need is the street number and street name and then either the city name or zip code.

- ✔ If you omit the city name or zip code, the Maps app looks for the closest matching address near your current location.

- ✔ Touch the X icon in the Search box to clear the previous search.

Finding a business, restaurant, or point of interest

You may not know an address, but you know when you crave sushi or bulgogi or perhaps the exotic flavors of Wyoming. Maybe you need a hotel or a gas station or you have to find a place that removes tattoos. To find a business entity or a point of interest, type its name in the Search box; for example:

```
Sports bar
```

This command flags taverns and community watering holes on the current Maps screen or nearby.

Or you can be specific and look for businesses near a certain location by specifying the city name, district, or zip code, such as

```
Tacos 92123
```

After typing this command and touching the Search button, you see a smattering of taco stands and restaurants found in my old neighborhood in San Diego, similar to the ones shown in Figure 14-4.

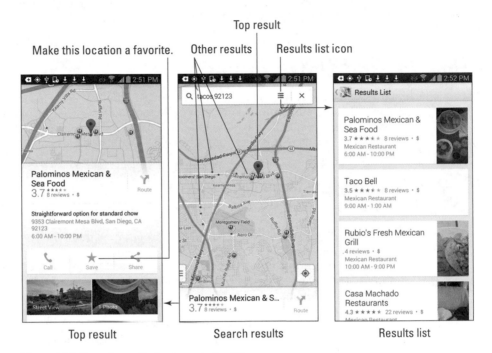

Figure 14-4: Search results for tacos in San Diego.

To see more information about a result, touch its card, such as the one for the Palominos Mexican & Sea Food in Figure 14-4. Or touch the Results List icon to see a whole swath of cards. After touching a card, you can view more details.

Route

You can touch the Route icon on the restaurant's (or any location's) Details screen to get directions; see the later section "Asking for directions." The Route icon can also shows up as a car (or another mode of transportation), as shown earlier, in Figure 14-3.

> ✔ Every letter or dot on the screen represents a search result (refer to Figure 14-4).
>
> ✔ Spread your fingers on the touchscreen to zoom in to the map.
>
> ✔ If you *really* like the location, touch the Save (Star) icon. It directs the Maps app to store the location as one of your favorite places. The location shows as a star on the Maps app screen. See the next section.

Searching for favorite or recent places

Just as you can bookmark favorite websites when using the Internet app, you can mark favorite places in the real world by using the Maps app. The feature is called Saved Places.

To visit your favorite places or browse your recent map searches, touch the Saved Places icon at the top of the Maps app screen. If you don't see the icon, touch the X button to clear the Search box.

The Saved Places window sports various categories of places you've *starred* (marked as favorites), locations you've recently searched for, or places you've been.

✔ Mark a location as a favorite by touching the Star icon when you view the location's details.

✔ The Recently Accessed Places list allows you to peruse items you've located or searched for recently.

✔ Touch the app icon (in the upper left corner of the screen) to return to the Maps app when you're done looking at saved places.

Locating one of your contacts

You can zero in on where a friend lives or works by using the Maps app. This trick functions only when you've specified an address for the contact — either home or work or another location. If so, your Galaxy Note can easily help you find that location or even give you directions.

The secret to finding a contact's location is the little icon by the contact's address. The icon looks like the standard "Here it is" Pushpin icon that's used in the Maps app and shown in the margin. Anytime you see this icon or a similar one while using the Contacts app, you can touch the icon to view that location in the Maps app.

How to Get There

Finding something is only half the job. The other half is getting there. Thanks to its various direction and navigation features, the Maps app stands at the ready to be your copilot. It's like having a backseat driver, but one who knows where he's going and — *bonus* — who has a Mute option.

Asking for directions

One command associated with locations found in the Maps app is for getting directions. The command is called Route, and it shows either the Route icon (see the margin) or a mode of transportation, such as a car, bike, or bus. Here's how it works:

Route

1. **Touch the Route icon in a location's card.**

   After touching the Route icon, you see a screen similar to the one shown in Figure 14-5.

Figure 14-5: Planning a trip.

2. **Choose a method of transportation.**

   The available options vary, depending on your location. In Figure 14-5, the items are (from left to right) Car, Public Transportation, Bicycle, and On Foot.

3. **Set a starting point.**

   You can type a location or choose from one of the locations shown on the screen, such as your current location, home location, or any location you've previously searched or saved. Touch the Starting Location item to choose another location.

4. **Ensure that the starting location and destination are what you want.**

   If they're backward, touch the Swap icon. (Refer to Figure 14-5.)

5. **Choose a route card.**

   One or more routes are listed on the screen, as shown in Figure 14-5. Touch one of the cards to see the details, which are shown in the right in the figure.

6. **Peruse the results.**

The map shows your route, highlighted as a blue line on the screen, as shown in Figure 14-5.

To see a list of directions, touch the results card, shown at the bottom of the screen. You see a scrolling list of turns, distances, and directions. Touch the Preview icon to get a bird's-eye view of your route.

✔ The Maps app alerts you to any toll roads on the specified route. As you travel, you can choose alternative, non-toll routes, if they're available. You're prompted to switch routes during navigation; see the next section.

✔ You may not get perfect directions from the Maps app, but for places you've never visited, it's a useful tool.

Navigating to your destination

Maps and lists of directions are so 20th century. I don't know why anyone would bother trying to unfold a map in the front seat of a car, especially when your Galaxy Note features a digital copilot, in the form of voice navigation.

To use navigation, obey these steps:

1. **Choose a location on the map.**

   It must be a spot other than your current location. You can search for a business, type a location, or long-press any part of the map.

2. **Choose a card from the search results.**

   This process works identically to finding any location; see the earlier section "How to Find Other Things."

Route

3. **Touch the Route icon.**

The Route icon can look like the icon shown in the margin, but most often it looks like a car.

4. **Ensure that My Location is chosen on the next screen, similar to what's shown in Figure 14-6.**

Your starting point, your current location

Figure 14-6: Plotting your course.

If you don't see My Location, touch the top entry (refer to Figure 14-6) where it should be, and then choose the My Location item from the next screen.

5. **Choose a card representing the route you want to take.**

Sometimes only one card is available, but others may appear. The variety depends upon traffic conditions, toll roads, swarms of locusts, and similar things you might want to avoid.

6. **Touch the Start icon.**

And you're on your way.

While navigating, the phone displays an interactive map that shows your current location and turn-by-turn directions for reaching your destination. A digital voice tells you how far to go and when to turn, for example, and gives you other nagging advice, such as to sit up, be nice to other drivers, and call your mother once in a while.

To exit navigation, touch the Close icon at the bottom of the screen.

- ✔ The neat thing about Navigation is that whenever you screw up, a new course is immediately calculated.

- ✔ When you tire of hearing the navigation voice, touch the Action Overflow icon in the lower right corner of the navigation screen. Choose the Mute Voice Guidance command.

- ✔ I refer to the navigation voice as Gertrude.

- ✔ You can touch the Action Overflow icon while navigating and choose Step By Step List to review your journey. The Route Preview command, on the same menu, lets you see the big picture.

- ✔ The phone stays in Navigation mode until you exit. A Navigation notification, similar to the Start icon (refer to Step 6) can be seen atop the touchscreen while the Galaxy Note is in Navigation mode.

- ✔ To exit Navigation mode, touch the X icon, found in the lower left corner of the navigation screen.

- ✔ In Navigation mode, your phone consumes a *ton* of battery power. I highly recommend that you plug the phone into your car's power adapter (the "cigarette lighter") for the duration of the trip.

15

Everyone Say "Cheese"

In This Chapter

▶ Taking a still picture

▶ Deleting the image you just shot

▶ Taking a panorama

▶ Turning on the flash

▶ Setting the resolution

▶ Viewing images and videos stored on your phone

▶ Sharing images

▶ Cropping or rotating an image

A phone without a camera is like a hair dryer without a cheese grater. I suppose it was the way digital cameras kept shrinking that led some mad phone scientist to consider merging the two technologies. They had room! So the phone camera was born.

The digital camera and cell phone do make a good combination: Oftentimes, picture-taking opportunities arise. You may not have a camera available, but you always have your cell phone. So whenever you spy a UFO or Bigfoot or your father-in-law actually picking up the dinner bill, you can snap a picture. You can even share that image for posterity on the Internet.

Smile for the Camera App

A camera snob will tell you that no true camera has a ringtone. You know what? He's correct: Top-quality cameras are not found in cell phones. Regardless, your phone has a camera. Why not make the best of it?

Capturing the moment

Picture-taking and video-recording duties on your Galaxy Note are handled by the same app — the Camera app. A shortcut dwells smack dab on the Home screen, but you can also locate the Camera app's icon on the Applications screen.

The Camera app controls both the main camera, which is on the phone's butt, and the front-facing camera, which is not on the phone's butt. The app takes still images and records videos, depending on how it's used.

After starting the Camera app, you see the main Camera screen, as illustrated in Figure 15-1.

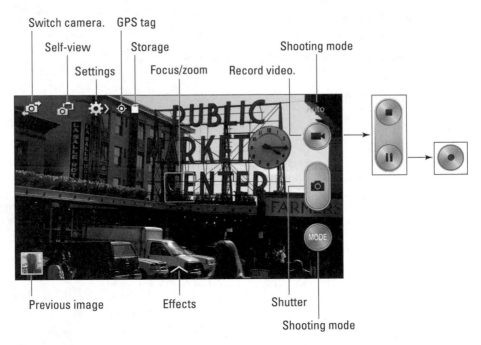

Figure 15-1: Your phone as a camera.

To take a still picture, touch the Shutter icon. The camera focuses, you may hear a mechanical shutter sound play, and the flash may go off. You're ready to take the next picture.

To record video, touch the Record icon, shown in Figure 15-1. As video is being recorded, two new icons appear: Stop and Pause. Touch the Stop icon to end the recording; touch Pause to suspend recording; touch the same button again, which is now the Record button, to continue. Then, finally, touch the Stop button to end the video.

To switch back to still photography from recording a video, touch the Camera button, shown in the margin.

To preview the image or video, touch the Previous Image icon that appears in the lower left corner of the screen, as shown in Figure 15-1. After viewing the preview, press the Back button to return to the Camera app.

- ✔ The Galaxy Note can be used as a camera in either landscape or portrait orientation.

- ✔ The camera focuses automatically. The rectangle at the center of the screen turns green when the image is in focus.

- ✔ Zoom by swiping or pinching the screen. The center rectangle changes its size to reflect the zoom factor. You can also zoom by using the Volume button: Up zooms in; down zooms out. A slider appears on the screen when you use the Volume button — and you can manually adjust the zoom by swiping the slider as well.

- ✔ You can take as many pictures or record as much video with your phone as you like, as long as you don't run out of internal or external storage. Speaking of which:

- ✔ The storage icon in Figure 15-1 indicates that images and recordings are saved to the phone's MicroSD card. To change storage locations, see the later section "Choosing the storage device."

- ✔ Hold steady when recording video! The camera still works when you whip the phone around, but wild gyrations render the video unwatchable.

- ✔ If your pictures appear blurry, ensure that the camera lens on the back of the phone isn't dirty.

- ✔ Use the Gallery app to preview and manage your pictures. See the later section "Where Your Photos Lurk" for more information.

- ✔ The Galaxy Note stores pictures in the JPEG image file format, using the jpg filename extension. Video is stored in the MPEG4 file format, using the .mp4 filename extension. Images and videos are stored in the DCIM/Camera folder on either internet storage or the MicroSD card. Internal storage is named sdcard0; external storage is named extSdCard.

Deleting immediately after you shoot

Sometimes, you just can't wait to delete an image. Either an annoyed person is standing next to you, begging that the photo be deleted, or you're just not happy and you feel the urge to smash into digital shards the picture you just took. Hastily follow these steps:

1. **Touch the previous image that appears on the screen.**

   Refer to Figure 15-1 for the previous image thumbnail's location. That icon appears whether you snapped a picture or shot a video.

2. Touch the Delete icon.

If you don't see the icon, tap the screen so that the icon shows up.

3. Touch the OK button to confirm.

The image or video has been eradicated.

For mass image extinction, open the Gallery app. See the later section "Deleting photos and videos."

Doing a self-portrait

Who needs to pay a ton of money for a mirror when you have the Galaxy Note? Well, forget the mirror. Instead, think about taking all those self-shots without having to second-guess whether the camera is pointed at your face.

To take your own mug shot, also known as a *selfie,* start the Camera app and touch the Switch Camera icon, as shown in the margin. When you see yourself, you've done it correctly. Smile. Click. You got it.

Touch the Switch Camera icon again to direct the phone to use the rear camera again.

Shooting a panoramic image

A *panorama* is a wide shot, like a landscape, a beautiful vista, or a family photograph where everyone should seriously lose some weight. You can take a picture as wide as you like using the Camera app, if you switch the camera into Panorama mode. Obey these steps:

1. Start the Camera app.

2. Touch the Shooting Mode icon.

Refer to Figure 15-1 for its location.

3. Swipe the modes left or right to choose Panorama.

Use Figure 15-2 as your guide.

4. Hold your arms steady.

5. Touch the Shutter button.

6. Pivot slightly to your left or right.

As you move the camera, a blue frame appears, helping you line up the next shot.

7. Continue pivoting as subsequent shots are taken.

The shots are snapped automatically, with the phone beeping every time an image is taken.

Select Auto mode.

View all shooting modes.

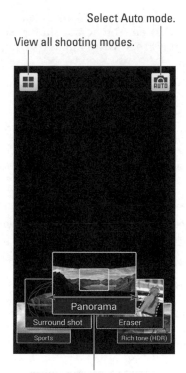

Panorama

Surround shot | Eraser

Sports | Rich tone (HDR)

Swipe modes left and right.

Figure 15-2: Selecting a shooting mode.

8. Touch the Shutter button again to end the panorama.

If you don't, the panorama ends by itself after a dozen or so beeps. Use the progress bar on the touchscreen to clue you in to how many shots remain.

The Camera app assembles all the shots, creating a panoramic image.

To restore the Camera app to normal, or Auto, shooting mode, repeat Steps 1 and 2 but choose Auto in Step 3.

The camera automatically captures the panoramic shot. You touch the Shutter button only to finish.

Taking a screen shot

A *screen shot*, also called a *screen cap* (for *cap*ture), is a picture of your phone's touchscreen. So if you see something interesting on the screen, or you just want to take a quick pic of your Galaxy Note life, you take a screen shot. Two techniques are available for capturing the screen.

The first screen shot method is to press and hold the S Pen button and then long-press the screen by using the S Pen. You hear a shutter sound, and then the screen shot is presented in the Screen Write app for saving or scribbling.

The second screen shot method is to activate the phone's Palm Motion feature. Heed these directions:

1. **Open the Settings app.**

2. **Touch the Controls tab.**

3. **Ensure that the master control switch by the Palm Motion item is on or green.**

   If it isn't, slide the Master Control icon to the right.

4. **Touch the Palm Motion item (not the master control switch), to see the Palm Motion screen.**

5. **Ensure that the Capture Screen item is active.**

   An active item features a green master control switch.

When the Capture Screen item is enabled, you create a screen shot by swiping left or right across the touchscreen with the side of your open palm. Upon success, you hear a clicking sound. The screen has been captured.

- ✓ As a bonus, the captured screen is saved to the phone's clipboard, where you can paste it into an app that accepts graphic input. See Chapter 4 for information on cut, copy, and paste.

- ✓ You can view the screen shots by using the Gallery app. They're found in the Screenshots album.

- ✓ Screen shots are kept in the `Pictures/Screenshots` folder on the phone's internal storage. They're saved in the PNG graphics file format.

Camera Settings and Options

The Galaxy Note's camera is much more than just a hole in the case. Taking a picture or shooting a video can involve more than just touching an icon. To help you get the most from the phone's cameras, various settings, options, and effects eagerly lurk beneath the Camera app's interface. This section describes some of its common features, the handy ones, and even the oddballs.

Finding the settings

To control the Camera app, you touch the Settings icon found on the Camera app's main screen. The icon is illustrated in Figure 15-1 and shown in the margin. Touching that icon displays a column (or row, depending on the phone's orientation) or additional Settings icons. Those icons are illustrated in Figure 15-3.

The icons themselves are switches that instantly change a setting or summon additional items or a menu. For example, touching the Flash icon changes the flash setting, as described in the next section. Touching the Settings icon displays an onscreen menu.

The following sections illustrate how to use several of the icons shown in Figure 15-3.

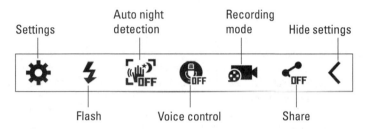

Figure 15-3: Camera app icon parade.

Setting the flash

The Camera app features three flash settings. The current setting is shown in the Camera app's icon parade, shown in Figure 15-3 and displayed by touching the Settings icon on the Camera app's main screen. The Galaxy Note features three flash settings, shown in Table 15-1.

Table 15-1		Galaxy Note Camera Flash Settings
Setting	*Icon*	*What Happens*
On		The flash always activates.
Auto		The flash activates during low-light situations.
Off		The flash never activates, even in low-light situations.

To change the flash setting, touch the Settings icon on the Camera app's screen, and then tap the current Flash icon. Every time you tap, the icon changes the setting, as shown in Table 15-1.

When you're shooting video, the On setting activates the phone's LED lamp the entire time you're recording video. The On setting for the flash must be set before you shoot video and, yes, it uses a lot of battery power.

A good time to turn on the flash is when taking pictures of people or objects in front of something bright, such as Aunt Betty holding her prized peach cobbler in front of an exploding volcano.

Changing image resolution

High-resolution images are great for printing photos. They're good for photo-editing. They're not required for images you plan to share with Facebook or send as e-mail attachments. Plus, the higher the resolution, the more storage space the image consumes. Therefore, I present you with my general rule for setting the image resolution:

You don't always need to use the highest resolution.

And another rule:

Set the image resolution before *you shoot the picture.*

Here's how to set the image resolution for the Galaxy Note camera when taking still images:

1. **In the Camera app, touch the Menu button.**

2. **Choose Settings.**

   The Settings window appears, as shown in Figure 15-4. You can also get there by choosing the Settings icon (refer to Figure 15-3), which is why the Settings icon shown in Figure 15-4 is the Settings Settings Settings icon.

3. **Touch the Camera icon.**

4. **Choose Photo Size.**

5. **Choose a resolution.**

   The numbers in the white circles on the menu represent megapixels. The other numbers represent the horizontal-by-vertical image resolution in pixels. The final numbers (in parentheses) are the aspect ratio, width to height.

   The list of resolutions can be scrolled up and down.

6. **Press the Back button to return to the Camera app's main screen.**

   All the images you shoot from this point on are at the resolution you set in Step 5.

Video settings

Still image settings   Settings

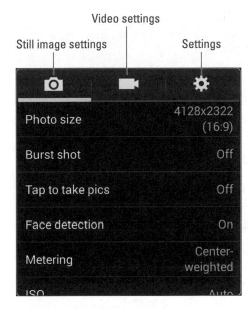

Figure 15-4: The window with the triple
Settings icon.

Check the video quality before you shoot!

✔ The phone's front-facing camera has different (and lower) resolutions than the rear camera. You must first switch to that camera to set its resolution.

✔ Yes, low resolutions are just fine for uploading to Facebook. The resolution of the output device (a computer monitor or tablet screen) is low; therefore, you don't need to waste storage and upload time sending high-resolution images or videos to Facebook.

✔ *Megapixel* is a measurement of the amount of information stored in an image. One megapixel is approximately 1 million *pixels,* or individual dots that compose an image. It's often abbreviated *MP.*

Setting video quality

Video recording uses image-quality settings, not resolution. To set the image quality for videos, choose the image-quality setting from the window shown in Figure 15-4: Follow the steps in the preceding section, but in Step 3 choose the Video icon. Use the Video Size item to choose the quality setting.

✔ As with setting single-shot resolution, the highest video quality isn't always required. For example, if you're shooting videos that you plan to upload to the Internet, select one of the lower qualities, if not the lowest quality.

✔ Set the resolution or video quality *before* you shoot! Especially when you know where the video will end up (on the Internet, on a TV, or in an e-mail), it helps to set the quality first.

Activating location information

The Galaxy Note not only takes a picture but also tracks where you're located on Planet Earth when you take the picture — if you've enabled that option. The feature is often called GPS Tag, although the command in the Galaxy Note's Camera app is titled Location Tag.

To confirm the Location Tag setting, follow these steps:

1. **While using the Camera app, press the Menu button.**

2. **Choose the Settings command.**

   An onscreen menu appears (refer to Figure 15-4).

3. **Touch the Settings tab.**

   It's the tab with the Gear icon (the Settings Settings Settings tab), shown earlier, in Figure 15-4.

4. **Ensure that the Location Tag item is set to On.**

   If it isn't, choose the Location Tag item and then touch On.

When the Location Tag setting is enabled, you see the GPS Tag icon appear on the Camera app's screen, as illustrated in Figure 15-1.

Not everyone is comfortable with having the phone record a picture's location, so you can turn off this option. Just repeat these steps, but in Step 4 choose the Off command.

See the later section "Navigating to an image's location" for information on how to use the GPS Tag feature.

Choosing the storage device

Images you take and videos you record on your Galaxy Note are stored on the primary storage device, also known as *internal storage*. You can change that location to the MicroSD card, or *external storage*. To do so, follow these steps while using the Camera app:

1. **Press the Menu button and choose the Settings command.**

2. **Touch the Settings Settings Settings tab.**

   Refer to Figure 15-4 for its location.

3. **Scroll down to choose the Storage item.**

4. **Choose Memory Card to direct the Camera app to use the Micro SD card for storing images and videos, or choose Device to use internal storage.**

When the memory card is chosen, the Memory Card icon appears on the Camera app screen (refer to Figure 15-1). When internal storage is chosen, the SD card icon doesn't appear.

Where Your Photos Lurk

The pictures and videos you take with your phone don't completely vanish after you touch the Camera app's Shutter icon. Though you can preview a previously shot picture or video, the place you go to look at the entire gamut of visual media is the app named Gallery.

Visiting the Gallery app

You can start the Gallery app by locating its icon on the Applications screen. Images (and videos) stored in the Gallery are organized into piles, or *albums,* as shown in Figure 15-5.

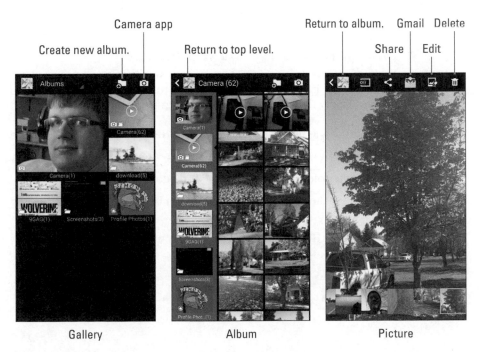

Figure 15-5: The Gallery app.

Choosing an album displays a stack of thumbnail images. Touch a thumbnail to see its full-screen image, as shown in the figure on the far right.

- ✔ Press the Back button or app icon (in the upper left corner of the screen) to back out of viewing an image and return to the album. Repeat that action to return to the main Gallery Library screen when you're done viewing an album.

- ✔ The Camera album contains pictures you've shot using the phone's camera. In Figure 15-5, two albums named Camera are shown: One represents images stored on the phone's internal storage, and the other represents images on the MicroSD card.

- ✔ The Download album contains images downloaded from the Internet.

- ✔ The Screenshots album holds screen captures you've taken on the Galaxy Note. Refer to the earlier section "Taking a screen shot."

- ✔ Albums from online photo-sharing sites also show up in the Gallery, as long as you've configured the Galaxy Note with your photo sharing account. Google's photo sharing service, Picasa Web, is one service that Galaxy Note can link to. Picasa Web albums are flagged by a special icon in the Gallery.

- ✔ Various apps may also create their own albums in the Gallery app.

- ✔ If you synchronize pictures between your phone and a computer, those programs that do the synchronizing also create their own albums.

Navigating to an image's location

When an image has a GPS tab, you can use the Gallery app to not only preview that image but also hunt down the location where the image was taken. Follow these steps in the Gallery app:

1. **Touch the image so that you can view it in Full-Screen mode.**

2. **Press the Menu button and choose the Get Directions command.**

   If you don't see the Get Directions command, the image lacks a GPS tag.

3. **Touch the route card that appears below the starting and ending destinations on the screen.**

   You see the location highlighted as a destination. You may have to zoom in to see the details.

At this point, you're using the Maps app on your Galaxy Note. Refer to Chapter 14 for information on navigation and finding locations.

Sharing from the Gallery

The key to getting images out of your phone and into the world is to look for the Share icon, shown in the margin. Touch that icon while viewing an image (refer to Figure 15-5), and peruse the apps shown on the list to choose a sharing method. Here are some of your choices:

Bluetooth: Send the picture or video to another device via the Bluetooth connection. That other device may be a printer, for example, in which case you can print the picture. See Chapter 19 for details on sharing with Bluetooth.

Gmail and Email: Attach the image to a new message you compose using either the Gmail or Email app. You can choose Gmail directly by touching the Gmail icon atop the image's screen, shown in Figure 15-5. (Tap the screen to make the icons appear.)

Facebook: Share the photo on the Facebook app.

Add to Dropbox: Save the photo in your Dropbox cloud storage.

The total number of apps available for sharing images depends on the variety of apps installed on your phone.

For sharing videos, choose the YouTube option. Fill in the information on the screen and touch the Upload button to publish your video.

Image Management

The Gallery app is more than just a photo album. It also sports features that let you perform minor image surgery. This section discusses a few of the more interesting options.

Cropping an image

One of the few true image-editing commands available in the Gallery app is Crop. You can use the Crop tool to slice out portions of an image, such as when removing ex-spouses and convicts from a family portrait. That probably leaves only you!

To crop an image, obey these directions while using the Gallery app:

1. **Summon the image you want to crop.**

   You must view the image on the screen by itself.

2. **Press the Menu button.**

3. **Choose Crop.**

   If the Crop command is unavailable, you have to choose another image. Not every album lets you modify images. For example, images imported from online photo-sharing sites cannot be edited on the phone.

4. **Work the crop-thing.**

   You can drag the rectangle around to choose which part of the image to crop. Drag an edge of the rectangle to resize the left and right or top and bottom sides. Or drag a corner of the rectangle to change the rectangle's size proportionally. Use Figure 15-6 as your guide.

Portion discarded

Drag rectangle.

Adjust sides and corners.

Portion kept

Figure 15-6: Working the crop-thing.

5. **Touch the Done button when you've finished cropping.**

   Only the portion of the image within the rectangle is saved; the rest is discarded.

Your Galaxy Note's Gallery app creates a new image when you crop. The original, uncropped image is retained. The new cropped image appears as its own image. That way, if you don't like the crop, you can delete that image and start over again with the original.

Rotating pictures

Showing someone else an image on your phone can be frustrating, especially when the image is a vertical picture that refuses to fill the screen when the phone is in a vertical orientation. You can fix that issue by rotating the picture.

To rotate, view the image in the Gallery app. Press the Menu button and choose either the Rotate Left or Rotate Right command. Repeat a command if you need to reorient the image more than 90 degrees.

To undo an image rotation, simply rotate the image again, but in the opposite direction.

Deleting photos and videos

It's entirely possible, and often desirable, to remove unwanted, embarrassing, or questionably legal images and videos from the Gallery. The limitation is that you can remove only those images copied to or created by the phone's camera. That includes all images in the Camera album, the Download album, and any albums you've synchronized from a desktop computer.

To delete an image, view it in the Gallery app. Touch the Delete icon and touch the OK button to confirm. Poof! It's gone.

   ✔ If the Delete icon doesn't show up, tap the screen.

   ✔ You can perform mass execution of images when viewing an album: Press the Menu button and choose the Select Item command. Touch images to select them, and then touch the Delete icon to rid yourself of the lot. Touch the OK button to confirm.

   ✔ You can't undelete an image you've deleted. There's no way to recover such an image using available tools on the Galaxy Note.

   ✔ Some images cannot be removed, such as images brought in from social networking sites or from online photo-sharing services. To remove those images, you must either stop synchronizing with the online album or visit the album sharing website and flag the photos as private — or just delete them.

Listen to the Music

In This Chapter

▶ Checking into music on your phone

▶ Listening to a song

▶ Copying music from your computer

▶ Purchasing music online

▶ Organizing your music into playlists

▶ Making a new playlist

▶ Listening to Internet radio

Musicians can be expensive. Years back, I would hire a band to follow me around and play music. The band had to be versatile: classical, jazz, show tunes, rock — no country. So you can imagine the money I've saved since I discovered that my Galaxy Note also serves as a portable music player. Not only that, but the phone is lighter, it eats a lot less than the musicians, and it's easier to get past the drug-sniffing dogs.

Your Top 40

To carry out portable-music-playing duties, your Galaxy Note comes with the Music app. It's your phone's digital jukebox, playing music that you buy, copy, or collect. It also handles general audio duties. So if you have any nonmusical sound files on your phone, they're played by the Music app as well.

Browsing your music library

To musically entertain yourself with the Galaxy Note, kick off your shoes, find a comfy place to relax, put on a set of headphones, and fire up the Music app. You'll find it on the Applications screen.

Oh, I suppose you could don your dancing booties and dance while you listen to tunes. Either way, Figure 16-1 shows the Music app in Album view. If you don't see any albums on your phone — or any music, for that matter — quickly flip forward to the section "The Hits Just Keep On Coming" for information on acquiring music for your phone.

Albums

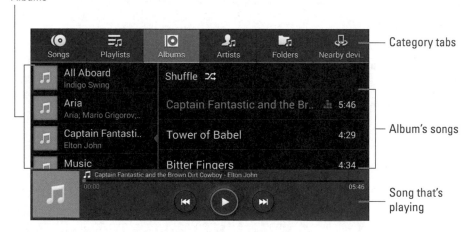

Figure 16-1: Albums in the music library.

The Music app organizes by category the music stored on your phone. The categories appear at the top of the app's screen, as shown in Figure 16-1. When the phone is held vertically, only a few of the categories show up; swipe the screen left or right to access them all. Here's the gamut:

Songs: All songs stored in the phone are listed alphabetically.

Playlists: Songs are presented according to *playlists,* which are groups of songs you create. See the later section "Music Organization."

Albums: Songs are organized by album. Choose an album to list its songs, as illustrated in Figure 16-1.

Artists: Songs are listed by recording artist or group. Choose this category, and then choose an artist to see their albums. Choosing an album displays the songs for that album. Some artists may have only one song, not in any particular album.

Folders: Getting nerdy, the songs are presented according to how they're stored on the phone. Typically, that's done by placing artists and albums into folders. You may find two Music folders, for example — one for music saved to the phone's internal storage and another for music on the MicroSD card.

Nearby Devices: Songs are accessed via the local network and any actively broadcasting media-sharing devices. Touch a computer, game machine, or media device to access and listen to the songs available on that device.

These categories (with the exception of Nearby Devices) are merely ways to organize the music — ways to make tunes easier to find when you may know an artist's name but not an album title or when you may want to hear a song but you don't know who recorded it.

- Any song that's playing appears on the screen, as shown earlier, in Figure 16-1. Use the onscreen controls to play, pause, or switch to another song.

- The size of the phone's storage limits the total amount of music you can keep on your phone. Also, consider that pictures and videos stored on your phone horn in on some of the space that can be used for music.

- Album artwork generally appears on imported music as well as on music you purchase online. If an album has no artwork, it cannot be manually added or updated (at least, not by using the Music app).

- When your phone is unable to recognize an artist, it uses the title *<Unknown>*. This happens with music you copy manually to the phone. Music that you purchase, or import or synchronize with a computer, generally retains the artist and album information. (Well, the information is retained as long as it was supplied on the original source.)

Playing a tune

To listen to music on your phone, first find a song in the Music app's library, as described in the preceding section. Then touch the song title. The song plays on its own screen, similar to the one shown in Figure 16-2.

While the song is playing, you're free to do anything else with the phone. In fact, the song continues to play even when the phone is locked. In that case, the song appears on the lock screen, along with Play/Pause and other controls.

After the song is done playing, the next song in the list plays. Touch the Show Song List button (refer to Figure 16-2) to review the songs in the list.

The next song doesn't play if you have activated the Shuffle feature. In this case, the phone randomizes the songs in the list, so who knows which one is next?

The next song might not play if you have the Repeat option on: The three Repeat settings are shown in Table 16-1, along with the Shuffle settings. To change a setting, simply touch either the Shuffle or Repeat icon.

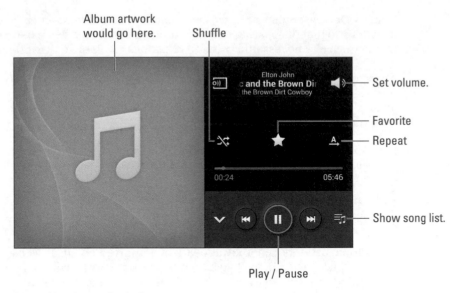

Album artwork would go here.

Shuffle

Set volume.

Favorite

Repeat

Show song list.

Play / Pause

Figure 16-2: A song is playing.

To stop the song from playing, touch the Pause button (refer to Figure 16-2).

Table 16-1	Shuffle and Repeat Icons	
Icon	*Setting*	*What Happens When You Touch the Icon*
	Shuffle Is Off	Songs play one after the other.
	Shuffle Is On	Songs are played in random order.
	Repeat Is Off	Song don't repeat.
	Repeat All Songs	All songs in the list play over and over.
	Repeat Current Song	The same song plays over and over.

When music plays on the phone, a notification icon appears, similar to the one shown in the margin. Pull down the notifications panel to access the music controls. Touch the Music button to quickly summon the Music app.

- The volume is set by using the Volume button on the side of the phone: Up is louder; Down is quieter.

- Determining which song plays next depends on how you chose the song that's playing. If you choose a song by artist, all songs from that artist play, one after the other. When you choose a song by album, that album plays. Choosing a song from the entire song list causes all songs in the phone to play.

- To choose which songs play after one another, create a playlist. See the section "Music Organization," later in this chapter.

- After the last song in the list plays, the phone stops playing songs — unless the Repeat All Songs option is set, in which case the song or list plays again.

- Touch the Favorite (Star) icon to add the song to the Favorites playlist. See the later section "Reviewing your playlists."

"What's this song?"

You might consider getting a handy, music-oriented widget called Sound Search for Google Play. You can obtain this widget from the Google Play Store and then add it to the Home screen, as described in Chapter 22. From the Home screen, you can use the widget to identify music playing within earshot of your phone.

To use the widget, touch it on the Home screen. The widget immediately starts listening to your surroundings, as shown in the middle of the sidebar figure. After a few seconds, the song is recognized and displayed. You can choose to either buy the song at the Google Play Store or touch the Cancel button and start over.

The Sound Search widget works best (exclusively, I would argue) with recorded music. Try as you might, you cannot sing into the thing and have it recognize a song. Humming doesn't work, either. I've tried playing the guitar and piano and — nope — that doesn't work, either.

But for listening to ambient music, it's a good tool for discovering what you're listening to.

The Hits Just Keep On Coming

Odds are good that your Galaxy Note came with no music preinstalled. It may have, though: Some resellers may have preinstalled a smattering of tunes, which merely lets you know how out of touch they are musically. Regardless, you can add music to your phone in a number of ways, as covered in this section.

Borrowing music from your computer

It may seem odd, but when you look for music in the 21st century, you look to your computer, not to a stereo system. Even the once ubiquitous stack of CDs or shelf full of albums is now replaced by the humble PC. So why not purloin a few of the tunes stored there and copy them to your phone? Here's how it works:

1. **Connect the phone to the PC.**

   Use the USB cable that comes with the phone.

   If you have trouble, ensure that your phone is connected as a media player or uses something called MTP. See Chapter 20 if you have difficulty making the connection.

   Over on the PC, the AutoPlay dialog box appears in Windows, prompting you to choose how best to mount the phone into the Windows storage system.

2. **On the PC, choose Windows Media Player from the AutoPlay dialog box.**

   The option may be labeled Sync Digital Media Files to This Device.

   If the AutoPlay dialog box doesn't appear, start the Windows Media Player program.

3. **On the PC, ensure that the Sync list appears, as shown in Figure 16-3.**

   Click the Sync tab or the Sync toolbar button to view the Sync list. Your phone should appear atop the list, similar to what's shown in the figure.

   If you have a MicroSD card installed in your Galaxy Note, you find two sync locations, as illustrated in Figure 16-3. Choose Card to save music to the MicroSD card; choose Phone to use internal storage. Either location is fine, but external storage (MicroSD or card) most likely has more room.

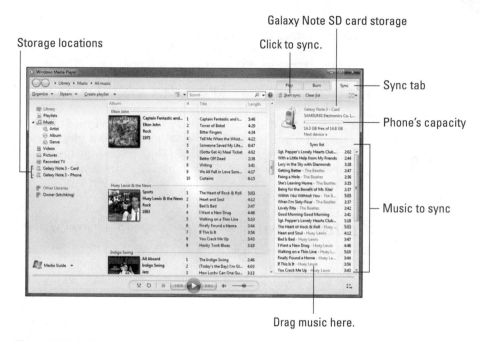

Figure 16-3: Adding music to your phone.

4. Drag to the Sync area the music you want to transfer to your phone.

In Figure 16-3, you see a list of songs that appear in the Sync list. To add more, drag an album or individual song into the Sync list. Dragging an album sets up all its songs for transfer.

5. Click the Start Sync button to transfer the music from the PC to your Galaxy Note.

The Start Sync button may be located atop the list, as shown in Figure 16-3, or it might be found on the bottom, depending on the version of Windows Media Player.

6. Close the Windows Media Player when the transfer is complete.

Or keep it open — whatever.

7. Unplug the phone from the USB cable.

You can unplug the USB cable from the computer as well. Chapter 20 specifically covers the phone-to-computer connection, if you need more information.

The steps for synchronizing music with other media jukebox programs work similarly to those I just outlined.

✔ You cannot use iTunes to synchronize music with your Galaxy Note.

✔ Another option for copying music is to use the Samsung Kies program. See Chapter 20.

✔ The phone can store only so much music! Don't be overzealous when copying over your tunes. In Windows Media Player (refer to Figure 16-3), a capacity-thermometer thing shows you how much storage space is used and how much is available on your phone. Pay heed to the indicator!

Getting music from the Google Play Store

It's possible to get music for your Galaxy Note from the same source where you buy apps — the Google Play Store. This music is not, however, available to the Music app. Instead, you must obtain Google's Play Music app, which can be downloaded from the Play Store to your Galaxy Note.

See Chapter 18 for information on obtaining apps such as Play Music. Should you do so, you can obtain music from the Play Store. Here's how it works:

1. **Open the Play Store app on your phone.**

   It can be found on the Home screen or, like all apps, on the Applications screen.

2. **Choose the Music category.**

   The Music category is found on the Store Home screen, the top level in the app. Choose Store Home from the sidebar; see Chapter 18 for specifics on how the Play Store app works.

3. **Use the Search command to locate music you want, or just browse the categories.**

   Keep an eye out for special offers at the Play Store. It's a great way to pick up some free tunes.

   Eventually, you see a page showing details about the song or album. Choose a song from the list to hear a preview. The button next to the song or album indicates the purchase price, or it says *FREE,* for free music.

4. **Touch the FREE button to get a free song; touch the BUY or price button to purchase a song or album.**

   Don't worry — you're not buying anything yet.

5. To buy music, choose your credit card or payment source.

If a credit card or payment source doesn't appear, touch the Continue button to set up a payment method. Sign up with Google Checkout and submit your credit card or other payment information.

You may be prompted to type your Google password.

6. Touch the Buy button or Confirm button.

The song or album is added to the Galaxy Note's music library.

The music you buy at the Play Store isn't downloaded to your phone. It shows up only in the Play Music app, and it plays over an Internet connection. You can retain the music on your phone by touching the Pushpin icon to "pin" the music. That way, it can be played without an Internet connection.

If you desire to buy music electronically, I can recommend the Amazon MP3 app. It lets you buy music from the Amazon website. To keep the music on your phone, it must be downloaded from the Amazon cloud to the Galaxy Note. All music you download by using the Amazon MP3 app is available instantly to your Galaxy Note's Music app.

✔ All music sales in the Google Play Store are final. Don't blame me — I'm just writing down Google's current policy for music purchases.

✔ If you plan to download an album or multiple songs, connect to a Wi-Fi network. That way, you don't run the risk of a data surcharge on your cellular plan. See Chapter 19 for information on activating the Galaxy Note's Wi-Fi.

✔ You eventually receive a Gmail message listing a summary of your purchase.

✔ Music you purchase from the Google Play Music store is available on any mobile Android device with the Play Music app installed — if you use the same Google account on that device. You can also listen to your tunes by visiting the `http://music.google.com` site on any computer connected to the Internet.

Music Organization

The Music app organizes your music by category, song, artist, album, and so on. Like most humans, however, you probably have favorite songs and tunes that match your mood. You have things that you like to hear in one setting or songs you prefer to listen to in another. Music is emotional, after all.

To fulfill your personal tastes and moods, you can organize your tunes into playlists. A *playlist* is a collection of tunes you create. You build the list by combining songs from whatever music you have on your phone. You can then listen to the playlist and hear the music you want to hear in the order you want to hear it.

Reviewing your playlists

The Music app automatically creates a cadre of playlists for you, including

Favorite: Songs you've flagged by touching the Star icon

Most Played: Songs you play most often — your obsessions

Recently Played: Songs you've listened to recently

Recently Added: Songs you've just copied to the phone or purchased online

Beyond these playlists, you can create your own. Build playlists to match your mood, to organize songs you like, to build a party list, and so on. To view all available playlists, choose the Playlists tab at the top of the Music app screen.

To listen to a playlist, chose it from the list of playlists and touch the first song in the playlist.

A playlist is a helpful way to organize music when a song's information may not have been completely imported into your phone. For example, if you're like me, you probably have a lot of songs by "Unknown." The quick way to remedy this situation is to build a playlist for the artist and then add those unknown songs to the playlist. See the next section.

Building playlists

To create your own, custom playlist, or to add songs to an existing playlist, follow these steps:

1. **Long-press the song, artist, or album that you want to add to the playlist.**

   When you choose Artist or Album, all songs associated with that artist or album are added to the playlist.

2. **Choose the Add to Playlist command.**

3. **Touch the Plus icon to create a new playlist, or choose the playlist to add the song(s) to that playlist.**

   If you choose to create a new playlist, type a short, descriptive name for it. Touch the OK button to create the playlist and to add songs to the playlist.

4. **Repeat Steps 1 through 3 to continue building or creating playlists.**

The songs appear in the playlist in the order you add them; you cannot rearrange the order afterward. That's a bummer.

You can continue adding songs to as many playlists as you like. Adding songs to a playlist doesn't noticeably affect the phone's storage capacity.

- To remove a song from a playlist, long-press the song in the playlist and choose the Remove command. Removing a song from a playlist doesn't delete the song from your phone. (See the next section for information on deleting songs from the music library.)

- To delete a playlist, long-press its name in the list of playlists. Choose the Delete command. Although the playlist is removed, none of the songs in the playlist has been deleted.

Deleting music

To purge unwanted music from your phone, follow these brief, painless steps while using the Music app:

1. **Long-press the music that offends you.**

    It can be an album, a song, or even an artist.

2. **Choose Delete.**

    A warning message appears.

3. **Touch the OK button.**

    The music is gone.

You cannot use your phone to delete music purchased at the Google Play Store for the Play Music app. You can, however, remove the songs by visiting the My Music website: http://music.google.com. Click the triangle menu next to an album title and choose the Delete Album command.

Galaxy Note Radio

Though they're not broadcast radio stations, some sources on the Internet — *Internet radio* sites — play music. Lamentably, your Galaxy Note doesn't come with any Internet radio apps, but that doesn't stop you from finding a few good ones at the Google Play Store. Two free services that I can recommend are

- TuneIn Radio
- Pandora Radio

The TuneIn Radio app gives you access to hundreds of Internet radio stations broadcasting around the world. They're organized by category, so you can find just about whatever you want. Many of the stations are also broadcast radio stations, so odds are good that you can find a local station or two, which you can listen to on your phone.

Pandora Radio lets you select music based on your mood and customizes, according to your feedback, the tunes you listen to. The app works like the Internet site www.pandora.com, in case you're familiar with it. The nifty thing about Pandora is that the more you listen, the better the app gets at finding music you like.

These apps are available at the Google Play Store. They're free, although paid versions might also be available.

✔ It's best to listen to Internet radio when your phone is connected to the Internet via a Wi-Fi connection. Streaming music can use a lot of your cellular data plan's data allotment.

✔ See Chapter 18 for more information about the Google Play Store.

✔ Internet music of the type delivered by the apps mentioned in this section is referred to by the nerds as *streaming* music. That's because the music arrives on your phone as a continuous download from the source. Unlike music you download and save, streaming music is played as it comes in and isn't stored long-term.

What Else Does It Do?

In This Chapter

▶ Setting alarms

▶ Using the calculator

▶ Checking your schedule

▶ Reading eBooks

▶ Playing games

▶ Using Google Now

▶ Scribbling on the screen

▶ Recording audio

▶ Enjoying YouTube

*W*hat do you call one gadget that serves many purposes? Years back, it would have been a *fantasy,* a *fake,* or a *Swiss army knife.* In the TV show *Star Trek,* it was the *tricorder,* which was a combination computer-recording device that made a loud, whistling noise even when Mr. Spock was sneaking around. Today, that device is called a Galaxy Note phone.

This chapter covers the smattering of apps included with the Galaxy Note that do interesting and useful things. It answers the question, "What else does it do?"

It's a Clock

The Galaxy Note keeps constant and accurate track of the time, which is displayed at the top of the Home screen as well as the unlock screen. Because the time is kept accurately, I would take the phone's time-keeping ability as a sure sign that you should toss out every clock in your house. Well, maybe not *every* clock, but you can do without your alarm clock, for certain.

The Clock app is the Galaxy Note's timekeeping headquarters. It features an alarm clock, 'round-the-world clocks, a stopwatch, a timer, and even a plain old desk clock. The only thing it can't do is time-travel, but that option is rumored to be included in the next release.

Here's what the four tabs in the Clock app do:

Alarm: Set or reset alarms and alerts or create new alarms and alerts.

World Clock: View the current time in various cities around the globe.

Stopwatch: Time events, such as how long it takes the lad to clean his room after you ask.

Timer: Set a quick timer that you can use for cooking or to wake up from a nap. I use the Timer to remind me to keep my laundry moving.

Figure 17-1 shows the Clock app's Alarm face, with several alarms created and two of them set.

Figure 17-1: The Clock app wakes you up.

You create alarms by touching the Create Alarm button. Fill in the various fields on the screen, setting the alarm time, day, and sound; whether it repeats; and so on. Give the alarm a descriptive name, and then tap the Save button.

Alarms must be set, or else they won't trigger. Set an existing alarm by touching its icon, shown in Figure 17-1.

✔ When an alarm is set, the Alarm status icon appears atop the screen, similar to the one that appears in the margin. The icon is your clue that an alarm is set and ready to trigger.

✔ For a larger time display, you can add the Clock widget to the Home screen. Refer to Chapter 22 for more information about widgets on the Home screen.

✔ Turning off an alarm doesn't delete the alarm.

✔ To delete an alarm, long-press the alarm and choose the Delete command. The alarm is gone.

✔ The alarm doesn't work when you turn off the phone. The alarm goes off, however, when the phone is locked. The alarm also sounds when you've silenced the phone.

✔ Consider getting a docking station so that you can use your phone as a nighttime music station and clock.

✔ So tell me: Do alarms go *off*, or do they go *on*?

It's a Calculator

One of the oldest, most traditional, and most frighteningly dull cell phone apps is Calculator. Please — don't let the math frighten you.

Start the Calculator app by choosing its icon from the Applications screen; it's found in the Samsung folder. The Calculator appears, as shown in Figure 17-2. Feel free to type various math problems; the phone does the math.

✔ The scary calculator buttons appear only when the phone is held in a horizontal orientation.

✔ Long-press the calculator's text (or results) to cut or copy the results.

✔ I use the Calculator most often to determine my tip at a restaurant. In Figure 17-2, a calculation is being made for an 18 percent tip on a tab of $56.24, which would have been less had my date not insisted on getting dessert.

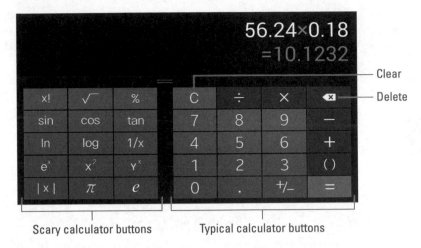

Scary calculator buttons   Typical calculator buttons

Figure 17-2: The Calculator.

It's a Calendar

Nothing beats keeping track of your appointments and schedule, especially when you become rich and famous. The mere act of having kids often requires that you make note of where you need to be and when. To help you stay on time, and to prevent little Molly from spending another tear-filled afternoon stranded at the roller rink, the Galaxy Note offers the handy S Planner app.

- The S Planner app works with your Google account to keep track of your schedule and appointments. You can visit Google Calendar on the web at

   `http://calendar.google.com`

- You automatically have a Google Calendar; it comes with your Google account.

- I recommend that you use the S Planner app on your phone to access Google Calendar. It's a better way to access your schedule than using the Internet app to reach Google Calendar on the web.

- Before you throw away your datebook, copy into the S Planner app some future appointments and info, such as birthdays and anniversaries.

- The S Planner app is known as the Calendar app on other Android phones. You may see it referred to as such in various Android phone documentation.

- You can install a Calendar widget on the Home screen for quick access to looming appointments in the S Planner app. See Chapter 22 for details on adding widgets to the Home screen.

Checking your schedule

To see your schedule or upcoming important events, or to know simply which day of the month it is, summon the S Planner app. It can be found on the Applications screen. Touch its icon to behold the magnificence of your schedule.

Figure 17-3 shows the S Planner app's three views: Month, Week, and Day. They look subtly different in the horizontal orientation, but it's the same information. Not shown is Agenda view, which displays only upcoming events. Each view is chosen from the View action bar, illustrated in the figure.

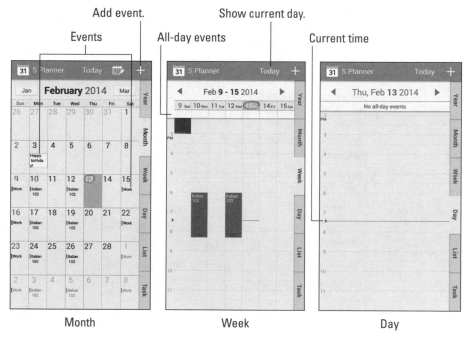

Month Week Day

Figure 17-3: The Calendar app.

- ✏ Use Month view to see an overview of what's going on, and use Week view or Day view to see your appointments.

- ✏ I check Week view at the start of the week to remind me of what's coming up.

- ✏ To scroll from month to month, swipe the screen up or down. In Week view or Day view, scroll from left to right.

- ✏ Touch the Today icon to be instantly whisked back to the current day.

✔ The current day is highlighted in Month view and Week view. A horizontal bar marks the current time (refer to Day view in Figure 17-3).

✔ Different colors flag your events. The colors represent a calendar category to which the events are assigned. See the later section "Creating a new event" for information on calendars.

Reviewing events

To see more detail about an event, touch it. When you're using Month view, touch the event's date to see Week view. Then choose the event again to see its details, similar to the event shown in Figure 17-4.

Review or change reminder warning.
Edit event.
Event details
Share event.
Touch to see event location in the Maps app.
Remove reminder.

Figure 17-4: Event details.

The details you see depend on how much information was recorded when the event was created. Some events have only a minimum of information; others may have details, such as a location for the event. When the event's location is listed, you can touch that location and the Maps app pops up to show you where the event is being held.

Touch the Back button to dismiss the event's details.

- ✔ Birthdays and a few other events on the calendar may be pulled from the phone's address book or from social networking apps. That probably explains why some events are listed twice; they're pulled in from two sources.

- ✔ The best way to review upcoming appointments is to choose the List tab on the right side of the screen.

- ✔ Google Now also lists any immediate appointments or events. See the later section "It's Google Now."

Creating a new event

The key to making the S Planner app work is to add events: appointments, things to do, meetings, or full-day events such as birthdays and lobotomies. To create a new event, follow these steps:

1. **Touch the Add Event button.**

   Refer to Figure 17-3 for its location, which is the same no matter which way you're viewing the calendar. Well, unless you hold the phone horizontally, in which case you must touch the New button.

2. **Ensure that the Add Event tab is chosen.**

   If not, you're creating a new task, which isn't a time-specific event.

3. **Type the event name.**

   For example, type **Colonoscopy**.

4. **Set the event's starting date and time and then the ending date and time.**

   If the event lasts all day, such as when your in-laws visit you for an hour, place a green check mark in the All Day box.

5. **Choose the calendar.**

   Calendars are a way to organize events by color, or to associate an event with a specific online account. If you're unsure, choose your Gmail account from the Calendar menu.

6. **If the event repeats, such as a regular meeting or appointment, touch the Repeat item to specify how and when the event reoccurs.**

7. **Set the location.**

   For the location, type a search item similar to one you'd type when searching for an address using the Maps app. If you have the full address, type it in, but often just a street address and zip code work.

8. Fill in other fields to further describe the event.

A good item to set is the event reminder. That way, the phone signals you for an impending date or appointment.

9. Touch the Save button to create the new event.

To change an event after it's been created, display its details and touch the Edit icon (refer to Figure 17-4).

To remove an event, display its details and press the Menu button. Choose the Delete command, and then touch the OK button to confirm.

When an event's day and time arrive, and as long as you've set an event reminder (refer to Step 8 in this section), an Event Reminder notification appears, similar to the one shown in the margin. You might also receive a Gmail notification, depending on how you chose to be reminded when the event was created.

- ✒ You can change an event at any time: Simply touch the event to bring up more information, and then touch the Edit icon to make modifications (refer to Figure 17-4).

- ✒ Calendar categories are handy because they let you organize and color-code your events. They can be confusing because Google calls them *calendars*. I think of them more as categories: I have different calendars (categories) for my personal and work schedules, government duties, clubs, and so on.

- ✒ Try to avoid using the My Calendar category for your events. Those events appear on your phone, but they aren't shared with your Google account.

- ✒ If you use a Microsoft Exchange Server account, choose that account to coordinate the event with other devices that also access the account.

- ✒ My advice is to type location information for an event as though you're typing a search query for the Maps app. When the event is displayed, the location becomes a link; touch the link to see where you need to go on the map.

- ✒ When the event lasts all day, such as a birthday or your mother-in-law's visit that was supposed to last for an hour, touch the All Day box to add a check mark.

- ✒ When you have events that repeat twice a month (say, on the first and third Mondays), you need to create two separate events — one for the first Monday and another for the third. Then have each event repeat monthly.

- ✒ You can set additional reminders by touching the green Plus icon by the Reminder heading.

- To remove an event, touch the event to display the details. Press the Menu button and choose the Delete command. Touch the OK button to confirm. When deleting repeating events, you need to specify whether all events are being removed or only the one.

- It's necessary to set an event's time zone only when that event takes place in another time zone or when an event spans time zones, such as an airline flight. In that case, the Calendar app automatically adjusts the starting and stopping times for events, depending on where you are.

- If you forget to set the time zone and you end up hopping around the world, your events are set according to the time zone in which they were created, not the local time.

It's an eBook Reader

An *eBook* is an electronic version of a printed book. The words, formatting, figures, pictures — all that stuff is simply stored digitally so that you can read it on something called an *eBook reader*. The Galaxy Note doesn't come with any eBook reader apps, but don't let that stop you from enjoying eBooks on your phablet.

Two eBook reader apps I can recommend are Google's own Play Books app and the Amazon Kindle app. Both are available at the Google Play Store. Installing apps from the Play Store is covered in Chapter 18.

After you obtain an eBook reader app, your next stop is an electronic bookstore to pick up some reading material.

For the Play Books app, eBooks are obtained at the Google Play Store. You use the same Play Store app to buy books as you do to obtain apps. The process works the same.

For the Amazon Kindle app, eBooks are obtained from Amazon's Kindle store. It helps if you already have an Amazon account, in which case you log in to that account to obtain your electronic texts.

Both eBook reader apps organize eBooks into a digital library, similar to what's shown in Figure 17-5 for the Play Books app. The library lists any titles you've obtained for your Google Books account. Or when you're returning to the Play Books app after a break, you see the current page of the eBook you were last reading. You can choose either mode from the sidebar, as shown in the figure.

Viewing options

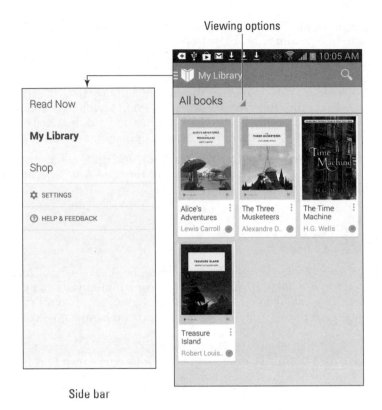

Side bar

Figure 17-5: The Play Books library.

Touch a book in the digital library to open it. If you've opened the book previously, you're returned to the page you last read. Otherwise, the first page you see is the book's first page.

To begin reading, touch a book to open it.

Figure 17-6 illustrates the basic book-reading operation in the Play Books app. You turn pages by swiping left or right, but probably mostly left. You can also turn pages by touching the far left or right side of the screen.

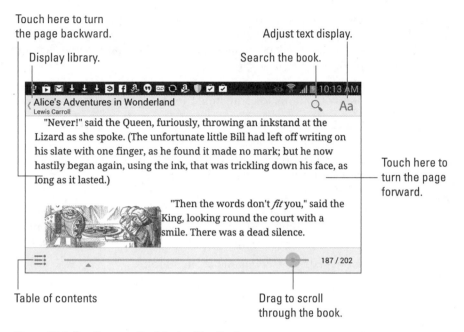

Touch here to turn
the page backward.

Display library.

Adjust text display.

Search the book.

Touch here to
turn the page
forward.

Table of contents

Drag to scroll
through the book.

Figure 17-6: Reading an eBook in the Play Books app.

The Play Books app also works in the vertical orientation, which you may find easier for reading, although you won't see all the icons shown in Figure 17-6.

- ✔ The advantage of an eBook reader is that you can carry an entire library of books with you without developing back problems.

- ✔ If you don't see a book in the library, press the Menu button and choose the Refresh command.

- ✔ To ensure that your reading material is always available in the Play Books app, touch the Action Overflow icon on a book's cover and choose the Keep On Device command. That way, the phone doesn't need an Internet connection to synchronize and download books to the library. I choose this command specifically before I leave on a trip where an Internet signal may not be available (such as in an airplane).

- ✔ To remove a book from the Play Books library, touch the Action Overflow icon on the book's cover and choose the Delete from Library command.

- ✔ If the onscreen controls (refer to Figure 17-6) disappear, touch the screen to see them again.

- eBooks do not have indexes. Some might, but because text size and phone orientation affect pagination, a traditional index doesn't make sense. Rather than rely on an index, use the eBook app's Search command to locate items of interest.

- The *Aa* icon is used to adjust the display. Touching this button displays a menu of options for adjusting the text on the screen and the brightness.

- To return to the library, touch the Play Books app icon in the upper left corner of the screen or press the Back button.

- Synchronization allows you to keep copies of your Google Books on all your Android devices as well as on the `http://books.google.com` website.

- Lots of eBooks are free, such as quite a few of the classics, including some that aren't boring. Current and popular titles cost money, though the cost is often less than the book's real-world equivalent.

- Not every title is available as an eBook.

- Yes, you need an Amazon account to purchase eBooks (or even to download freebies) for the Kindle eBook reader app. I highly recommend that you visit Amazon.com to set up an account, if you don't already have one.

- To ensure that you get your entire Kindle library on your Galaxy Note, turn on the Wi-Fi connection (see Chapter 19), press the Menu button, and choose the Archived Items command.

It's a Game Machine

The secret is out: You can use your Galaxy Note to play games. Not just the old, boring cell phone games but also the sophisticated games that eagerly consume your valuable time.

As far as I can tell, not a single game is prepackaged on the phone. Well, unless you consider the Google Finance app a game.

Plenty of understandable and enjoyable games are available at the Google Play Store, including zillions of titles that are popular, free, and captivating. Visit the Google Play Store and choose the Games category. Slide the screen to the left until you see the Top Free category. Have fun.

See Chapter 18 for details on using the Google Play Store to obtain thrill-a-minute apps for your phone.

It's Google Now

Don't worry about the Galaxy Note controlling too much of your life: It harbors no insidious intelligence, and the Robot Revolution is still years away. Until then, you can use your phone's listening abilities to enjoy the feature called Google Now. It's not quite like having your own, personal Jeeves, but it's on its way.

Activate Google Now by using the Google Search widget on the Home screen. You can also start the Google app, nestled in the Google folder on the Applications screen. After the brief, first-time tutorial ends, you're ready to use Google Now.

Figure 17-7 illustrates a typical Google Now screen. Below the Search text box, you'll find cards. You cannot manually add cards. If you want more, keep using Google Now. The more it learns about you, the more cards appear.

Cards

Search for something.

Ask a question.

Swipe a card to the right to dismiss it.

Figure 17-7: Google Now is ready for business. Or play.

You can use Google Now to search the Internet, just as you would use Google's main web page. More interesting than that, you can ask Google Now questions; see the nearby sidebar, "Barking orders to Google Now."

Barking orders to Google Now

One way to have a lot of fun is to use the Google Now app verbally. Just say, "Okay, Google." Say it out loud. Anytime you see the Google Now app, it's listening to you. Or, when the app is being stubborn, touch the Microphone icon.

You can speak simple search terms, such as "Find pictures of Megan Fox." Or you can give more complex orders, among them:

✔ Will it rain tomorrow?

✔ What time is it in Frankfurt, Germany?

✔ How many euros equal $25?

✔ What is 103 divided by 6?

✔ How can I get to Disneyland?

✔ Where is the nearest Canadian restaurant?

✔ What's the score of the Lakers–Celtics game?

✔ What is the answer to life, the universe, and everything?

When asked such questions, Google Now responds with a card and a verbal reply. When a verbal reply isn't available, you see Google search results displayed.

It's a Scribble Pad

When you're desperate to use the S Pen, you need only summon the Action Memo app. It's the primary app on the Galaxy Note to take advantage of the S Pen, by letting you doodle, draw, or mark up documents, which you can then save or share to make all the other smartphone owners jealous.

Using the Action Memo app

To play or, um, work with the S Pen, start the S Memo app. You can summon this app in two ways.

The clever, S Pen way is to use the Air Command whatsis: While pressing the S Pen button, bring the S Pen close to the phone's touchscreen. Choose the Action Memo item, the first one on the right. Or you can just hold the S Pen button and tap the screen twice. Either way, the Action Memo pad appears on the screen.

The not-as-clever, un-S Pen way is to open the Action Memo app on the Applications screen. It's found in the Samsung folder. When you open the Action Memo app, you can peruse and manage previous memos, as well as scribble new ones, similar to what's shown in Figure 17-8.

Figure 17-8: The S Memo app.

To create a new document, touch the Add icon. Start scribbling. Use the icons atop the memo pad, shown in Figure 17-8, to help craft your message. Touch the Save icon to save.

Saved memos appear on the main S Memo screen. You can choose a saved memo for editing or just view it in a larger format.

- Opening the Action Memo app allows you to review and manage your memos. The S Pen-screen-tap method merely pops up a quick window for taking notes.

- You don't need to use the S Pen to draw your masterpieces. Your finger works but lacks the refinement of the pen — which I suppose explains the difference between painting with a brush and finger painting.

- See Chapter 3 for more information on the Air Command whatsis.

Capturing and scribbling

A common thing to do with the S Pen is to capture a screen image, scribble on that image, and then send the image off, sharing it with friends, enemies, and co-workers. Here's how this operation works:

1. **Summon the screen upon which you want to scribble.**

   It can be anything you see on the Galaxy Note's screen, any app, any window, anything that shows up — even the lock screen (though it doesn't capture well).

2. **Press the S Pen button, and then long-press the touchscreen using the S Pen.**

   You hear a shutter sound, and the screen blinks. You've just captured the screen, which is now saved. Your next step is to mark up that screen-capture image, which looks similar to the one shown in Figure 17-9.

Figure 17-9: Scribbling on a screen capture.

3. **Scribble.**

   Use the controls, illustrated in Figure 17-9, to mess with the image.

4. **Touch the Share icon to send the image elsewhere.**

   Choose an app to use for sharing, such as Gmail, Facebook, or any of the other apps or options displayed.

5. **Touch the Save button to save the image.**

Scribbles that you capture in this manner are saved in the Gallery. Look in the Screenshots album.

It's a Tape Recorder

It makes sense that your Galaxy Note should be able to record your voice. It has a microphone. It has a speaker. It has storage. All it needs is the smarts — the app — to record, and voilà! The app is the Voice Recorder, and it comes preinstalled on your phone, dwelling in the Samsung folder on the Applications screen.

After opening the Voice Recorder, you see the main screen, shown in Figure 17-10. Touch the Record button to begin recording your voice or your surroundings. (In the figure, the app is recording, so the Record button has changed to the Pause button.)

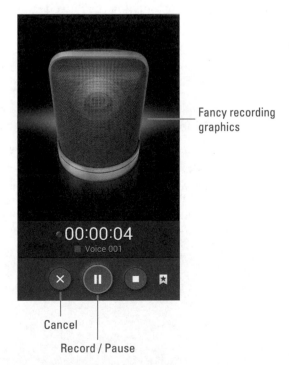

Fancy recording graphics

Cancel

Record / Pause

Figure 17-10: The phone is listening.

When you're done, touch the Stop button. The recording is saved to the library (not shown in Figure 17-10). Long-press an entry and choose the Rename command to apply a better, more descriptive name to your recordings.

- ✔ To get the recording out of your phone, long-press it. Choose the Share Via command, and then select the appropriate app, such as Gmail, to send the recording elsewhere.

- ✔ Recordings are saved in the Sounds folder on the phone's internal storage. They're saved in the MPEG-4, audio-only file format, with the `.m4a` filename extension.

- ✔ *Tape recorders* were mechanical devices used to record audio. Your elders may still have a tape recorder handy so that you may look at it with nostalgic awe. Either that, or you can find a tape recorder in any nearby technology museum or antique store.

It's a Video Player

It's not possible to watch "real" TV on your phone, but a few apps come close. The YouTube app is handy for watching random, meaningless drivel, which I suppose makes it a lot like TV.

Search for videos in the YouTube app by touching the Search icon. Type the video name, a topic, or any search terms to locate videos. Zillions of videos are available.

The YouTube app displays suggestions for any channels you're subscribed to, which allows you to follow favorite topics or YouTube content providers.

- ✔ Use the YouTube app to view YouTube videos, rather than use the Internet app to visit the YouTube website.

- ✔ Orient the phone horizontally to view the video in a larger size.

- ✔ Because you have a Google account, you also have a YouTube account. I recommend that you log in to your YouTube account when using the YouTube app: Touch the Action Overflow icon and choose the Sign In command. Log in if you haven't already. Otherwise, you see your account information, your videos, and any video subscriptions.

- ✔ Not all YouTube videos are available for viewing on mobile devices.

18

The Apps Chapter

In This Chapter

▶ Using the Play Store app

▶ Managing apps

▶ Searching for apps

▶ Downloading a free app

▶ Getting a paid app

▶ Reviewing apps you've downloaded

▶ Sharing an app

▶ Updating an app

▶ Organizing the Apps menu

*T*he Windows operating system didn't come to rule the PC world because of Microsoft's ruthless sales. Well, perhaps, but what Windows really had going for it was a wealth of available software, those programs that make a computer worth more than the sum of its parts. When it comes to technology, the gauge of success is software, not computer hardware.

As software makes a computer, apps make a decent smartphone. To meet this end, your Galaxy Note has access to hundreds of thousands of apps, all available for the horde of Android phones. You can get new apps to expand the phone's abilities, apps to entertain and distract you, and apps to help you get work done. Welcome to the apps chapter.

2. Pandora® internet r̶a̶
Pandora ◇
★★★★★

3. Facebook Messenger
Facebook ◇
★★★★☆

4. Instagram
Instagram
★★★★★

5. Candy Crush Saga

The Google Play Store

Your Galaxy Note shipped with several dozen apps preinstalled. It's a pittance. You'll find zillions more apps at the Google Play Store. Each of them extends the abilities of what your phone can do. Some cost money. Most are free. They're all waiting for you to try, and it starts by visiting the Play Store.

- Officially, it's called the Google Play Store. It may also be referenced as Google Play. The app is named Play Store.

- The Google Play Store was once known as Android Market, and you may still see it referred to as the Market.

- This section talks about getting apps for your phone. For information on getting music, see Chapter 16. Chapter 17 mentions buying books.

- *App* is short for application. It's a program, or software, that you can add to your phone to make it do new, wondrous, or useful things.

- All apps you download can be found on the Applications screen. Further, apps you download have shortcut icons placed on the Home screen. See Chapter 22 for information on moving apps on the Home screen.

- I highly recommend that you connect your phone to a Wi-Fi network if you plan to obtain apps, books, or other digital goodies at the Play Store. Wi-Fi not only gives you speed, but it also helps you avoid data surcharges. See Chapter 19 for details on connecting your phone to a Wi-Fi network.

- The Play Store app is frequently updated, so its look may change from what you see in this chapter. Updated information on the Google Play Store is available on my website:

      www.wambooli.com/help/android/google-play

Visiting the Play Store

Your new app experience begins by opening the Play Store app. It's found on the Applications screen, with a shortcut icon on the primary Home screen.

After opening the Play Store app, you see the main screen, similar to the one shown in Figure 18-1. Categories appear that help you browse for apps, games, books, and so on. The rest of the screen highlights popular or recommended items.

Find apps by choosing the Apps category from the main screen, also known as Store Home (refer to Figure 18-1). The next screen lists popular and featured items plus categories you can browse by swiping the screen from right to left. The category tabs appear toward the top of the screen.

When you have an idea of what you want, such as an app's name or even what it does, searching works fastest: Touch the Search icon at the top of the Play Store screen (refer to Figure 18-1). Type all or part of the app's name or perhaps a description.

To see more information about an item, touch it. Touching doesn't buy anything. Instead, you see a more detailed description, screen shots, and perhaps a video preview.

Figure 18-1: The Google Play Store.

Return to the main Google Play Store screen at any time by touching the Google Play app icon in the upper left corner of the screen.

- ✔ The first time you open the Play Store app, you have to accept the terms of service; touch the Accept or OK button.

- ✔ You can be assured that all apps that appear in the Play Store can be used with your Galaxy Note. There's no way to download or buy one that's incompatible.

- ✔ Pay attention to an app's ratings. Ratings are added by people who use the apps — people like you and me. Having more stars is better. You can see additional information, including individual user reviews, by choosing the app.

- ✔ Another good indicator of an app's success is how many times it's been downloaded. Some apps have been downloaded tens of millions of times. That's a good sign.

- ✔ See Chapter 22 for more information on widgets and live wallpapers.

Obtaining an app

After you locate an app you want, the next step is to download it from the Google Play Store into your Galaxy Note. The app is installed automatically, building up your collection of apps and expanding what the phone can do.

Good news: Most apps are available for free. Better news: Even the apps you pay for don't cost dearly. In fact, it seems odd to sit and stew over whether paying 99 cents for a game is "worth it."

I recommend that you download a free app first, to familiarize yourself with the process. Then try your hand at a paid app.

The process of obtaining an app, free or not, works pretty much the same. Follow these steps:

1. **Open the Play Store app.**

2. **Find the app you want and open its description.**

   The app's description screen looks similar to the one shown on the right side in Figure 18-2.

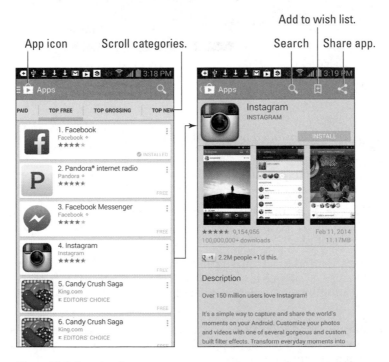

Figure 18-2: App details.

The difference between a free app and a paid app is found on the button used to obtain the app. For a free app, the button says *Install.* For a paid app, the button shows the price.

You may find three other buttons when viewing an app that's already installed on your phone: Open, Update, and Uninstall. The Open button opens it; the Update button updates it; and the Uninstall button removes it. See the later sections "Updating an app" and "Removing an app" for more information on using the Update and Uninstall buttons.

3. **Touch the Install button to get a free app; for a paid app, touch the button with the price on it.**

   The next screen describes the app's permissions. The list isn't a warning, and it doesn't mean anything bad. It's just that the Play Store is informing you which of phone features the app has access to.

4. **Touch the Accept button.**

   For a paid app, you may have to choose a method of payment or input a new method, if one isn't on file. Choose a credit card, if you have one set up with Google Wallet. If not, you can input credit card information per the directions on the screen.

5. **For a paid app, touch the Buy button.**

   The Downloading notification appears atop the screen as the app is downloaded. You're free to do other things on your phone while the app is downloaded and installed.

6. **Touch the Open button to run the app.**

   Or, if you were doing something else while the app was downloading and installing, choose the Successfully Installed notification, shown in the margin. The notification features the app's name with the text *Successfully Installed* beneath it.

Never buy an app twice

Any apps you've already purchased from the Google Play Store — say, for another phone or mobile device — are available for download on your Galaxy Note at no charge. Simply find the app. You see it flagged as *Purchased* in the Play Store. Touch the Install button to install it, as described in this chapter.

You can review any already purchased apps in the Play Store: Choose the My Apps item from the sidebar (shown in Figure 18-1). Choose the All tab from the top of the screen. You see all the apps you've ever obtained at the Google Play Store, including apps you've previously paid for. Those apps are flagged as *Purchased.* Choose that item to reinstall the paid app.

At this point, what happens next depends on the app you've downloaded. For example, you may have to agree to a license agreement. If so, touch the I Agree button. Additional setup may involve setting your location, signing in to an account, or creating a profile, for example.

After you complete the initial app setup, or if no setup is necessary, you can start using the app.

✔ Apps you download are added to the Applications screen, made available like any other app on your phone.

✔ When you dither over getting an app, consider adding it to your wish list. Touch the Wish List icon when viewing the app. (The icon is shown in the margin.) You can review your wish list by choosing the My Wishlist item from the Play Store app's sidebar (shown earlier, in Figure 18-1).

✔ Some apps add shortcut icons on the Home screen after they're installed. See Chapter 22 for information on removing the icon from the Home screen, if that is your desire.

✔ For a paid app, you receive a Gmail message from the Google Play Store, confirming your purchase. The message contains a link you can click to review the refund policy in case you change your mind about the purchase.

✔ Be quick on that refund: Most apps allow you only 15 minutes to get your money back. You know when the time limit is up because the Refund button on the app's description screen changes its name to Uninstall.

✔ Also see the section "Removing an app," later in this chapter.

Manage Your Apps

The Play Store app does two important jobs: It's not only where you obtain new apps for your Galaxy Note but also the place you return to for performing app management. This task includes reviewing apps you've downloaded, updating apps, organizing apps, and removing apps that you no longer want or that you severely hate.

Reviewing your apps

To peruse the apps you've downloaded from the Google Play Store, follow these steps:

1. **Start the Play Store app.**

2. **Choose My Apps from the sidebar.**

   Touch the Play Store app icon, illustrated in Figure 18-1, to view the navigation drawer.

3. **Peruse your apps.**

Your apps are presented in two categories: Installed and All, as shown in Figure 18-3. Installed apps are found on your phone; apps in the All category include apps you have downloaded that may not currently be installed.

Apps in need
of an update   Update button

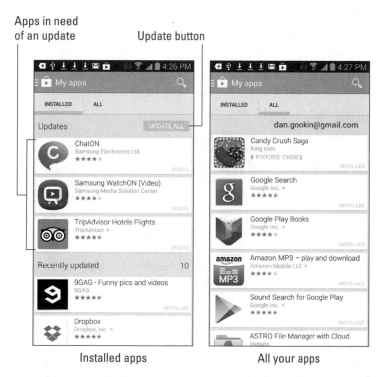

Installed apps   All your apps

Figure 18-3: Your apps.

Touch an app to see its details. Touch the Open button to run the app; the Update button to update to the latest version; or the Uninstall button to remove the app. Later sections in this chapter describe the details for updating and uninstalling apps.

- ✔ While viewing an app's details, you can activate automatic updating: Press the Menu button and choose the Auto-Update item. When a check mark is by that item, the Auto-Update feature has been activated. Not every app features automatic updating.

- ✔ Uninstalled apps remain on the All list because you did, at one time, download the app. To reinstall them (and without paying a second time for paid apps), choose the app from the All list and touch the Install button.

Sharing an app

When you love an app so much that you just can't contain your glee, feel free to share it with your friends. You can easily share a link to the app in the Play Store by obeying these steps:

1. **In the Play Store, choose the app to share.**

   You can choose any app, though you need to be at the app's Details screen with the Free or price button or the Details screen on an app you've installed (refer to Figure 18-2).

2. **Touch the Share icon.**

   A menu appears, listing various apps and methods for sharing the app's Play Store link with your pals.

3. **Choose a sharing method.**

   For example, choose Gmail to send a link to the app in an e-mail message.

4. **Use the chosen app to send the link.**

   What happens next depends on which sharing method you've chosen.

The end result of these steps is that your friend receives a link. That person can touch the link on their mobile Android device and be whisked instantly to the Google Play Store, where the app can be viewed and installed.

Updating an app

Whenever a new version of an app is available, you see it flagged for updating, as shown in Figure 18-3. Don't worry if it's been a while since you've been to the My Apps screen; apps in need of an update also display the App Update notification, shown in the margin.

To update an individual app, view its information screen: Choose the app from the My Apps screen (refer to Figure 18-3). Touch the Update button, and then touch Accept to download the new version. Or, from the list of installed apps, touch the Update All button to update a slew of apps at one time. This step still involves touching the Accept button for each app.

The updating process often involves downloading and installing a new version of the app. That's perfectly fine; your settings and options aren't changed by the update process.

Look for the App Update notification to remind yourself that apps are in need of an update. You can choose this notification to be taken instantly to the app's details screen, where the Update button eagerly awaits your touch.

Removing an app

I can think of a few reasons to remove an app. It's with eager relish that I remove apps that don't work or that somehow annoy me. It's also perfectly okay to remove redundant apps, such as when you have multiple eBook readers that you don't use. And if you're desperate for an excuse, removing apps frees up a modicum of storage.

Whatever the reason, remove an app by following these directions:

1. **Open the Play Store app.**

2. **Choose My Apps from the sidebar.**

   Figure 18-1 illustrates the navigation drawer; touch the App icon to view it.

3. **In the Installed list, touch the app that offends you.**

4. **Touch the Uninstall button.**

5. **Touch the OK button to confirm.**

   The app is removed.

The app continues to appear on the All list even after it's been removed. That's because you downloaded it once. That doesn't mean, however, that the app is still installed.

✔ You can always reinstall paid apps that you've uninstalled. You aren't charged twice for doing so.

✔ You can't remove apps that are preinstalled on the Galaxy Note by either the phone's manufacturer or your cellular service provider. I'm sure there's probably a technical way to uninstall the apps, but seriously: Just don't use the apps if you want to remove them and discover that you can't.

Controlling your apps

The Play Store app isn't your final destination for truly managing the apps installed on your phone. To really get your hands dirty, you need to visit the Application Manager. Be forewarned: The Applications screen isn't the friendliest location on your Galaxy Note.

Follow these steps to find the Applications screen:

1. **Open the Settings app.**

   At the Home screen, press the Menu button and choose the Settings command.

2. **Touch the General tab and choose the Application Manager item.**

   Behold the Applications Manager screen.

Avoiding Android viruses

How can you tell which apps are legitimate and which might be viruses or evil apps that do odd things to your Galaxy Note? Well, you can't. In fact, most people can't, because most evil apps don't advertise themselves as such.

The key to knowing whether an app is evil is to look at what it does, as described in this chapter. If a simple grocery-list app uses the phone's text messaging service and the app doesn't need to send text messages, it's suspect.

In the history of the Android operating system, only a handful of malicious apps have been distributed, and most of them were found on phones used in Asia. Google routinely removes malicious apps from the Play Store, and a feature of the Android operating system even lets Google remotely wipe such apps from your phone. So you're pretty safe.

Generally speaking, avoid "hacker" apps, porn apps, and apps that use social engineering to make you do things on your phone that you wouldn't otherwise do, such as text an overseas number to see racy pictures of politicians or celebrities.

All the apps installed on your phone are displayed according to four categories, each represented as a tab at the top of the screen:

Downloaded: This screen lists all apps you've obtained and downloaded from the Google Play Store.

SD Card: On this screen you find either apps installed on the MicroSD card or apps that can be transferred to that storage location. An app currently on the MicroSD card features a green check mark in its box.

Running: You see all apps actively running on the Galaxy Note. This list includes services and other items that don't show up as apps but that are required for the phone to function properly.

All: This screen lists all apps on the phone, including services, Android functions, and lots of things you can look at but should never touch.

To view more information about an app, choose a category and then touch the app. For example, to witness the details of a running app, touch or swipe to the Running tab and choose an app from the list. You see details about the app, most of which are technical in nature.

Various buttons show up on the app's Details screen. The variety of buttons you see depend on which category is chosen. Here are some of the buttons and what they do:

Stop/Force Stop: Touch this button to halt a program run amok. For example, I had to stop an older Android app that continually made noise and offered no other option to exit.

Report: This button helps you inform Google of suspect software or other problems with the app.

Uninstall: Touch the Uninstall button to remove the app, which is another way to accomplish the same steps described in the preceding section.

Refund: Freshly purchased apps feature the Refund button rather than the Uninstall button. Touch the Refund button to uninstall the paid app *and* get your money back. Be quick, though: After a given amount of time, anywhere between 15 minutes and 24 hours, the Refund button transforms itself back into the Uninstall button.

Move to SD Card: Touch this button to transfer the app from the phone's internal storage to the MicroSD card. Doing so can help free capacity on the phone's internal storage.

Move to Storage Device: Touch this button to transfer an app from the MicroSD card to the phone's internal storage. (This button replaces the Move to SD Card button when an app already dwells on the MicroSD card.)

Clear Data: Touch this button to erase any information stored by the app. This information includes items you've created (text and pictures, for example), settings, accounts, and other information stored by the app.

Clear Cache: I've used this button to fix an app that doesn't work or that just sits all stubborn on the screen. This trick doesn't work every time, but it's worth a try when an app seems slow or suddenly stops working.

Clear Defaults: This button disassociates the app from certain file types. It's a reset switch for the Always/Just Once prompt, so when you've selected an app to always open a certain type of file — music, picture, or whatever — touching this button removes that choice. See Chapter 24 for more details.

Controversy is brewing in the Android community about whether to store apps on the phone's internal storage or its MicroSD card. I prefer internal storage because the app stays with the phone and is always available. Further, Home screen shortcuts to apps stored on the MicroSD card may disappear from time to time. That can be frustrating. My advice: Keep the apps on the phone's internal storage.

Applications Screen Organization

You have all the apps you want, or at least the ones you know you want. Where are they? Where do they dwell? And, seriously, how badly can you mess with them? This section answers those and other basic questions regarding app management.

Changing the Applications screen view

The Applications menu sports three views, as illustrated in Figure 18-4:

Customizable Grid: This view can be modified, as described in the next section.

Alphabetical Grid: This view is probably the one you use now. All apps appears in alphabetical order on a grid. New apps are inserted into the grid alphabetically, which jumbles everything.

Alphabetical List: I believe that no one uses this view. Apps appear in a simple list, requiring endless scrolling that leads to finger fatigue.

Customizable grid

Alphabetical grid

Alphabetical list

Figure 18-4: Different views of the Applications screen.

To change the Applications screen view, press the Menu button and choose the View Type command. Select a new view from the list.

Rearranging apps on the Applications screen

The Customizable Grid option for viewing the Applications screen lets you rearrange and order all your phone's apps. Unlike in the alphabetical views, the apps stay where you put them. You can even add panels to the Applications screen and create folders to help keep things organized.

To begin redecorating the Applications screen, press the Menu button and choose the Edit command.

Move an app by dragging its icon with your finger or the S Pen: Long-press the icon, and drag it to a blank part of the same page or to another page, right or left. Touch the Save button when you're done.

Working with Applications screen folders

The Galaxy Note comes preconfigured with a few app folders on the Applications screen. To build a new folder, obey these steps:

1. **Press the Menu button and choose the Create Folder command.**

2. **Type a name for the folder.**

   Be short and sweet so that the name fits beneath the folder icon.

3. **Touch the OK button to create and name the folder.**

   The folder appears empty — just a dull circle. To use the folder, you have to drag app icons into it. To do that, you must edit the Applications screen.

4. **Press the Menu button and choose the Edit command.**

5. **Long-press an icon and drag it over the folder icon. Lift your finger to "drop" the app icon into the folder.**

6. **Repeat Step 5 to continue placing apps into the folder.**

To remove an item from a folder, edit the Applications screen. Open the folder, and then long-press an icon to drag it out of the folder and place it elsewhere on the screen.

To remove the folder, long-press its icon and drag it up to the Remove icon atop the screen. You don't need to empty the folder before removing it, but any app icons inside the folder are removed and placed directly on the Applications screen after the folder is gone.

Touch the Save button when you're done working with folders; otherwise, all your work is lost.

✔ I use folders on the Applications screen primarily to hide the app icons I seldom use, such as those preinstalled by the cellular carrier. That way, they are put out of the way and don't interfere when I'm browsing the Applications screen for apps I really do use.

✔ Folders can also be created on the Home screen, which is a far better way to organize your apps. See Chapter 22 for details.

Part V
Nuts and Bolts

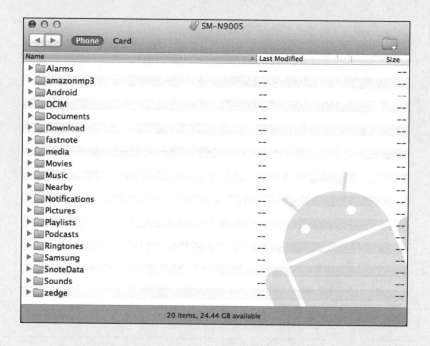

Learn how to synchronize photos with Dropbox on the Internet at www.dummies.com/extras/samsunggalaxynote3.

In this part...

- ✓ Understand wireless networking and devices
- ✓ Work with connecting, sharing, and storing information
- ✓ Explore the world with your Galaxy Note
- ✓ Discover how to customize and configure your phone
- ✓ Get the lowdown on maintaining and troubleshooting

19

Wireless Wizardry

In This Chapter

▶ Using the mobile data network

▶ Setting up Wi-Fi

▶ Connecting to a Wi-Fi network

▶ Establishing a mobile hotspot

▶ Sharing the Internet connection

▶ Configuring and using Bluetooth

▶ Printing on your Galaxy Note

▶ Sharing with Android Beam

*P*hones were born with wires attached. Telephone wires marched from coast to coast. Wires dwelled in the walls of your home. Wires connected the phone to the wall and connected the handset to the phone's base. Wires were such a big deal that wireless phones of the 1980s were known by the moniker *cordless*. It was the dawn of a new age.

What's the point of having a truly mobile phone if you tether it to something by a wire? Although the Galaxy Note isn't completely wire-free, it's quite close. In fact, all the phone's basic forms of communications are accomplished using wireless methods, including the digital cellular signal, Wi-Fi networking, Bluetooth, and the wireless wizardry covered in this chapter.

Bluetooth

ly device

☐ Galaxy Note 3
Only visible to paired devices

Paired devices

✆ Nica
Connected to phone audio

ilable devices

ch Ultrathin KB Cov

It's a Wireless Life

Don't duck — although you would, if you could see all the wireless communications going on around you. An entire spectrum of wireless activity is darting about everywhere, unseen by human eyes. These wireless signals come from all over, even from satellites orbiting the earth. They let you talk, but (most importantly) they let you communicate with the Internet. This section explains how it's all done on the Galaxy Note.

Understanding the mobile data network

Of the many fees and charges on your monthly cell phone bill, the heftiest one is probably for the mobile data network. It isn't the wireless service you talk on (which is a much smaller charge), but it's important for a smartphone because your Galaxy Note uses the mobile data network to talk with the Internet.

Several types of mobile data network are available to your phone. The current network being used sports a special icon that appears on the status bar. Here's a description of the variety of network types and their speed values:

4G LTE: The speed of this fourth generation of digital cellular network is comparable to standard Wi-Fi Internet access. It's fast. It also allows for both data and voice transmission at the same time.

4G / HSPA+: It isn't as fast as the full 4G LTE, but it's still faster than the 3G network. The speed is tolerable for surfing the web, watching YouTube videos, and downloading information from the Internet.

3G: The third generation of wide-area data networks is several times faster than the previous generation of data networks.

E / EDGE: The slowest data connection is the original. It's also known as *1X* because it's the first generation.

The Galaxy Note always uses the fastest network available. Whenever a 4G LTE signal abounds, the phone uses it. Otherwise, the 4G data network is chosen, followed by E. Or, when no mobile data network is available, that part of the status bar is blank.

- ✓ The digital cellular signal may still appear when you're using Wi-Fi. That's because some apps use that signal exclusively. Or something.

- ✓ You can still make phone calls when no data network is available. As long as the signal-strength bars on the phone's status bar show that a signal is present, you can receive and make phone calls.

- ✓ Accessing the digital cellular network isn't free. You likely signed up for some form of subscription plan for a certain quantity of data when you first received your Android phone. When you exceed that quantity, the cost can become prohibitive.

- ✓ The data subscription is based on the *quantity* of data you send and receive. At 4G LTE speeds, the prepaid threshold can be crossed quickly.

Understanding Wi-Fi

The mobile data connection is nice, and it's available pretty much all over, but it costs you money. A better option, and one you should seek out when it's available, is *Wi-Fi,* or the same wireless networking standard used by computers for communicating with each other and the Internet.

Making Wi-Fi work on your Galaxy Note requires two steps. First, you must activate Wi-Fi, by turning on the phone's wireless radio. The second step is connecting to a specific wireless network. The next two sections cover these steps.

✔ When your phone is connected to a Wi-Fi network, it uses that network rather than the digital cellular network.

✔ Wi-Fi stands for *wir*eless *fi*delity. It's brought to you by the numbers 802.11 and the letters B, N, and G.

Activating Wi-Fi

Follow these steps to activate Wi-Fi on your Galaxy Note:

1. **At the Home screen, touch the Apps icon.**

2. **Open the Settings app.**

3. **Touch the Connections tab.**

4. **Ensure that the Wi-Fi master control icon is on.**

   If it isn't, slide the master control to the right to activate the phone's Wi-Fi radio. The switch is green when it's on.

If you've already configured your phone to connect to an available wireless network, the phone is connected automatically. Otherwise, you have to connect to an available network, which is covered in the next section.

To turn off Wi-Fi, repeat the steps in this section but in Step 4 slide the master control switch to the left. Turning off Wi-Fi disconnects your phone from any wireless networks.

✔ You can quickly activate or deactivate the Galaxy Note's Wi-Fi radio by choosing the Wi-Fi Quick Action. See Chapter 3 for more information on the Quick Actions.

✔ Using Wi-Fi to connect to the Internet doesn't incur data usage charges.

Connecting to a Wi-Fi network

After activating the Galaxy Note's Wi-Fi radio, you can connect to an available wireless network. Heed these steps:

1. **Open the Settings app.**

2. **Touch the Connections tab and choose Wi-Fi.**

   Don't touch the master control icon, which turns the Wi-Fi radio on or off; touch the *Wi-Fi* text on the left side of the screen.

   You see a list of Wi-Fi networks displayed, similar to what appears in Figure 19-1. Any previously connected networks that are not in range appear at the bottom of the list (not shown in Figure 19-1).

   In Figure 19-1, the Imperial Wambooli network is now connected. That's my office network.

3. **Choose a wireless network from the list.**

   When no wireless networks are shown, you're sort of out of luck regarding Wi-Fi access from your current location.

   In Figure 19-1, I chose the Imperial Wambooli network, which is my office network.

Available
Wi-Fi networks   Wi-Fi connected

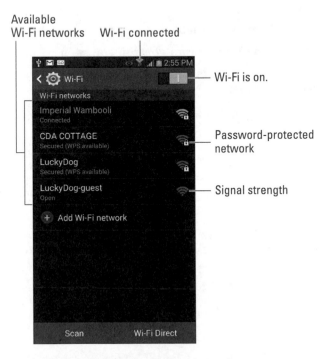

Wi-Fi is on.

Password-protected
network

Signal strength

Figure 19-1: Hunting down a wireless network.

4. **If prompted, type the network password.**

   Putting a check mark in the box by the Show Password option makes it easier to type a long, complex network password.

5. **Touch the Connect button.**

   You should be immediately connected to the network. If not, try the password again.

When the phone is connected, you see the Wi-Fi status icon appear atop the touchscreen, as shown in the margin. This icon indicates that the phone's Wi-Fi is on, connected, and communicating with a Wi-Fi network.

Some wireless networks don't broadcast their names, which adds security but also makes accessing them more difficult. In these cases, choose the Add Wi-Fi Network command (refer to Figure 19-1) to manually add the network. You need to input the network name, or *SSID,* and the type of security. You also need the password, if one is used. You can obtain this information from the unfocused young lady with the lip ring who sold you coffee or from whoever is in charge of the wireless network at your location.

✔ Not every wireless network has a password. They should! Generally speaking, I don't avoid connecting to any public network that lacks a password, but I don't use that network for shopping, banking, or any other secure online activity.

✔ Some public networks are open to anyone, but you have to use the Internet app to get on the web and find a login page that lets you access the network: Simply browse to any page on the Internet, and the login page shows up.

✔ The phone automatically remembers any Wi-Fi network it's connected to and its network password. The network is automatically connected as soon as the Galaxy Note is within range.

✔ To disconnect from a Wi-Fi network, simply turn off Wi-Fi on the phone. See the preceding section.

✔ Use Wi-Fi whenever you plan to remain in one location for a while. Unlike a mobile data network, a Wi-Fi network's broadcast signal has a limited range. If you wander too far away, your phone loses the signal and is disconnected.

Connecting via WPS

Many Wi-Fi routers feature WPS, which stands for Wi-Fi Protected Setup. It's a network authorization system that's really simple and quite secure. If the wireless router features WPS, you can use it to quickly connect your phone to the network.

To make the WPS connection, follow these steps:

1. **Touch the WPS connection button on the router.**

   Either the button is labeled WPS or it uses the WPS icon, shown in the margin.

2. **On your Galaxy Note, visit the Wi-Fi screen in the Settings app.**

   Refer to Steps 1 and 2 in the preceding section.

3. **Press the Menu button.**

4. **Choose the WPS Push Button command.**

   The Wi-Fi connection is made.

Some WPS Wi-Fi routers may feature a PIN instead of a push button. In that case, choose the WPS Pin Entry command in Step 4 and type the PIN on your phone.

A Connection to Share

Your Galaxy Note deftly accesses the mobile network signal. It can get on the Internet from any location where that signal is available. Your other mobile devices, such as a laptop computer? Well, unless these gizmos sport their own cellular modems, it's tough luck. That is, unless you bother to *share* the Galaxy Note's Internet connection. This section explains how it's done.

Before proceeding, be aware that the Mobile Hotspot and Internet Tethering options must be enabled on your cellular data plan. Yes, that's an extra cost, one that you probably skipped over when you signed up for the service. If the features aren't enabled, your Galaxy Note cannot perform the tasks described in this section.

Creating a mobile hotspot

The Mobile Hotspot feature allows your Galaxy Note to share its mobile data connection by creating its own Wi-Fi network. Other Wi-Fi devices — computers, laptops, other mobile devices — can then access that Wi-Fi network to enjoy a free ride on the Internet, courtesy of your Galaxy Note.

Well, it may not be free, because the feature comes at a premium price, but you get my point.

To set up a mobile hotspot on your phone, heed these steps:

1. **Turn off the Wi-Fi radio.**

   There's no point in creating a Wi-Fi hotspot where one is already available.

2. **Plug the phone into a power source.**

   The Mobile Hotspot feature draws a lot of power.

3. **Open the Settings app.**

4. **Touch the Connections tab and choose the Tethering and Portable Hotspot.**

5. **Slide the master control by the Portable Wi-Fi Hotspot option to the On position.**

   The master control turns green when it's activated.

   The hotspot is on and available, but you probably want to do some additional customization, such as giving the hotspot a better name and setting up a password.

6. **Choose the Portable Wi-Fi Hotspot item.**

   Touch the left side of the item, not the master switch.

7. **Touch the Configure button, found at the bottom of the screen.**

8. **Type a name for the hotspot into the Network SSID text box.**

9. **Type a password into the Password box.**

   Place a check mark by the Show Password item to see the password as you type.

   Don't forget the password! Well, if you do, just type a new one.

10. **Touch the Save button to save the hotspot network's name and password.**

    You're done.

When the mobile hotspot is active, the Mobile Hotspot notification appears on the phone's status bar, as shown in the margin.

To turn off the mobile hotspot, slide the master control switch to the left (Step 5), and it's disabled. The settings (SSID or network name and password) are retained for the next time you activate the Wi-Fi hotspot.

✐ The range of the mobile hotspot is about 30 feet. Things such as walls and molten lava can interfere with the signal, shortening its range.

✐ Data usage fees apply when you use the mobile hotspot, and you pay them on top of the fee that your cellular provider may charge for the mobile hotspot service. These fees can add up quickly.

✐ Don't forget to turn off the mobile hotspot when you're done using it.

Tethering the Internet connection

A more intimate and direct way to share the Galaxy Note's digital cellular connection is to connect the phone directly to a computer and activate the USB tethering feature.

Yes, I am fully aware that tethering goes against the wireless theme of this chapter. Still, it remains a solid way to provide Internet access to another gizmo, such as a laptop or desktop computer.

Follow these steps to set up Internet tethering:

1. **Connect the Galaxy Note to another mobile device by using the USB cable.**

   I've had the best success with this operation when the computer is a PC running Windows.

2. **On the phone, open the Settings app.**

3. **From the Connections tab, choose Tethering and Portable Hotspot.**

4. **Place a green check mark by the USB Tethering item.**

   Internet tethering is activated. Well, unless your data plan doesn't support it, in which case nothing happens.

The other device should instantly recognize your Galaxy Note as a "modem" with Internet access. Further configuration may be required, which depends on the device using the tethered connection. For example, you may be prompted on the PC to locate and install software for your phone. Do so: Accept the installation of new software when you're prompted by Windows.

- ✔ When Internet tethering is active, the Tethering Active notification appears, as shown in the margin. Choose that notification to further configure tethering.

- ✔ To end Internet tethering, repeat Steps 2 through 4 to remove the green check mark. You can then disconnect the USB cable.

- ✔ Sharing the digital network connection incurs data usage charges against your cellular data plan. Be mindful of your data usage when you're sharing a connection.

The Bluetooth Way

If the terms *Wi-Fi* and *digital cellular connection* don't leave you completely befuddled, I have another term for you. It's *Bluetooth*, and it has nothing to do with the color blue or dental hygiene.

Bluetooth is a wireless protocol for communication between two or more Bluetooth-equipped devices. Your Galaxy Note just happens to be Bluetooth-equipped, so it too can chat it up with Bluetooth devices, such as those earphone-speakers that make you look like you have a tiny robot parasite on the side of your head.

Understanding Bluetooth

Bluetooth is a peculiar name for a wireless communications standard. Unlike Wi-Fi networking, with Bluetooth you simply connect two gizmos. One would be your Galaxy Note; the other would be some type of peripheral, such as a keyboard, printer, or speakers. Here's an overview of how the operation works:

1. **Turn on the Bluetooth wireless radio on both gizmos.**

2. **Make the gizmo you're trying to connect to discoverable.**

3. **On your phone, choose the peripheral gizmo from the list of Bluetooth devices.**

4. **Optionally, confirm the connection on the peripheral device.**

   For example, you may be asked to input a code or press a button.

5. **Use the device.**

When you're done using the device, you simply turn it off. Because the Bluetooth gizmo is paired with your phone, it's automatically reconnected the next time you turn it on (that is, if you have Bluetooth activated on the phone).

 Bluetooth devices are marked with the Bluetooth logo, shown in the margin. It's your assurance that the gizmo can work with other Bluetooth devices.

 Bluetooth was developed as a wireless version of the old RS-232 standard, the serial port on early personal computers. Essentially, Bluetooth is wireless RS-232, and the variety of devices you can connect to and the things you can do with Bluetooth are similar to what you could do with the old serial port standard.

Activating Bluetooth

You must turn on the phone's Bluetooth radio before you can use one of those Borg-earpiece implants and join the ranks of the walking connected. Here's how to turn on Bluetooth:

1. **Open the Settings app.**

2. **Choose the Connections tab.**

3. **Slide the Bluetooth master control to the right.**

   When the master control is green, Bluetooth is on.

When Bluetooth is on, the Bluetooth status icon appears. It uses the Bluetooth logo, shown in the margin.

To turn off Bluetooth, repeat the steps in this section but slide the master control to the left — the Off position.

✔ You can also turn on Bluetooth by choosing the Bluetooth Quick Action.

✔ When the Power Control widget is installed on the Home screen, touch the Bluetooth icon to turn it on. See Chapter 22 for more information on installing Home screen widgets.

✔ Activating Bluetooth puts an extra drain on the phone's battery. Be mindful to use Bluetooth only when necessary, and remember to turn it off when you're done.

Pairing with a Bluetooth device

To make the Bluetooth connection between your phone and some other gizmo, such as a Bluetooth headset, follow these steps:

1. **Ensure that Bluetooth is on.**

   Refer to the preceding section.

2. **Turn on the Bluetooth gizmo or ensure that its Bluetooth radio is on.**

   Some Bluetooth devices have separate power and Bluetooth switches.

3. **Open the Settings app.**

4. **Touch the Connections tab and choose the Bluetooth item.**

   Touch the text that says *Bluetooth,* not the master control icon on the right.

5. **Touch the Scan button.**

   You see a list of available and paired devices, similar to the ones shown in Figure 19-2. Don't fret if the device you want doesn't yet appear in the list.

6. **If the other device has an option to become visible, select it.**

   For example, some Bluetooth gizmos have a tiny button to press that makes the device visible to other Bluetooth gizmos.

   Likewise, if the other device needs to see the phone, touch the phone's name at the top of the Bluetooth screen (refer to Figure 19-2). This action makes the phone visible to the other device.

7. **Choose the device.**

   The phone and Bluetooth device attempt to pair. You may be required to type the device's passcode or otherwise acknowledge the connection.

Headset   Bluetooth status

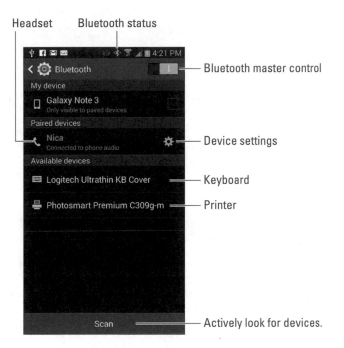

— Bluetooth master control

— Device settings

— Keyboard

— Printer

— Actively look for devices.

Figure 19-2: Finding Bluetooth gizmos.

After pairing, you can begin using the device.

To break the connection, you can either turn off the gizmo or disable the Bluetooth radio on your Galaxy Note. Because the devices are paired, when you turn on Bluetooth and reactivate the device, the connection is instantly reestablished.

- ✔ How you use the device depends on what it does. For example, you use a Bluetooth headset to talk and listen on the phone. As long as the headset is paired with the phone and powered on, you can use it.

- ✔ Use the Headset button on the In-call screen to switch between a Bluetooth headset and the phone's microphone and speaker while you're on the phone.

- ✔ You can turn the Bluetooth earphone on or off after it has been paired.

- ✔ To unpair a device, touch the Settings icon by the device's entry in the Bluetooth screen (refer to Figure 19-2). Choose the Unpair command to break the Bluetooth connection and stop using the device.

- ✔ Only unpair devices you don't plan to use again. Otherwise, simply turn off the Bluetooth device.

- ✔ Bluetooth can use a lot of power. Especially for battery-powered devices, don't forget to turn them off when you're no longer using them with your phone.

Printing to a Bluetooth printer

One of the common ways to print pictures or even documents on your Galaxy Note is to pair the phone with a Bluetooth printer. The secret is to find and use the Share icon, choose Bluetooth, and then select a Bluetooth printer. As you may suspect, the actual steps for this process can be more complicated. That's why I list them here:

1. **View the document, web page, or image you want to print.**

   You can print from the Internet app or Gallery app or from a number of apps.

2. **Touch the Share icon.**

   If a Share icon isn't visible in the app, press the Menu button and look for the Share command or Share Via command.

3. **Choose Bluetooth.**

   If the Bluetooth option isn't available, you may not be able to print from the app. Even so, check out the nearby sidebar, "Printing from the cloud."

4. **Choose your Bluetooth printer from the list of items on the Bluetooth screen.**

5. **If a prompt appears on the printer, confirm that your phone is printing a document.**

   The document is uploaded (sent from the phone to the printer), and then it prints. You can view the upload status by checking the phone's notifications.

Not everything on your phone can be printed on a Bluetooth printer. When you can't find the Share icon or the Bluetooth item isn't available on the Share menu, you can't print using Bluetooth.

TIP

Printing from the cloud

Another way to print from your Galaxy Note is to obtain the Google Cloud Printing app from the Play Store. By coordinating between your Google account on a desktop computer, the Chrome web browser, and the phone, you can print on one of your home or office printers — no Bluetooth required.

For more information on Google Cloud Print, refer to my website at

    www.wambooli.com/blog/?p=4736

Android Beam It to Me

Your Galaxy Note features an NFC radio, where *NFC* stands for Near Field Communications and *radio* is a type of vegetable. NFC allows your phone to communicate with other NFC devices. That connection is used for the quick transfer of information. The technology is called *Android Beam.*

Turning on NFC

You can't play with the Android Beam feature unless the phone's NFC radio has been activated. To confirm that it has, or to activate it, follow these steps:

1. **Open the Settings app.**

2. **Touch the Connections heading.**

3. **Ensure that the master control by the NFC item is on or green.**

    If not, slide the master control icon to the right.

With NFC activated, you can use your phone to communicate with other NFC devices. These include other Galaxy Note phones, Galaxy Note and Galaxy Tab tablets, as well as payment systems for various merchants.

To disable NFC, repeat these steps but in Step 3 remove the check mark.

Using Android Beam

The Android Beam feature works when you touch your phone to another NFC device, such as another Android phone or tablet. As long as the two devices have an NFC radio and the Android Beam feature is active, they can share information. You can beam contacts, map locations, web pages, YouTube videos, and lots of other things. Generally speaking, if the app features the Share icon, you can probably use Android Beam and other content as easily as touching the two gizmos.

When two Android Beam devices touch — usually, back-to-back — you see a prompt appear on the screen: Touch to Beam. Touch the screen, and the item you're viewing is immediately sent to the other device. That's pretty much it.

Using Jim Beam

Follow these steps to enjoy a bottle of Kentucky straight bourbon whiskey:

1. **Unscrew cap.**

2. **Pour.**

3. **Enjoy.**

It isn't truly necessary to pour the whiskey into another container for consumption, though many users find a glass, mug, or red Solo cup useful.

Alcohol and social networking do not mix.

Sync, Share, and Store

In This Chapter

▶ Understanding the USB connection

▶ Connecting the phone to a computer

▶ Synchronizing files

▶ Using cloud storage

▶ Perusing storage information

▶ Formatting the MicroSD card

*Y*ou have a phone. You have a computer. How do you start them talking? Better still, how can you get a picture from your phone into your computer, or vice versa? The answer is that you bind the two with vines from a medieval castle, hire a Druid, and sing songs of the tree spirits. Sometimes it seems that steps like these are required.

It's not that difficult to put a Galaxy Note and a computer on speaking terms. After they're connected, you can share information back and forth, copying files hither and thither, possibly yon. The notion is to keep everything synchronized. I've written down the details in this chapter so that you don't have to memorize anything or hire a Druid.

Back up/Restore

name
Galaxy Note 3

Phone number
12087551167

Internal memory   1.91 GB / 26.34 GB

External memory   528 MB / 14.83 GB

ware information

the latest firmware.

ent firmware version : PDA:MK1 / PHONE:MJ9 / CSC:MK1 (TGY)
firmware version : PDA:MK1 / PHONE:MJ9 / CSC:MK1 (TGY)

The USB Connection

The most direct way to mate your phone with your computer is to use the USB cable that comes with the Galaxy Note. It's a match made in heaven, but, like many matches, it often works less than smoothly. Rather than hire a counselor to put the phone and computer on speaking terms, I offer you some good USB connection advice in this section.

in Contacts.

Connecting the USB cable

The USB connection is made by using a USB cable, similar to the one that comes in the box with your Galaxy Note. In fact, it's exactly like that cable. The cable's A end plugs into the computer. The other end, which looks like two connectors side-by-side (the *USB 3.0 Micro-B plug*), gets shoved into the multipurpose jack at the bottom of the phone.

The connectors are shaped differently and cannot be plugged in either backward or upside down.

- ✔ When the USB connection has been made successfully, the USB notification appears, similar to the one shown in the margin.

- ✔ The phone-computer connection works best with a powered USB port. If possible, plug the USB cable into the computer itself or into a powered USB hub.

- ✔ The Galaxy Note's USB cable is a USB 3.0 cable. You can still use the old-style USB 2.0 micro-USB cables, popular with other Android phones on your Galaxy Note: Simply plug the micro-USB connector into the right side of the multipurpose jack on the bottom of the phone.

- ✔ For data transfer to take place at top speeds on the Galaxy Note, you must connect its USB 3.0 cable into a USB 3.0 port on a computer. These ports are color-coded blue.

- ✔ A flurry of activity takes place when you first connect an Android phone to a Windows PC. Notifications pop up about new software that's installed. Don't fret if you see a message about software not being found. That's okay. If you see the AutoPlay dialog box, prompting you to install software, do so.

Configuring the USB connection

The USB connection is configured automatically whenever you connect your Galaxy Note to a computer. Everything should work peachy. When it doesn't, you can try manually configuring the USB connection: Swipe down the notifications panel and choose the USB notification.

The USB Computer Connection screen lists two options for configuring the USB connection:

Media Device (MTP): When this setting is chosen, the computer believes the Galaxy Note to be a portable media player, which it is, kinda. This option is the most common option.

Camera (PTP): In this setting, the computer is misled into thinking that the phone is a digital camera. Select this option only when the MTP option fails to make the connection.

See the later section "Synchronize Your Stuff" to see how to use the basic, USB MTP connection.

✔ No matter which USB connection option you've chosen, the phone's battery charges whenever it's connected to a computer's USB port — as long as the computer is turned on, of course.

✔ If your Galaxy Note has a MicroSD card, its storage is also mounted to the computer, as well as the phone's internal storage. You do not need to configure that storage separately to make the USB connection.

✔ PTP stands for Picture Transfer Protocol. MTP stands for Media Transfer Protocol.

Connecting to a Mac

You need special software to deal with the Galaxy Note-to-Macintosh connection. That's because the Mac doesn't natively recognize Android phones. Weird, huh? It's like Apple wants you to buy some other type of phone. I just don't get it.

To help deal with the USB connection on a Mac, obtain the Android File Transfer program. On your Mac, download that program from this website:

```
www.android.com/filetransfer
```

Install the software. Run it. From that point on, whenever you connect your Galaxy Note to the Mac, you see a special window appear, similar to the one shown in Figure 20-1. It lists the phone's folders and files. Use this window for file management, as covered later in this chapter.

View internal storage.

View MicroSD storage.

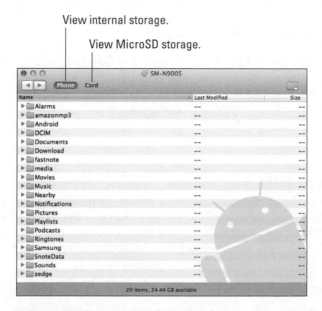

Figure 20-1: The Android File Transfer program.

✔ The Kies program can also be used to transfer files between the Galaxy Note and a Mac. See the later section "Connecting with Samsung Kies."

✔ Cloud storage can also be used to transfer files between your phone and a Macintosh (and a PC). See the later section "Sharing files with the cloud."

Disconnecting the phone from the computer

The process is cinchy: When you're done transferring files, music, or other media between your PC and the phone, close all programs and folders you have opened on your computer — specifically, those you've used to work with the phone's storage. Then you can disconnect the USB cable. That's it.

✔ It's A Bad Idea to unplug the Galaxy Note while you're transferring information or while a folder window is open on your computer. Doing so can damage the phone's storage, rendering unreadable some of the information that's kept there. To be safe, close those programs and folder windows you've opened before disconnecting.

✔ Unlike other external storage on the Macintosh, there's no need to eject the phone's storage when you're done accessing it. Simply disconnect the phone. The Mac doesn't get angry when you do so.

Synchronize Your Stuff

The point of making the USB connection between your Galaxy Note phone and a computer is to exchange files. You can't just wish the files over. Instead, I recommend following the advice in this section.

File transfer works best when you have a good understanding of basic file operations. You need to be familiar with file operations such as copy, move, rename, and delete. It also helps to know what folders are and how they work. The good news is that you don't need to manually calculate a 64-bit cyclical redundancy check on the data, nor do you need to know what a parity bit is.

Transferring files

I can think of plenty of files you would want to copy from a computer to your Galaxy Note: pictures, videos, and audio files. You can also copy vCards exported from your e-mail program, which helps to build the phone's address book. Likewise, you may want to copy files from the phone to the computer. Either way, it works the same. Follow these steps:

1. **Connect the phone and computer by using the USB cable.**

   Specific directions are offered earlier in this chapter.

2. **On a PC, if the AutoPlay dialog box appears, choose the option Open Folder/Device to View Files.**

When the AutoPlay dialog box doesn't appear, you can view files manually: Open the Computer window, and then open the phone's icon, found at the bottom of that window. Open the Storage icon to view files.

The phone's folder window that you see looks like any other folder in Windows. The difference is that the files and folders in that window are on your Galaxy Note, not on the computer.

On a Macintosh, the Android File Transfer program should start, appearing on the screen as shown earlier, in Figure 20-1.

3. **Open the source and destination folder windows.**

Open the folder that contains the files you want to copy. The folder can be found on the computer or on the phone. Then open the folder on the computer or phone where you want the file copies. Have both folder windows — computer and phone — visible on the screen, similar to what's shown in Figure 20-2.

Figure 20-2: Copying files to an Android phone.

4. **Drag the file icon from one folder window to the other.**

Dragging the file copies it, either from phone to computer or from computer to phone.

If you want to be specific, drag the file to the phone's download folder or to the root folder (refer to Figure 20-2).

On the PC, drag icons from the phone's storage to the My Documents, My Pictures, or My Videos folder, as appropriate. You can also drag directly to the desktop and decide later where to store the file.

The same file-dragging technique can be used for transferring files from a Macintosh. You need to drag the icon(s) to the Android File Transfer window, which works just like any folder window in the Finder.

5. **Close the folder windows and disconnect the USB cable when you're done.**

Refer to the specific instructions earlier in this chapter.

Though this manual technique works, the best way to transfer media to the phone is to use a media program, such as the Windows Media Player. See Chapter 16 for information on synchronizing music. You can also synchronize pictures and videos in the same way, by using a media program on the computer.

✔ When your Galaxy Note has a MicroSD card installed, you see Windows display two AutoPlay dialog boxes. Each dialog box represents a different storage source — internal storage as well as the MicroSD card.

✔ Files you've downloaded on the phone are stored in the download folder.

✔ Pictures and videos on the phone are stored in the DCIM/Camera folder.

✔ Music on the phone is stored in the Music folder, organized by artist.

Connecting with Samsung Kies

The Samsung way to connect your phone to a computer is to obtain and use the Samsung Kies program. A copy can be downloaded to your computer (PC or Mac) from the following website:

```
www.samsung.com/us/kies
```

Ensure that you download the proper version of Kies for the Galaxy Note 3. Run the program to install it on the computer.

When you run Samsung Kies, it begs you to connect the Galaxy Note to the computer by using the USB cable. Do so. If the phone uses a sophisticated screen lock, such as a PIN or password, unlock the phone so that the Kies program on the computer can access the phone's information.

After Kies starts, you see its main screen, similar to the one shown in Figure 20-3. You can synchronize music, photos, and videos by using Kies, although the methods described elsewhere in this book will probably work more effectively for you.

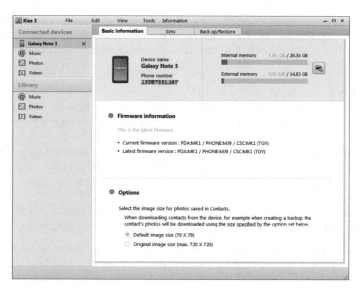

Figure 20-3: Kies for the Galaxy Note 3.

- To copy files to the phone by using Kies, use the File menu. Choose File➪Add File to Galaxy Note 3➪Internal (or External) and then choose the file to send over.

- Using Kies doesn't prevent you from transferring files as described in the preceding section, which I believe is a more effective way to move files back and forth between phone and computer. In fact:

- If you don't like Kies, don't use it. Simply close the program's window after it starts.

- If an update is looming for the Galaxy Note, the Kies program alerts you. Follow the directions on the computer screen to update the phone's software. Also see Chapter 23 for additional information on updates.

Sharing files with the cloud

A handy way to share files between a computer and your Galaxy Note is to use _cloud storage._ That's just fancy talk for storing files on the Internet.

Many choices are available for cloud storage, including Google's own Google Drive and Microsoft's SkyDrive. I'm fond of the Dropbox service.

All files saved to cloud storage are synchronized instantly with all devices that access the storage. Change a file on a computer and it's updated on your phone. The files are also available directly on the Internet from a web page. Even so, I recommend that you use a specific cloud storage app on your phone to access the files.

To make the file transfer from the computer to the phone, save a file in the cloud storage folder. On your phone, open the cloud storage app, such as Drive or Dropbox. Browse the folders to touch a file icon and view that file on your phone.

To transfer a file from your phone to a computer, view the file or media and then touch the Share icon. Choose the Drive or Dropbox icon to share the item via Google Drive or Dropbox, respectively.

Because all devices that share the cloud storage are instantly synchronized, you don't need to worry about specific file transfers. All files saved to cloud storage are available to all devices that can access that storage.

✔ The Google Drive app is named Drive. You must download this app from the Play Store because it's not preinstalled on the Galaxy Note.

✔ The Dropbox app is preinstalled on your Galaxy Note, but you must still configure it to hook into your Dropbox account. You'll find the Dropbox app in the Galaxy Plus folder on the Applications screen.

✔ These cloud storage services are free for a limited amount of storage. Beyond that, you need to pay a monthly fee.

Galaxy Note Storage Mysteries

Information on your phone (pictures, videos, music) is stored in two places: on the removable MicroSD card or on the phone's internal storage. That's about all you need to know, though if you're willing to explore the concept further — including the scary proposition of file management on a cell phone — keep reading.

Generally speaking, you use specific apps to access the stuff stored on your phone — for example, the Gallery app to view pictures or the Music app to listen to tunes. Beyond that, you can employ some nerdy apps to see where stuff dwells on your phone.

Reviewing storage stats

To see how much storage space is available on your phone, open the Settings app and choose the Storage category, found on the General tab. The Storage screen details information about storage space, similar to what's shown in Figure 20-4.

Items consuming storage

Used space   Free space

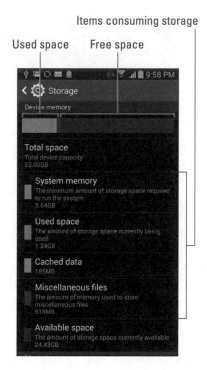

Figure 20-4: Phone storage information.

If you phone has external storage, look for the SD Card category at the bottom of the Storage screen (not shown in Figure 20-4).

Touch a category on the Storage screen to view details on how the storage is used or to launch an associated app. For example, touching Used Space (refer to Figure 20-4) displays a list of items occupying that chunk of storage.

✔ Things that consume the most storage space are videos, music, and pictures, in that order.

✔ To see how much storage space is not being used, refer to the Available Space item.

Managing files

You probably didn't get an Android phone because you enjoy managing files on a computer and wanted another gizmo to hone your skills. Even so, you can practice the same type of file manipulation on a phone as you would on a computer. Is there a need to do so? Of course not! But if you want to get dirty with files, you can.

The main tool for managing files on the Galaxy Note is the My Files app. It's found in the Samsung folder on the Applications screen. It's an okay file manager; better tools are available at the Play Store. One of my favorites is the ASTRO File Manager.

Dealing with MicroSD storage

The basic installation and removal of the Galaxy Note's MicroSD card is covered in Chapter 1. Once installed, the MicroSD card's storage is available to the phone for saving pictures, apps, and other information. Before you can use the MicroSD card, it must be formatted. Here are the steps necessary to accomplish that task:

1. **Open the Settings app.**

2. **From the General category, choose the Storage item.**

3. **Touch the Format SD Card command.**

   The command is found at the bottom of the Storage screen. If the phone is connected to a computer, the command isn't available; disconnect the phone in that case.

4. **Touch the Format SD Card button.**

   All data on the MicroSD card is erased by the formatting process.

5. **Touch the Delete All button.**

   The MicroSD card is unmounted, formatted, mounted again, and then made ready for use.

After the card is formatted, you can use it to store information, music, photos, and even apps.

- The Galaxy Note's Camera app automatically stores images on the MicroSD card. This setting can be changed; see Chapter 15.

- When copying music to the phone, choose the Galaxy Note's "Card" storage when using programs such as the Windows Media Player. Refer to Chapter 16.

- Apps can be relocated to the MicroSD card storage. See Chapter 18.

- The Unmount SD Card command is also found on the Storage screen in the Settings app. It allows you to remove the MicroSD card without turning off the Galaxy Note. Seeing how you must remove the phone's battery to get at the MicroSD card, I recommend that you simply turn off the phone and remove the card; unmounting isn't necessary.

- See Chapter 1 for information on inserting and removing the MicroSD card.

21

Take It Elsewhere

In This Chapter

▶ Understanding roaming
▶ Disabling data-roaming features
▶ Entering Airplane mode
▶ Contacting friends abroad
▶ Using Skype
▶ Using your phone overseas

*Y*ou can take your phone with you wherever you go. It's small and portable. But whether you can *use* the phone is another question. Wander too far from your cellular provider's signal and you witness the curiosity of roaming. Then there's the ability to make calls both to and from strange and distant locales. Yep, plenty of issues are involved when you take your Galaxy Note elsewhere.

Where the Phone Roams

The word *roam* takes on an entirely new meaning when it's applied to a cell phone. It means that your phone receives a cell signal whenever you're outside your cell phone carrier's operating area. In that case, your phone is *roaming*.

Roaming sounds handy, but there's a catch: It almost always involves a surcharge for using another cellular service — an *unpleasant* surcharge.

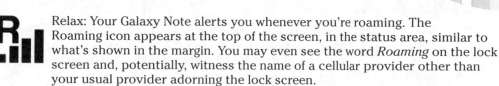

Relax: Your Galaxy Note alerts you whenever you're roaming. The Roaming icon appears at the top of the screen, in the status area, similar to what's shown in the margin. You may even see the word *Roaming* on the lock screen and, potentially, witness the name of a cellular provider other than your usual provider adorning the lock screen.

There's little you can do to avoid incurring roaming surcharges when making or receiving phone calls. Well, yes: You can wait until you're back in an area serviced by your primary cellular provider. You can, however, altogether avoid using the other network's data services while roaming. Follow these steps:

1. **Open the Settings app.**

   It's found on the Applications screen, although from the Home screen you can press the Menu button and choose the Settings command.

2. **Touch the Connections tab.**

3. **Choose More Networks and then Mobile Networks.**

4. **Ensure that the Data Roaming option isn't selected.**

   Remove the green check mark by Data Roaming.

Your phone can still access the Internet over the Wi-Fi connection while it's roaming. Setting up a Wi-Fi connection doesn't make you incur extra charges, unless you have to pay to get on the wireless network. See Chapter 19 for more information about Wi-Fi.

Another network service you might want to disable while roaming has to do with multimedia, or *MMS,* text messages. To avoid surcharges from another cellular network for downloading an MMS message, follow these steps:

1. **Open the Messages app.**

2. **If the screen shows a specific conversation, press the Back button to return to the main messaging screen.**

   The main screen lists all your conversations.

3. **Touch the Menu button and choose the Settings command.**

4. **Choose the SMS/MMS tab.**

5. **Remove the green check mark by the Auto-Retrieve option.**

   Or, if the item isn't selected, you're good to go — literally.

When the phone is roaming, you may see the text *Emergency Calls Only* displayed on the lock screen.

Airplane Mode

The rules about flying on an airplane with a cell phone are changing. Whereas it was once outright forbidden to even look at a cell phone while the plane was aloft, governments around the world have left it up to the airline to determine in-flight usage.

Generally speaking, follow the flight crew's direction when it comes to using your Galaxy Note whilst in the air. They'll let you know when and how you can use the phone — specifically, whether it needs to be turned off for takeoff and landing and, once in the air, whether you can use it to make phone calls or enable any wireless features, such as Wi-Fi and GPS.

Traditionally, cell phones are placed into what's commonly called Airplane mode during a flight. In this mode, it's okay to use the phone and access many of its features, except for cellular network access. So you can listen to music, play games, or use the in-flight Wi-Fi if your bankroll can afford it.

The most convenient way to place the Galaxy Note in Airplane mode is to obey these quick steps, which don't even require that you unlock the phone:

1. **Press and hold the phone's Power/Lock button.**

   The Device Options menu appears.

2. **Choose Airplane Mode.**

3. **Touch the OK button to confirm.**

The most inconvenient way to put the phone into Airplane mode is to use the Settings app. Follow these steps: On the Connection tab, touch the square by Airplane Mode to set the green check mark. Touch the OK button to confirm — and Airplane mode is active.

When the phone is in Airplane mode, a special icon appears in the status area, similar to the one shown in the margin. You might also see the text *No Service* appear on the phone's lock screen.

To exit Airplane mode, repeat the steps in this section: Choose Airplane Mode from the Device Options menu, or remove the green check mark by the Airplane Mode item in the Settings app.

- The Airplane mode Quick Action button can also be used to take the phone into or out of Airplane mode.

- Bluetooth networking is disabled in Airplane mode. See Chapter 19 for more information on Bluetooth.

- You can compose e-mail while the phone is in Airplane mode. No messages are sent until you disable Airplane mode and connect again with a data network. Unless:

- Many airlines feature onboard wireless networking. You can turn on wireless networking for your Android phone and use a wireless network in the air: Simply activate the Wi-Fi feature, per the directions in Chapter 19, after placing the phone in Airplane mode — well, after the flight attendant tells you that it's okay to do so.

Galaxy Note air-travel tips

I don't consider myself a frequent flyer, though I travel several times a year. I do it often enough that I wish the airports had separate lines for security: one for seasoned travelers, one for families, and one, of course, for frickin' idiots. The last category would have to be disguised by placing a Bonus Coupons sign or a Free Snacks banner over the metal detector. That would weed 'em out.

Here are some of my tips for traveling with your cell phone on an airline:

✔ **Charge your phone before you leave.** This tip probably goes without saying, but you'll be happier with a full cell phone charge to start your journey.

✔ **Take a cell phone charger with you.** Many airports feature USB chargers, so you might need only a USB-to-micro–USB cable. Still, why risk it? Bring the entire charger with you.

✔ **At the security checkpoint, place your phone in a bin.** Add to the bin all your other electronic devices, keys, brass knuckles, grenades, and so on. I know from experience that leaving your cell phone in your pocket most definitely sets off airport metal detectors.

✔ **If the flight crew asks you to *turn off* your cell phone for takeoff and landing, obey the command.** That's *turn off,* as in power off the phone or shut it down. It doesn't mean that you place the phone in Airplane mode. Turn it off.

✔ **Use the phone's Calendar app to keep track of flights.** The combination of airline and flight number can serve as the event title. For the event time, I insert take-off and landing schedules. For the location, I add the origin and destination airport codes. Remember to input the proper time zones. Referencing the phone from your airplane seat or a busy terminal is much handier than fussing with travel papers. See Chapter 17 for more information on the Calendar app.

✔ **Some airlines feature Android apps you can use while traveling.** Rather than hang on to a boarding pass printed by your computer, for example, you just present your phone to the scanner.

International Calling

You can use your Galaxy Note to dial up folks who live in other countries. You can also take your cell phone overseas and use it in another country. Completing either task isn't as difficult as properly posing for a passport photo, but it can become frustrating and expensive when you don't know your way around.

Dialing an international number

A phone is a bell that anyone in the world can ring. To prove it, all you need is the phone number of anyone in the world. Dial the number using your phone, and, as long as you both speak the same language, you're talking!

To make an international call from your phone, you merely need to know the foreign phone number. The number includes the international country-code prefix, followed by the number.

Before dialing the international country-code prefix, you must first dial a plus sign (+) when using the Dialer app. The + symbol is the country *exit code,* which must be dialed in order to flee the national phone system and access the international phone system. For example, to dial Finland on your phone, you dial +358 and then the number in Finland. The +358 is the exit code (+) plus the international code for Finland (358).

To produce the + code in an international phone number, press and hold the 0 key on the Phone app's keypad. Then input the country prefix and the phone number. Touch the green Dial button to complete the call.

- Most cellular providers surcharge when sending a text message abroad. Contact your cellular provider to confirm the text message rates. Generally, you'll find two rates: one for sending and another for receiving text messages.

- If texting charges vex you, remember that e-mail has no associated per-message charge. There are also alternative ways to chat, such as Google Hangouts and Skype, both covered in Chapter 13.

- In most cases, dialing an international number involves a time zone difference. Before you dial, be aware of what time it is in the country or location you're calling. The Clock app can handle this job for you: Summon a clock for the location you're calling, and place it on the Clock app's World Clock tab (see Chapter 17).

- Dialing internationally also involves surcharges, unless your cell phone plan already provides for international dialing.

- The + character isn't a separator character, it's a prefix. When you see an international number listed and it shows the + character, as in 011+20+xxxxxxx, do not insert the + character when you type that number. Instead, dial +20 and then the rest of the international phone number without the + character.

- International calls fail for a number of reasons. One of the most common is that the recipient's phone company or service blocks incoming international calls or calls from cell phones.

- Another reason that international calls fail is the zero reason: Oftentimes, you must leave out any zero in the phone number that follows the country code. So, if the country code is 254 for Kenya and the phone number starts with 012, you dial +254 for Kenya and then 12 and the rest of the number. Omit the leading zero.

- Know which type of phone you're calling internationally — cell phone or landline. The reason is that an international call to a cell phone often involves a surcharge that doesn't apply to a landline.

Making international calls with Skype

One of the easiest, and cheapest, ways to make international calls on your Galaxy Note is to use the Skype app. The phone doesn't come with this app preinstalled, so you have to pick up a copy from the Google Play Store. See Chapter 13 for details on using Skype.

Because Skype uses the Internet, you can also use Skype to contact overseas Skype users without incurring any extra costs (well, beyond your normal data plan). You can, however, use your Skype account to dial internationally, from the United States to a foreign country as well as from a foreign country to your home. All you need is some Skype Credit.

The easiest way to add Skype Credit is to visit Skype on the Internet using a computer: www.skype.com. Sign into your account and surrender a credit card to add a few pennies of credit. Though that may seem disappointing, remember that Skype's rates are far cheaper than placing a call by using your cellular provider.

To make an international call, log in to Skype as you normally would. At the main Skype screen, touch the Call Phone icon to summon the phone dialpad. Punch in the number, including the plus sign (+) symbol for international access. Touch the Call icon to place the call. When you're finished with the call, touch the End button.

✔ You're always signed In to Skype unless you sign out. Pressing the Home button to switch from Skype to another app doesn't sign you out.

✔ To sign out of Skype, press the Menu button while viewing the main Skype screen and choose the Sign Out command.

✔ Check with your cellular provider to see whether you're charged connection minutes for using Skype. Even though the international calling with Skype is free, you might still be dinged for the minutes you use on Skype to make the call.

Taking your Galaxy Note abroad

The easiest way to use a cell phone abroad is to rent or buy one in the country where you plan to stay. I'm serious: Often, international roaming charges are so high that it's cheaper to buy a simple throwaway cell phone wherever you go, especially if you plan to stay there for a while.

When you opt to use your own phone rather than buy a local phone, things should run smoothly — if a compatible cellular service is in your location. Not every cell phone uses the same network as the Galaxy Note, and, of course, not every foreign country uses the same cellular network. Things must match before the phone can work. Plus, you may have to deal with foreign-carrier roaming charges.

The key to determining whether your phone is usable in a foreign country is to turn it on. The name of that country's compatible cellular service should show up at the top of the phone, where the name of your carrier appears on the main screen. So, where your phone once said *AT&T,* it may say *Wambooli Telcom,* for example, when you're overseas.

✔ You receive calls on your cell phone internationally as long as the phone can access the network. Your friends need only dial your cell phone number as they normally do; the phone system automatically forwards your calls to wherever you are in the world.

✔ The person calling you pays nothing extra when you're off romping the globe with your Galaxy Note. Nope — *you* pay extra for the call.

✔ While you're abroad, you dial internationally. When calling the United States, you use a ten-digit number (phone number plus area code). You may also be required to type the country exit code when you dial.

✔ When in doubt, contact your cellular provider for tips and other information specific to whatever country you're visiting.

✔ Be sure to inquire about texting and cellular data (Internet) rates while you're abroad.

✔ Using your phone over a Wi-Fi network abroad incurs no extra fees (unless data roaming is on, as discussed earlier in this chapter). In fact, you can use the Skype app on your phone over a Wi-Fi network to call the United States or any international number at inexpensive rates.

22

Customize Your Phone

In This Chapter

▶ Changing the Home screen background

▶ Putting your favorite apps on the Home screen

▶ Adding and removing icons and widgets

▶ Setting the phone's locks

▶ Exploring sound options

▶ Modifying display settings

*I*figure that only a small portion of people bother customizing anything. And just about all of them work in the technology field. Fulfilling their desires, they make everything customizable, probably because they figure everyone else wants to do so. The problem they run into is that the majority of humanity relies upon consistency. Sure, it may be mediocre and dull, but boring old uniformity is reliable and comforting.

You'll find plenty of things to customize on your phone. You can change the look of the Home screen, add extra security, change this, fiddle with that, and modify all sorts of things. Nothing is required, but if you're curious, consider reading this chapter to learn the limits of what's possible. Or never change a thing. That's entirely okay.

It's Your Home Screen

The Galaxy Note sports a roomy Home screen. It features up to seven Home screen panels that you can adorn with icons, widgets, and wallpapers. As the phone ships, examples of icons, widgets, and wallpaper festoon five of the seven panels. Most people never mess with them, but each of those items is completely customizable. After all, it's *your* Home screen. Why not make it the way you want?

Editing the Home screen

The key to changing the Home screen is the *long-press:* Press and hold your finger on a blank part of the Home screen (not on an icon). Upon success, you see the Home Screen menu, shown in Figure 22-1.

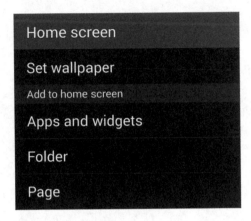

Home screen

Set wallpaper

Add to home screen

Apps and widgets

Folder

Page

Figure 22-1: The Home Screen menu.

The items controlled by the Home Screen menu are described here:

Set Wallpaper: Change the background image on the Home screen, lock screen, or both.

Apps and Widgets: Add shortcut icons (apps) and widgets to the Home screen.

Folder: Create folders for multiple apps on the Home screen.

Page: Add, remove, or manage multiple Home screen pages.

Later sections in this chapter describe how to use each command.

✔ You cannot summon the Home Screen menu when the Home screen panel is already full of icons or widgets. Display or add another panel and try again.

✔ Use folders to help organize apps on the Home screen, especially when the Home screen starts to overflow with icons. See the later section "Building app folders."

Changing wallpaper

The Home and lock screen background can be draped with two types of wallpaper:

Traditional: The wallpaper is chosen from a selection of still images. They can be images preloaded as wallpapers on the phone, or you can pluck an image from the phone's Gallery, such as a photo you've taken.

Live: The wallpaper image is animated, either displaying a changing image or reacting to your touch.

To set a new wallpaper for the Home screen, obey these steps:

1. **Long-press the Home screen.**

   The Home Screen menu appears (refer to Figure 22-1).

2. **Choose the Set Wallpaper command.**

3. **Choose whether to set the Home screen, Lock screen, or both Home and Lock screens.**

   When you choose the Home and Lock Screens item, the image is set for both; otherwise, you can set different wallpaper images for the Home and lock screens.

4. **Use the Select Wallpaper From menu to choose an app or a source for the wallpaper.**

   Among your choices, you'll find these options:

   Gallery: Choose a still image stored in the Gallery app.

   Live Wallpapers: Choose an animated or interactive wallpaper from a list.

   Photos: Choose a still image accessed via Google's Photos app. (These are pretty much the same as the Gallery.)

   Wallpapers: Choose a wallpaper from a range of stunning images that come with the Galaxy Note.

5. **Choose the wallpaper.**

   When you choose the Gallery option, you see a preview of the wallpaper, where you can select and crop part of the image. When setting both Home and lock screens, you need to crop both horizontally and vertically at the same time.

   For certain live wallpapers, the Settings button may appear. The settings let you customize certain aspects of the interactive wallpaper.

6. **Touch the Set Wallpaper button to confirm your selection.**

The new wallpaper takes over the Home screen, lock screen, or both.

✔ Live wallpaper features some form of animation. Sometimes, it's interactive, reacting to your touch.

✔ The Zedge app has some interesting wallpaper features. Check it out at the Google Play Store; see Chapter 18.

✔ See Chapter 15 for more information about the Gallery, including information on how cropping an image works.

Adding apps to the Home screen

You need not live with the unbearable proposition that you're stuck with only the apps that come preset on the Home screen. Nope — you're free to add your own apps. Just follow these steps:

1. **Visit the Home screen panel on which you want to stick the app icon.**

   The screen must have room for the icon.

2. **Touch the Apps icon to display the Applications screen.**

3. **Long-press the icon of the app you want to add to the Home screen.**

   The phone vibrates slightly, and then you see a preview of the Home screen.

4. **Drag the icon to a blank spot on the Home screen.**

   A copy of the app's icon is placed on the Home screen.

The app hasn't moved: What you see is a copy; a *shortcut.* You can still find the app on the Applications screen, but now the app is available — more conveniently — on the Home screen.

✔ Note that not every app needs a shortcut on the Home screen. I recommend placing only those apps you use most frequently.

 ✔ The best icons to place on the Home screen are those that show updates, such as new messages, similar to the icon shown in the margin. These icons are also ideal to place on the Favorites tray, as covered in the next section.

✔ See the later section "Rearranging and removing icons and widgets" for information on moving the app icon around on the Home screen or from one panel to another. That section also covers removing apps from the Home screen.

✔ You can also add apps to the Home screen by choosing the Apps and Widgets command from the Home Screen menu, shown earlier, in Figure 22-1. Choosing this command merely skips over Steps 1 and 2 in this section; you still have to long-press the icon and drag it to a Home screen page.

Putting an app on the Favorites tray

The Galaxy Note features the *Favorites tray:* It's a row of app icons that floats along the bottom of every Home screen panel. It includes the Apps icon, as well as up to four other icons, such as the Phone app icon or any other app you use frequently. The Favorites tray icons appear the same no matter which Home screen panel is displayed.

To add an icon to the Favorites tray, drag the icon from elsewhere on the Home screen: Long-press the icon and drag it to the Favorites tray. Any icon already on the Favorites tray swaps positions with the icon you're moving.

> ✔ The Favorites tray can hold only four icons and the Apps icon. You cannot remove the Apps icon.

> ✔ You can drag all icons off the Favorites tray, leaving only the Apps icon. I do, however, recommend you have at least the Phone app icon on the Favorites tray.

> ✔ You can also place folder icons on the Favorites tray. The folder must be created on the Home screen and then dragged to the Favorites tray. See the later section "Building app folders."

Slapping down widgets

The Home screen is the place where you can find *widgets,* or tiny, interactive information windows. A widget often provides a gateway into another app or displays information such as status updates, the song that's playing, or the weather forecast. To add a widget to the Home screen, heed these steps:

1. **Switch to a Home screen panel that has room enough for the new widget.**

   Unlike app icons, some widgets can occupy more than a postage-stamp-size piece of real estate on the Home screen.

2. **Long-press the Home screen and choose Apps and Widgets.**

   You're taken to the Applications screen, which you could have also arrived at by touching the Apps icon on the Home screen.

3. **Touch the Widgets tab.**

4. **Scroll the list of widgets to choose the one you want to add.**

   For example, choose the Calendar widget to see an overview of your schedule on the Home screen.

5. **Drag the widget to the Home screen.**

   At this point, the operation works just like adding an app. One major difference, however, is that some widgets can be very big. Room must be available on the Home screen panel or you won't be able to add the widget.

Some widgets may require additional setup after you add them, such as setting a few quick options. You might also see a resize rectangle around the widget, similar to the one shown in Figure 22-2. Drag the edges or corners of that rectangle to resize the widget.

Figure 22-2: Arranging a widget.

> ✔ The variety of available widgets depends on the apps you have installed. Some applications come with widgets, some don't.
>
> ✔ To remove, move, or rearrange a widget, see the later section "Rearranging and removing icons and widgets."

Building app folders

The Galaxy Note has room for only seven Home screen panels, maximum. Each panel has room for 16 icons. That's 7 x 16 (or 112) app icons, plus four more icons on the Favorites tray, for 116 total app icons. For some people, that's just not enough. For those people, or even those who aren't into cramming apps on the Home screen, I present the app folder.

An *app folder* is simply a collection of two or more apps, both in the same spot on the Home screen. Figure 22-3 illustrates an app folder on the Home screen, shown both closed and open.

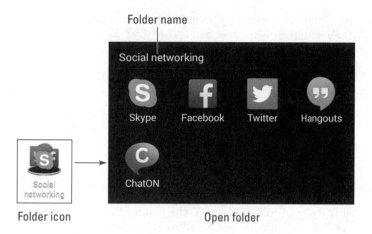

Figure 22-3: Anatomy of an app folder.

Create a folder by following these steps:

1. **Long-press the Home screen to display the Home Screen menu.**
2. **Choose the Folder command.**
3. **Type a short, descriptive name for the folder.**

   The name should reflect the folder's contents but also be short enough to fit under the Folder icon on the Home screen.
4. **Touch the OK button.**

The folder is created, but it's empty! Your next task is to drag similar app icons into the folder: Long-press an icon, which can be on any Home screen panel, and then drag it over the folder's icon. Lift your finger to add that icon to the folder. You can even drag icons from the Applications screen into a folder.

To use the folder, open it: Touch the folder's icon. You can then touch an app icon in the folder to start that app.

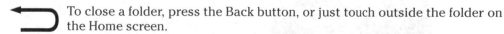

To close a folder, press the Back button, or just touch outside the folder on the Home screen.

✓ Folders are managed just like other icons on the Home screen. You can long-press them to drag them around.

✓ Folders are deleted just like icons and widgets, described in the later section "Rearranging and removing icons and widgets." Be aware that when you remove a folder, you also remove all icons held within that folder. (They aren't, however, uninstalled.)

✔ Change a folder's name by opening the folder and then touching the folder's name, shown earlier, in Figure 22-3. Type the new name by using the onscreen keyboard.

✔ Add more apps to the folder by dragging them over the folder's icon.

✔ To remove an icon from a folder, open the folder and drag out the icon.

✔ When the last icon is dragged out of a folder, the folder is empty. The empty folder can be removed from the Home screen, just like any other icon, as covered in the next section.

Rearranging and removing icons and widgets

Icons and widgets aren't fastened to the Home screen. If they are, it's day-old chewing gum that binds them, considering how easily you can rearrange and remove unwanted items from any Home screen panel.

Long-press an icon on the Home screen to move it. Eventually, the icon seems to lift and break free, as shown in Figure 22-4.

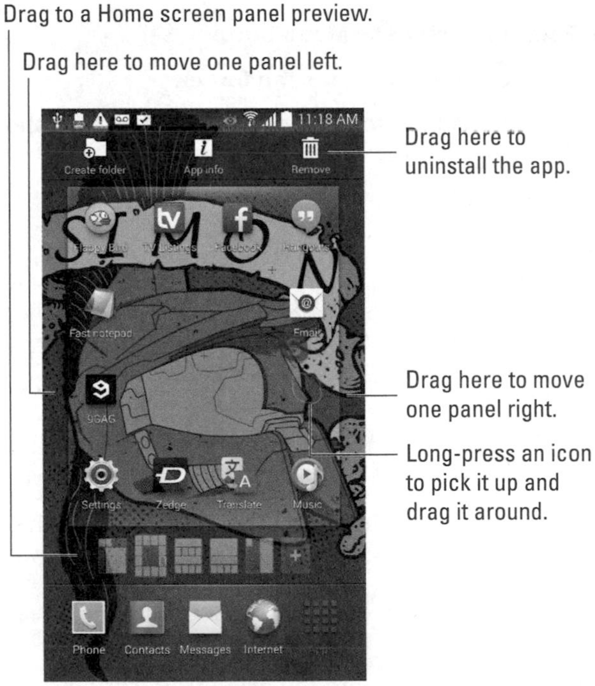

Drag to a Home screen panel preview.

Drag here to move one panel left.

Drag here to uninstall the app.

Drag here to move one panel right.

Long-press an icon to pick it up and drag it around.

Figure 22-4: Moving an icon.

You can drag a free icon to another position on the Home screen or to another Home screen panel (left or right), or you can drag the icon to the

Remove icon that appears on the Home screen, which deletes the shortcut (refer to Figure 22-4).

Widgets and folders can also be moved or removed in the same manner as icons.

✔ Dragging a Home screen icon or widget to the Remove icon doesn't uninstall the app or widget.

✔ When an icon hovers over the Remove icon, ready to be deleted, its color changes to red.

✔ See Chapter 18 for information on uninstalling apps.

Adding and removing Home screen panels

Did I write that the Galaxy Note has seven Home screen panels? My bad — it can have *up to* seven Home screen panels. You're free to remove panels you don't need. And, if you need to have seven panels again in the future, you can add them again.

To add or remove Home screen panels, heed these directions:

1. **At the Home screen, press the Menu button.**

2. **Choose Edit Page.**

   You see an overview of all Home screen panels, similar to the one shown in Figure 22-5.

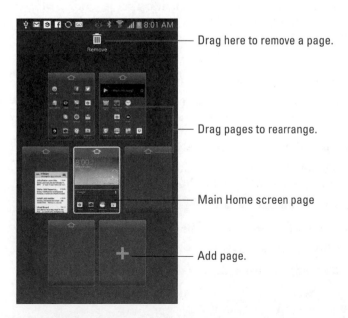

Figure 22-5: Manipulating Home screen panels.

3. **Work the Home screen panels.**

You can do these three things:

Remove: To remove a Home screen panel, drag it to the Remove icon. If the panel has icons or widgets, you see a warning. Touch the OK button to confirm the deletion.

Add: To add a Home screen panel, touch the thumbnail with the Plus Sign icon on it, as illustrated in Figure 22-5. If you don't see a thumbnail with the Plus Sign icon on it, you cannot add more panels.

Rearrange: Drag a panel around to change the order in which it appears. The thumbnail with the white border is the primary Home screen panel.

4. **Press the Back button when you're done editing.**

The phone needs a Home screen, so it must have at least one Home screen panel.

There's no way to undo a Home screen panel deletion. You have to add a new, blank panel and then repopulate it with icons and widgets.

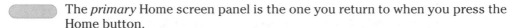 The *primary* Home screen panel is the one you return to when you press the Home button.

Galactic Screen Security

The Galaxy Note features a rudimentary screen lock: Swipe the lock screen and you're in. That's hardly true security, but it's not the end of your options when it comes to locking the screen, as described in this section.

Finding the screen locks

You'll find the Galaxy Note's screen locks in a single location: on the Select Screen Lock screen. Heed these steps to visit that screen:

1. **Open the Settings app.**

It's found on the Applications screen. A shortcut to the Settings app appears at the top of the Notifications panel.

2. **Touch the Device tab.**

3. **Choose the Lock Screen item.**

4. **Choose Screen Lock.**

5. **If prompted, work the screen lock.**

You're required to work screen locks other than the Swipe, Signature, and None settings to confirm that you're authorized to change this setting: Trace the pattern or type the PIN or password to continue.

Upon success, you see the Select Screen Lock screen. It lists the type of screen locks available on your phone. The standard Android screen locks are known as Swipe, Pattern, PIN, and Password. Samsung adds the Signature and None options. Using these items is covered in the next few sections.

> ✔ The lock you apply affects the way you unlock your phone. See Chapter 2.

> ✔ No locks appear when you answer an incoming phone call. You are, however, prompted to unlock the phone if you want to use its features while you're on a call.

> ✔ See the nearby sidebar "The lock doesn't show up!" for information on setting the Lock Automatically timer, which affects when the screen locks appear after you put the phone to sleep.

Removing a lock

To disable the pattern, PIN, or password screen lock on your phone, choose the Swipe or None options from the Select Screen Lock screen. The swipe lock is the standard screen lock preset when you first used your phone.

> ✔ Refer to the preceding section for information on finding the Swipe or None options.

> ✔ When the None option is chosen, the phone unlocks when you press the Power/Lock button or touch the Home button.

The lock doesn't show up!

The Galaxy Note features a few options that control when the screen lock kicks in. These options are presented on the lock screen, which you see immediately after setting a screen lock.

The first option is Lock Instantly with Power Key. Choose this item to ensure that pressing the Power/Lock button instantly locks the phone. When this item is off, the phone waits a few moments before the screen locks.

The Lock Automatically setting on the lock screen controls how long the phone waits to lock when the touchscreen times out. (The display time-out setting is covered elsewhere in this chapter.) Choose Lock Automatically to set the delay, which is normally 5 seconds. Choose the Immediately option to have the phone lock instantly when the display times out, or set another value if you prefer a longer delay.

Applying a password

The most secure way to lock the phone's screen is to apply a full-on password. Just like on a computer, the phone's lock screen password contains a combination of numbers, symbols, and uppercase and lowercase letters.

Set the password by choosing Password from the Select Screen Lock screen; refer to the earlier section "Finding the screen locks" for information on getting to that screen.

The password you create must be at least four characters long. Longer passwords are more secure but easier to mistype.

You type the password twice to set things up, which confirms to the Galaxy Note that you know the password and will, you hope, remember it in the future. Touch the OK button to set the password.

You need to type the password whenever you unlock the phone, as described in Chapter 2. You also type the password whenever you change or remove the screen lock, as discussed in the section "Finding the screen locks," earlier in this chapter.

Setting a PIN

A *PIN lock* is a code between 4 and 16 numbers long. It contains only numbers, 0 through 9. To set the PIN lock, follow the directions in the earlier section "Finding the screen locks" to reach the Select Screen Lock screen. Choose PIN from the list.

Type your PIN twice to confirm to the doubting Galaxy Note that you know it. The next time you need to unlock your phone, type the PIN by using the onscreen keyboard that appears on the lock screen. Touch the OK button to proceed.

    ✔ The PIN lock is considered secure, but it's not as secure as the Password screen lock.

    ✔ PIN stands for *p*ersonal *i*dentification *n*umber.

Creating an unlock pattern

The *unlock pattern* is perhaps the most popular, and certainly the most unconventional, way to lock your phone's screen. The pattern must be traced on the touchscreen to unlock the phone. Keep in mind that this option isn't as secure as the PIN or password, which is why a PIN is required as a backup when you choose the pattern lock.

To set the unlock pattern, follow these steps:

1. **Summon the Select Screen Lock screen.**

   Refer to the earlier section "Finding the screen locks."

2. **Choose Pattern.**

   If you haven't yet set a pattern, you may see a tutorial describing the process; touch the Next button to skip merrily through the dreary directions.

3. **Trace an unlock pattern.**

   Use Figure 22-6 as your guide. You can trace over the dots in any order, but you can trace over a dot only once. The pattern must cover at least four dots.

I began the pattern here.

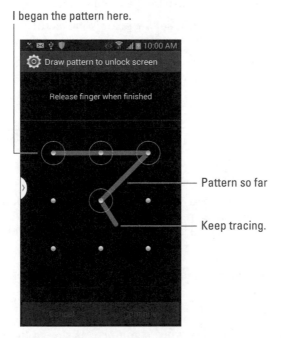

Pattern so far

Keep tracing.

Figure 22-6: Setting the unlock pattern.

4. **Touch the Continue button.**

5. **Redraw the pattern again, just to confirm that you know it.**

6. **Touch the Confirm button to set the pattern.**

Because the Pattern lock is insecure, a PIN is required:

7. **Type a backup PIN.**

Type a secret number at least four digits long.

8. **Confirm the PIN and touch the OK button.**

The pattern unlock is now set, along with its PIN backup.

Ensure that a check mark appears by the option Make Pattern Visible, found on the lock screen. That way, the pattern shows up when you need to unlock the phone. For even more security, you can disable this option, but you *must* remember how and where the pattern goes.

- Although it's popular, the pattern lock is not considered a secure screen lock. If you want security, use the Password lock.

- To remove the pattern lock, set Swipe or None as the lock type, as described in the preceding section.

- The pattern lock can start at any dot, not necessarily at the upper left dot, shown earlier, in Figure 22-6.

- The unlock pattern can be as simple or as complex as you like. I'm a big fan of simple.

- Wash your hands! Smudge marks on the display can betray your pattern.

Unlocking the phone with your signature

Time to put that S Pen to work! You can unlock your Galaxy Note by scribbling your signature on the touchscreen. As with the pattern lock, this type of screen lock also requires a PIN as a security backup. Here's how to configure the Signature lock:

1. **Choose the Signature item from the Select Screen Lock screen.**

Refer to the earlier section "Finding the screen locks" for details on hunting down the Select Screen Lock screen.

2. **Use the S Pen to jot down your signature, as shown in Figure 22-7.**

Of course, you don't have to write your name; I suppose any scribbling works.

3. **Carefully craft the same (or similar) signature three times.**

After the first two tries, touch the Continue button.

4. **Touch the Confirm button to set your signature or scribbling.**

5. **Type a PIN as a backup.**

The PIN must be at least four digits long.

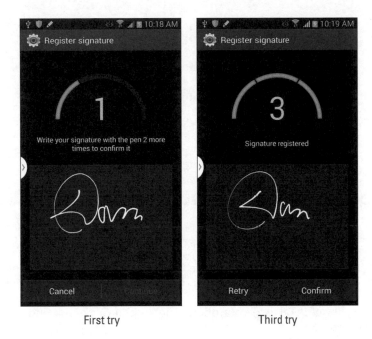

First try   Third try

Figure 22-7: Creating an unlock signature.

6. **Touch the OK button after confirming the PIN.**

    The signature lock is set.

The phone gives you two tries to use your signature to unlock the phone. When you fail, you must type the PIN to gain access to the phone. Likewise, you need to type the PIN to access the Select Screen Lock screen.

✔ If you find the Galaxy Note too fussy to recognize your sloppy John Hancock, you can direct it to be more forgiving: With the signature lock set, visit the lock screen and choose the Accuracy Level item. Choose the Low setting. And practice your penmanship.

✔ I'm pleased that the folks at my bank are more forgiving than the Galaxy Note when it comes to recognizing my signature.

Adding owner info text

Screen locks add security to your Galaxy Note, but what happens when a good Samaritan finds your phone? My guess is that he'd probably pick up the phone and turn it on. Whether your phone is locked or not, the Good Samaritan would probably appreciate some text right on the lock screen that says who the phone belongs to and how to contact them. That makes sense.

To add owner-info text to your phone's lock screen, follow these steps:

1. **Visit the Settings app.**

2. **Choose the Device tab.**

3. **Touch the Lock Screen category.**

4. **Choose Owner Information.**

5. **Type text into the box.**

   You can type more than one line of text, though the information is displayed on the lock screen as a single line.

6. **Ensure that there's a check mark in the box by the Show Owner Info on Lock Screen option.**

7. **Touch the OK button.**

Whatever text you type into the box appears on the lock screen. Therefore, I recommend typing something useful, as the command suggests: your name, address, another phone number, and an e-mail address, for example. This way, should you lose your phone and an honest person finds it, he can get it back to you.

Some Fine-Tuning

Your Galaxy Note features a plethora of options and settings for you to adjust. You can fix things that annoy you or make things better, to please your tastes. The whole idea is to make your phone more usable for you. Or just ignore making changes, and tolerate all the presets. It's up to you.

Setting sound and vibration options

Whether the phone rings, vibrates, or explodes depends on how you've configured it to signal you. Various sound and notification settings are manipulated by following these initial steps:

1. **Open the Settings app.**

2. **Choose the Device tab.**

3. **Choose Sound.**

Behold some of the many options you can change:

Volume master control: Choose the Volume command to adjust the sound levels for several different items in the phone. For example, you can turn up the ringtone volume for incoming calls, but keep the notifications and other volume levels set low.

Turn Over to Mute

One of the Galaxy Note's motion tricks is called Turn Over. You can use this trick to have the phone silence itself by simply flipping it over (gently, of course) on its face. To make this setting, touch the Controls tab in the Settings app. Ensure that the master control for the Motions item is set to On (green). Choose Motions, and then confirm that the master control by the Mute/Pause item is also green.

After the Turn Over to Mute function is active, it works when you simply lay the phone on its face. So when you receive an incoming call during a meeting or at some fine dining establishment, simply flip over your phone. This trick works for those times when you forget to silence your phone or when you're just being a cad.

Incoming-call vibration: You can make the phone vibrate for all incoming calls, which works in addition to any ringtone you've set (and still works when you've silenced the phone). To activate the incoming-call vibration, place a check mark by the item Vibrate When Ringing.

Vibration type: What is a vibration, anyway? Does the phone wiggle? You can set the vibration type by choosing the Vibrations command. Touch an item on the Vibrations menu to experience the variety. Touch the Create button to craft your own vibes.

Vibration intensity: Choose the Vibration Intensity command to adjust how violently the Galaxy Note vibrates for various phone tasks. Three settings are available. The Haptic Feedback item refers to vibrations when you touch the screen. Speaking of which:

Vibration when touching the Back, Home, or Menu buttons: Place a check mark by the Haptic Feedback item to have the phone vibrate when these buttons are touched.

Silent mode: Silent mode disables all sounds from the phone, except for music and YouTube and other types of media, as well as alarms that have been set by the Clock and Calendar apps.

Changing display settings

The Display item in the Settings app deals with touchscreen settings. To peruse the various display options, visit the Display screen by following these initial steps:

1. **Open the Settings app.**

2. **Choose the Device tab.**

3. **Choose Display.**

Here are some of the more popular items you can adjust on the Display screen:

Screen brightness: Choose the Brightness item to set the screen's brightness level, from dim to searchlight. The Automatic Brightness option lets the phone set its own brightness level as determined by the ambient light at your location. This item ticks people off because the screen tends to change its intensity while you're using it. Simply uncheck that item to avoid being ticked off.

Automatic lock timer: The Screen Timeout item is used to determine the inactivity span after which the phone automatically locks. Values range from 15 seconds up to 10 minutes.

The Screen Timeout value is based on physical interaction with the phone. You can, however, activate the Smart Screen feature so that the phone doesn't lock as long as you're looking at it. In the Settings app, tap the Controls tab and choose the Smart Screen item. Ensure that a check mark is placed by the Smart Stay item.

Auto Rotate: Place a check mark by the Auto Rotate Screen item so that certain apps, such as the Internet app, can reorient themselves between horizontal and vertical screen presentations. This setting can also be changed by using the Screen Rotation Quick Action.

You can override the Auto Rotate Screen command by using another Galaxy Note Smart Screen feature: Smart Rotation. In the Settings app, touch the Controls tab and choose Smart Screen. Place a check mark by the item Smart Rotation. Once active, the phone orients itself to your face, which overrides any Auto Rotate Screen setting.

23

Keep It Running

In This Chapter

▶ Checking the phone's battery usage

▶ Making the battery last

▶ Cleaning the phone

▶ Keeping the system up-to-date

▶ Dealing with problems

▶ Finding support

▶ Getting answers to common questions

You remember maintenance, don't you? It's the thing you're supposed to do to the lawn mower once or twice a year. It's the reason that businesses exist only to change your car's oil. It's why the coffee maker clogs — because (and you probably didn't know this) you have to clean it out with vinegar at least once a year. That's maintenance.

For your Galaxy Note, maintenance isn't much of a big deal, but as with all maintenance, you avoid it at your own peril. You'll never have to change the oil in your phone, rotate its tires, or pour vinegar into the speaker hole to unclog its pipes. Nope, all you really need to do is read this chapter.

Battery Care and Feeding

Perhaps the most important item you can monitor and maintain on your Galaxy Note is its battery. The battery supplies the necessary electrical juice by which the phone operates. Without battery power, your phone is about as useful as a tin-can-and-a-string for communications. Keep an eye on the battery.

Monitoring the battery

Your phone's current battery status is displayed at the top of the screen, in the status area, next to the time. The icons used to display the battery status are similar to those shown in Figure 23-1.

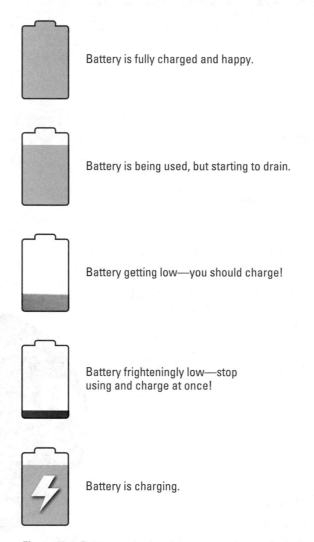

Battery is fully charged and happy.

Battery is being used, but starting to drain.

Battery getting low—you should charge!

Battery frighteningly low—stop using and charge at once!

Battery is charging.

Figure 23-1: Battery status icons.

You might also see the icon for a dead or missing battery, but for some reason, I can't get my phone to turn on and display it.

✔ Heed those low-battery warnings! The phone sounds a notification whenever the battery power gets low. (See the third Battery icon, shown in Figure 23-1.) The phone sounds another notification when the battery gets very low. (See the fourth Battery icon in Figure 23-1.)

✔ When the battery is too low, the phone shuts itself off.

✔ The best way to deal with a low battery is to connect the phone to a power source: Either plug the phone into a wall socket or connect the phone to a computer by using a USB cable. The phone charges itself immediately; plus, you can use the phone while it's charging.

✔ The phone charges more efficiently when it's plugged into a wall socket rather than a computer.

✔ You don't have to fully charge the phone to use it. If you have only 20 minutes to charge and the power level returns to only 70 percent, that's great. Well, it's not great, but it's far better than a 20 percent battery level.

✔ Battery percentage values are best-guess estimates. Just because you talked for two hours and the battery shows 50 percent doesn't mean that you're guaranteed two more hours of talking. Odds are good that you have much less than two hours. In fact, as the percentage value gets low, the battery appears to drain faster.

Determining what is drawing power

A nifty screen on your phone reviews which activities have been consuming power when the phone is operating from its battery. This informative screen is shown in Figure 23-2.

To get to this screen, follow these steps:

1. **Open the Settings app.**

2. **Touch the General tab.**

3. **Choose Battery.**

   You see a screen similar to the one shown in Figure 23-2.

Touch an item in the list to view specific details. For some items, such as Screen (shown in Figure 23-2), the details screen contains a button that lets you adjust the setting.

The number and variety of items listed on the battery-use screen depend on what you've been doing with your phone between charges and how many different programs are active.

Current battery
charge and state   Usage and time chart

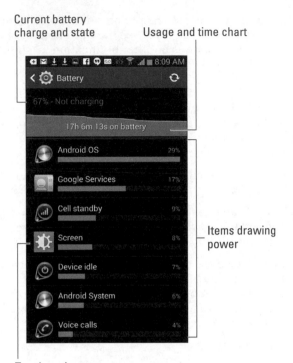

Items drawing
power

Touch to view usage
and change settings.

Figure 23-2: Things that drain the battery.

Using Power Saving mode

The Galaxy Note comes with a handy power-saving feature that you can employ to help squeeze extra juice out of the battery. To use these power-saving tools, follow these steps:

1. **Open the Settings app.**

2. **Touch the General tab.**

3. **Slide the master control by the item Power Saving Mode to the On position.**

   If the master control is already green, you're good to go.

4. **Choose the Power Saving Mode item.**

5. **Ensure that all items on the Power Saving Mode screen are checked.**

   Power saving is enabled.

The power-saving feature automatically disables certain phone features — specifically, power-draining features. It also throttles the screen brightness.

Choose the item Learn About Power Saving on the Power Saving Mode screen to review some tips and tricks for extending battery life.

Extending battery life

Here's a smattering of things you can do to help prolong the battery life in your Galaxy Note:

Turn off vibration options. The phone's vibration is caused by a teensy motor. Though you don't see much battery savings by disabling the vibration options, it's better than no savings. To turn off vibration, follow these steps:

1. **Open the Settings app.**
2. **Tap the Device tab.**
3. **Choose Sound.**
4. **Choose Vibration Intensity.**
5. **Throttle each setting down to the lowest possible position.**

   Or you can slide the control all the way over to the left, which disables vibration for each item.

Additionally, consider lowering the volume of notifications by choosing the Volume option. This option also saves a modicum of battery life, though in my travels, I've missed important notifications by setting the volume too low.

Dim the screen. The display is capable of drawing down quite a lot of battery power. Though a dim screen can be more difficult to see, especially outdoors, it definitely saves on battery life. See Chapter 22 for information on adjusting the screen brightness.

Turn off Bluetooth. When you're not using Bluetooth, turn it off. Or, when you *really* need that cyborg Bluetooth ear-thing, try to keep your phone plugged in. See Chapter 19 for information on turning off Bluetooth.

Turn off Wi-Fi. Wi-Fi networking on the phone keeps you on the Internet at top speeds but drains the battery as it's being used. Because I tend to use Wi-Fi when I'm in one place, I keep my phone plugged in. Refer to Chapter 19 for information on turning off the phone's Wi-Fi.

Regular Maintenance

There are only two tasks that you can do for regular maintenance on your phone: Keep it clean, and keep important information backed up.

Keeping it clean

You probably already keep your phone clean. I must use my sleeve to wipe the touchscreen at least a dozen times a day. Of course, better than your sleeve is something called a *microfiber cloth*. This item can be found at any computer- or office-supply store.

✔ Never use ammonia or alcohol to clean the touchscreen. These substances damage the phone. Use only a cleaning solution specifically designed for touchscreens.

✔ If the screen continually gets dirty, consider adding a *screen protector*. This specially designed cover prevents the screen from getting scratched or dirty but also lets you use your finger on the touchscreen. Be sure that the screen protector is intended for use with your specific phone brand.

✔ You can also find customized cell phone cases, belt clips, and protectors, though I've found that these add-on items are purely for decorative or fashion purposes and don't even prevent serious damage if you drop the phone.

Backing up your phone

A *backup* is a safety copy of the information on your phone. It includes any contact information, music, photos, videos, and apps you've installed, plus any settings you've made to customize your phone. Copying this information to another source is one way to keep the information safe, in case anything happens to the phone.

On your Google account, information is backed up automatically. This information includes your contacts list, Gmail messages, and Calendar app appointments. Because Android phones automatically sync this information with the Internet, a backup is always present.

To confirm that your Google account information is being backed up, heed these steps:

1. **Open the Settings app.**

2. **Tap the General tab and choose the Accounts item.**

3. **Choose Google.**

4. **Touch the green Sync icon by your Gmail address.**

   The Sync icon is shown in the margin.

5. **Ensure that a green check mark appears by every option.**

   When no check mark is there, touch the gray square to add one.

If you have more than one Google account synchronized with the phone, repeat these steps for every account.

You can also back up your phone by using the Kies program. After connecting your phone to a computer, one that has the Kies program installed, touch the Back Up/Restore tab. Place a check mark by the option Select All Items, and then click the Backup button to archive the selected items on your phone, saving a copy on the computer.

See Chapter 20 for more information on using Kies with your Galaxy Note 3.

Updating the system

Every so often, a new version of your phone's operating system becomes available. It's an *Android update* because *Android* is the name of the phone's operating system, not because your phone thinks that it's some type of robot.

Whenever an update occurs, you see an alert or a message appear on the phone, indicating that a system upgrade is available. You can touch the Install button to attempt to have the phone update itself. That operation will probably fail, however; Samsung prefers that you use the Kies program on a computer to update your phone.

See Chapter 20 for information on obtaining and installing the Kies 3 program. After it's installed, you connect the Galaxy Note to the computer by using a USB cable. At that point (with the Kies 3 program running), the update proceeds automatically. Heed the directions on the computer's screen.

You can manually check for updates, if you like, although the operation pretty much fails every time it's tried. Obey these steps:

1. **Open the Settings app.**

2. **On the General tab, choose About Device.**

3. **Choose Software Update.**

4. **Choose Update.**

5. **Touch the OK button because no updates are available.**

You could always be surprised, of course. If an update is available, attempt to install it. Otherwise, you can try this futile exercise again whenever you're bored.

- ✔ Updates can be distributed by either your cellular provider or Samsung, the phone's manufacturer.

- ✔ Historically speaking, Samsung doesn't update older devices with newer versions of the Android operating system. And, yes, your Galaxy Note 3 is considered an "older device."

Help and Troubleshooting

Things aren't as bad as they were in the old days. Back then, you could try two sources for help: the atrocious manual that came with your electronic device or a phone call to the guy who wrote the atrocious manual. It was unpleasant. Today, things are better. You have many resources for solving issues with your gizmos, including your Galaxy Note.

Getting help

The Galaxy Note features a Help app. It's found on the applications screen, and it actually contains information. Whether you find that information helpful is left to be determined; the actual Help files must be obtained over the Internet, so whenever you run the Help app, ensure that your phone is connected via Wi-Fi so as not to incur any data surcharges.

- ✔ In addition to the Help app, many apps feature the Help command: Press the Menu button and look for the Help item. Choose it to coax the phone into helping you.

- ✔ Some items in the Settings app, particularly on the Controls tab, feature the Try It button, which lets you demonstrate particular phone features.

Fixing random and annoying problems

Aren't all problems annoying? There isn't really such a thing as a welcome problem, unless the problem is welcome because it diverts attention from another, preexisting problem. And random problems? If problems were predictable, they would serve in office. Or maybe they already are?

Here are some typical problems and my suggestions for a solution:

Your phone has general trouble. For just about any problem or minor quirk, consider restarting the phone: Press and hold the Power/Lock button to summon the Device Options menu. Choose the Restart command. The phone turns off, solves the problem, and then turns itself back on again.

When restarting doesn't work, consider removing the phone's battery. Wait about 15 seconds, and then reinstall the battery and turn on the phone again. See Chapter 1 for details on removing and reinserting the phone's battery.

The data connection needs to be checked. Sometimes, the data connection drops but the phone connection stays active. Check the status bar. If you see bars, you have a phone signal. When you don't see either the 4G LTE, H+, H, 4G, E, or Wi-Fi icon, the phone has no data signal.

Occasionally, the data signal suddenly drops for a minute or two. Wait, and it comes back around. If it doesn't, the cellular data network might be down, or you may simply be in an area with lousy service. Consider changing your location.

For wireless connections, you have to ensure that the Wi-Fi is set up properly and working. Setup usually involves pestering the person who configured the Wi-Fi signal or made it available, such as the cheerful person in the green apron who serves you coffee.

An app has run amok. Sometimes, apps that misbehave let you know. You see a warning on the screen, announcing the app's stubborn disposition. Touch the Force Stop button to shut down the errant app.

When you see no warning or when an app appears to be unduly obstinate, you can shut 'er down the manual way, by following these steps:

1. **Open the Settings app.**
2. **Touch the General tab.**
3. **Choose Application Manager.**
4. **Swipe to the Running tab at the top of the Application Manager screen.**
5. **Choose the app that's causing you distress.**

   For example, a program doesn't start or it says that it's busy or has some other issue.
6. **Touch the Stop button.**

   The app stops.

After stopping the app, try opening it again to see whether it works. If it continues to run amok, contact the developer: Open the app's description screen in the Google Play Store app: Choose My Apps from the sidebar, and choose the app from the list of apps you've installed. Scroll down to the bottom of the description screen, and choose the option Send Email. Send the developer a message describing the problem.

The phone's software must be reset (a drastic measure). When all else fails, you can do the drastic thing and reset all the phone's software, essentially returning it to the state it was in when it first arrived. Obviously, you need not perform this step lightly. In fact, consider finding support (see the next section) before you start:

1. **Open the Settings app.**

2. **Tap the General tab and choose the item Backup and Reset.**

3. **Choose Factory Data Reset.**

   Nothing is wiped yet.

4. **Touch the Reset Device button.**

   Nothing is wiped yet.

5. **Touch the Delete All button to confirm.**

   All the information you've set or stored on the phone is purged.

Again, *do not* follow these steps unless you're certain that they will fix the problem or you're under orders to do so from someone in tech support.

You can, however, follow these directions if you decide to sell, give away, or return your phone. In that case, erasing all your personal information makes a lot of sense.

Getting support

Never discount these two sources of support: your cellular provider and the phone's manufacturer, Samsung. Even so, I recommend phoning your cellular provider first, no matter what the problem.

Contact information for both the cellular provider and phone manufacturer is found in the material you received with the phone. I recommend that you save those random pieces of paper in Chapter 1, which you obviously have read, and then follow my advice so that you can easily find that information.

Okay, so you don't want to go find the box, or you didn't heed my admonition and you threw out the box. In that event, Table 23-1 lists contact information on U.S. cellular providers. The From Cell column has the number you can call using your Galaxy Note; otherwise, you can use the toll-free number from any phone.

Table 23-1	U.S. Cellular Providers		
Provider	From Cell	Toll-Free	Website
AT&T	611	800-331-0500	www.att.com/esupport
Sprint Nextel	*2	800-211-4727	http://mysprint.sprint.com
T-Mobile	611	800-866-2453	www.t-mobile.com/Contact.aspx
Verizon	611	800-922-0204	http://support.vzw.com/clc

Your cellular provider's Help phone number might already be found in the phone's address book — the Contacts app. Look for it there if it's not listed here.

For hardware support, you can contact Samsung on the web at this address: www.samsung.com/us/mobile/cell-phones.

If you have an issue with the Google Play Store, you can visit its support website: http://support.google.com/googleplay.

Galaxy Note Q&A

I love Q&A! That's because not only is it an effective way to express certain problems and solutions but some of the questions might also cover areas I've been wanting to ask about.

"The touchscreen doesn't work!"

A touchscreen, such as the one used on your phone, requires a human finger for proper interaction. The phone interprets complicated electromagnetic physics between the human finger and the phone to determine where the touchscreen is being touched.

You can use the touchscreen while wearing special touchscreen gloves. Yes, they actually make such things. But for regular gloves? Nope.

The touchscreen might also fail when the battery power is low or when the phone has been physically damaged.

For precise interaction with the touchscreen, use the S Pen.

"I lost the S Pen!"

You can get a replacement for the S Pen at the Phone Store where you bought the Galaxy Note, though it isn't cheap, or at least not as cheap as you might think it could be. Even so, any stylus designed for use on a touchscreen works with the Galaxy Note. I recently tried the stylus that came with my laptop-tablet convertible, and it worked fine on the phone.

The only drawback to getting a stylus not designed for the Galaxy Note is that it doesn't fit into the S Pen compartment on the phone.

"The screen is too dark!"

Modern cell phones feature a teensy light sensor on the front. This sensor is used to adjust the touchscreen's brightness based on the ambient light of your location. If the sensor is covered, the screen can get very, very dark.

Ensure that you don't unintentionally block the light sensor. Avoid buying a case or screen protector that obscures the sensor.

Also see Chapter 22 for information about disabling the automatic brightness setting on your phone.

"The screen turns off during a call"

The screen is supposed to turn off during a call, which prevents your cheek from muting the phone or disconnecting the call. You can, however, override this setting: In the Settings app, touch the Device tab and choose the Call item. Remove the check mark by the item Turn Off Screen During Calls. That way, the screen remains on, which I don't recommend, but if you want it on, that's how it's done.

"The battery doesn't charge!"

Start from the source: Is the wall socket providing power? Is the cord plugged in? The cable may be damaged, so try another cable.

When charging from a USB port on a computer, ensure that the computer is turned on. Computers don't provide USB power when they're turned off.

"The phone gets so hot that it turns itself off!"

Yikes! An overheating phone can be a nasty problem. Judge how hot the phone is by seeing whether you can hold it in your hand: When the phone is too hot to hold, it's too hot. If you're using the phone to fry an egg, the phone is too hot.

Turn off the phone. Take out the battery, and let it cool.

If the overheating problem continues, have the phone looked at for potential repair. The battery might need to be replaced.

"The phone won't do Landscape mode!"

Not every app takes advantage of the phone's ability to orient itself in Landscape mode. For example, the Home screen doesn't "do landscape."

One app that definitely does Landscape mode is the Internet app, described in Chapter 11. So, just because an app doesn't enter Landscape mode doesn't mean that it *can't* enter Landscape mode.

Just to be sure, check the Screen Rotation option. The quick way to check is to pull down the notifications. Screen Rotation is a Quick Actions button that appears atop the notifications list. Ensure that Screen Rotation is on. If the problem persists, you know for certain that the app doesn't change orientation.

Part VI
The Part of Tens

 Enjoy another Part of Tens chapter online at www.dummies.com/extras/samsunggalaxynote3.

In this part...

- Understand ten tips, tricks, and shortcuts
- Work with ten things to remember

Ten Tips, Tricks, and Shortcuts

In This Chapter

▶ Customizing the lock screen

▶ Activating motion features

▶ Perfecting the phone's sound

▶ Setting new display fonts

▶ Unlocking dirty words on voice input

▶ Selecting and fixing default apps

▶ Avoiding data surcharges

▶ Watching the phone dream

▶ Finding a lost phone

▶ Nerding out with Task Manager

A tip is a handy suggestion, like "Don't climb the barbed-wire fence naked." A *trick* is an impressive skill that you can show off to others, like "Watch how I can shove two dimes and a nickel in one nostril and pull a quarter out the other." A *shortcut* is a quick way of doing an otherwise time-consuming task, like breaking up via Twitter instead of spending money on a fancy dinner first and then having to sit through all that crying and stuff.

This chapter contains a total of ten tips, tricks, and suggestions for using your Galaxy Note. The idea is to make life easier and more productive for you and your beloved phone so that you can get the most from your investment.

Spruce Up the Lock Screen

O how plain the lock screen! It doesn't have to be so. You can adorn the lock screen with various widgets, app launchers, a palette of your favorite apps, or a quick shortcut to the phone's Camera app. Such useful decoration begins by following these steps:

1. **Open the Settings app.**

   At the Home screen, press the Menu button and choose the Settings command.

2. **Touch the Device tab.**

3. **Choose the Lock Screen item.**

   You see various commands and options for the Galaxy Note's lock screen.

The Shortcuts item allows you to add a row of apps to the bottom of the lock screen, shown in Figure 24-1. You can run an app by swiping the app icon upward as you unlock the phone. That app immediately launches.

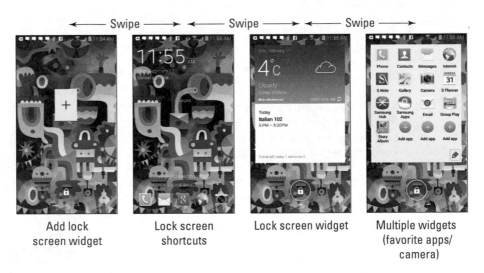

| Add lock screen widget | Lock screen shortcuts | Lock screen widget | Multiple widgets (favorite apps/camera) |

Figure 24-1: A well-decorated lock screen.

After choosing the Shortcuts item, slide its master control to the right. When the master control is green, lock screen shortcuts are active. You can then choose which shortcuts to use: Touch a shortcut icon on the Shortcuts screen to replace it with another, favorite app.

To activate lock screen widgets, choose the Multiple Widgets item. Slide the master control to the On, or green, setting. You can choose to use the Favorite Apps widget or Camera widget. Figure 24-1 shows the Favorite Apps widget.

To add new widgets, touch the Add button (refer to Figure 24-1). Choose a new lock screen widget from the scrolling list.

The lock screen widgets are accessed by swiping the lock screen left and right. You must swipe on the displayed time, which appears at the top of the lock screen. Otherwise, your swipe may just unlock the phone. Also, when viewing a widget, swipe the lock icon at the bottom of the screen to unlock the phone.

To remove a lock screen widget, long-press it. Drag the widget up to the Remove icon and it's gone. You can even remove the Clock widget, in which case only the large plus-sign icon appears on the Lock screen.

Use Galaxy Note Motion Features

The Galaxy Note features an array of interesting and even quirky commands that take full advantage of the phone's accelerometer and motion-sensing abilities. These commands all fall under the category of motion control.

To peruse motion options, follow these steps:

1. **Open the Settings app.**
2. **Tap the Controls tab.**

   The various motion commands are listed in the Motion Control part of the screen.

3. **Touch the Motions item.**

   The Motions screen is displayed.

4. **Slide the master control icon to the right.**

   When the icon is green, the master control is on and you have activated the phone's motion abilities.

Individual motion commands are listed on the Motions screen. Here are a few of the interesting things you can do with the motion commands on your Galaxy Note phone:

Direct call: View a contact on the screen, and then bring the phone up to your ear. That contact is immediately dialed.

Zoom: Touch the screen with your thumbs, and tilt the phone away or toward you to zoom in or out in an app such as the Internet (web browser) app or the Maps app.

Browse an image: Touch an object on the screen, and shift the phone left or right to move the object.

Mute/Pause: Flip the phone over on its face, and the sound is instantly silenced.

You can try out the motions by choosing one and then touching the Try It button.

Personalize the Sound

The Galaxy Note can adapt itself to your acoustical environment. To enable this feature, follow these steps:

1. **Locate yourself in a quiet environment.**

   Find a spot where you would typically use the phone.

2. **Put on the headset.**

   Sound adaptation works best when you use a pair of headphones.

3. **Stop any music or other apps that play music.**

   You can't run the sound test while the phone is playing music.

4. **Open the Settings app.**

5. **Tap the Device tab and choose the Sound command.**

6. **Choose the Adapt Sound item.**

7. **Tap the Start button.**

8. **As the phone plays various beeps, confirm whether you hear them.**

   Don't fret: You're not taking a hearing test, although in a way you are. The purpose of the test is to determine whether you can identify certain tones in your environment, not to see whether you're going deaf.

9. **Touch the Done button when you've completed the test.**

   Okay, it's not a test.

After the sound has been personalized, the Galaxy Note modifies the music and other sounds you hear so that it plays well in your environment — so that you can hear it best.

You can run through these steps again if your acoustical environment changes.

Change Screen Fonts

Here's something whimsical: You don't have to suffer through viewing all the text on your Galaxy Note using the same, dreary screen font. Nope, you can make all those other Android phone owners jealous because you can change fonts. Here's how:

1. **Open the Settings app.**
2. **Tap the Device tab.**
3. **Choose the Font item.**
4. **Use the Font Style item to select another font.**

   My Galaxy Note shows only two fonts available: Kaiti and ShaoNV. You can touch the Get Fonts Online button to obtain more fonts from Samsung, although they all cost money (typically, 99 cents) and you need a Samsung account to purchase the fonts.

5. **Touch the Yes button to apply the font to your phone.**

   Figure 24-2 shows the Settings app with the ShaoNV font applied.

Figure 24-2: The ShaoNV font.

To restore the original font, repeat these steps but choose Default Font in Step 4.

You can also set the font size by choosing the Font Size item. The size affects all text displayed by the Android operating system.

The default Android text font is named Roboto.

Add Spice to Dictation

I feel that too few people use dictation, despite how handy it can be — especially for text messaging. Anyway, if you've used dictation, you might have noticed that it occasionally censors some of the words you utter. Perhaps you're the kind of person who doesn't put up with that kind of s***.

Relax. You can revoke the vocal censorship by following these steps:

1. **Open the Settings app.**
2. **From the Controls tab, choose the Language and Input command.**
3. **Touch the Settings icon by the Google Voice Typing item.**
4. **Remove the check mark by the Block Offensive Words option.**

And just what are offensive words? I would think that *censorship* is an offensive word. But no — apparently, only a few choice words fall into this category. I won't print them here, because the phone's censor retains the initial letter and generally makes the foul language easy to guess. D***.

Choose Default Apps

Every so often, you may see the Complete Action Using menu, similar to the one shown in Figure 24-3.

Figure 24-3: The Complete Action Using question is posed.

The Galaxy Note has discovered multiple apps that can deal with your request. You pick one and then choose either Always or Just Once.

When you choose Always, the same app is always used for whatever action took place: listening to music, choosing a photo, navigation, and so on.

When you choose Just Once, you see the Complete Action Using prompt again and again.

My advice is to choose Just Once until you're sick of seeing the Complete Action Using prompt. At that point, after choosing the same app over and over, choose Always.

The fear, of course, is that you'll make a mistake. Fret not, gentle reader. The settings you choose can always be undone. For example, if you chose Crop Picture from Figure 24-3, you can undo that setting by following these steps:

1. **Open the Settings app.**

2. **Tap the General tab and choose Application Manager.**

3. **Scroll over the All tab so that you can see all your apps.**

4. **Locate the app you chose to "always" use.**

   This is the tough step, in that you may not remember your choice. The way I can tell is when the same app opens, such as the Gallery when I want the Photos app.

5. **Touch the app to display its detailed information screen.**

6. **Touch the Clear Defaults button.**

   The phone immediately forgets to always use that app.

You can screw up by following these steps. That's because the Complete Action Using prompt appears again. The next time you see it, however, make a better choice.

Also see the later section "Visit Task Manager."

Avoid Data Overages

An important issue for everyone using an Android phone is whether you're about to burst through your monthly data quota. Mobile data surcharges can pinch the wallet, but your Android phone has a handy tool to help you avoid data overages. It's the Data Usage screen, shown in Figure 24-4.

Figure 24-4: Data usage.

To access the Data Usage screen, follow these steps:

1. **Open the Settings app.**

2. **Choose the Connections tab.**

3. **Choose Data Usage.**

The main screen is full of useful information and handy tools. The line chart (refer to Figure 24-4) informs you of your data usage over a specific period. You can touch the Data Usage Cycle button to set that timespan, for example, matching it up with your cellular provider's monthly billing cycle.

The orange and red bars are used to remind you of how quickly you're filling your plan's data quota. Warning messages appear when total data usage passes one of the lines.

To set the limits, touch the graph on the screen. Use the tabs that appear to drag the limit lines (orange and red) up or down and to drag the data usage cycle lines left or right. You do need to activate the Set Mobile Data Limit item, shown in Figure 24-4.

To review access for a specific app, scroll down the screen and choose it from those shown on the data usage screen. Only apps that access the network appear. After choosing the app, detailed information shows up, similar to what's shown on the right in Figure 24-4. If you notice that the app is using more data than it should, touch the View App Settings button. You may be able to adjust some of the settings to curtail unintended Internet access.

Watch the Phone Dream

Does the Galaxy Note lock, or does it fall asleep? I prefer to think that the phone sleeps. That begs the question of whether it dreams.

Of course it does! You can even see the dreams, as long as you activate the Daydream feature — and you keep the phone connected to a power source or in a docking station. Heed these steps:

1. **Start the Settings app.**
2. **Choose the Device tab.**
3. **Choose Display and then Daydream.**
4. **Ensure that the Daydream master control is in the On position.**

   The master control icon is green when it's on.

   If the Desk Home Screen option is set, you need to touch the OK button to disable it. The Desk home screen appears only when you insert the Galaxy Note into a desktop docking stand. So it's okay to disable this option if you want the phone to daydream.

5. **Choose which type of daydream you want displayed.**

   I'm fond of Colors.

6. **Touch the Select Dream Time button.**
7. **Choose the All option.**

The daydreaming begins when the screen would normally time-out and lock. So if you've set the phone to lock after 1 minute of inactivity, it daydreams instead — if it's plugged in or docked.

- To disrupt the dream, swipe the screen.
- The phone doesn't lock when it daydreams. To lock the phone, press the Power/Lock key.

Find Your Lost Cell Phone

Someday, you may lose your beloved Galaxy Note. It might be for a few panic-filled seconds, or it might be for forever. The hardware solution is to weld a heavy object to the phone, such as an anvil or a rhinoceros, yet that strategy kind of defeats the entire mobile/wireless paradigm. (Well, not so much the rhino.) The software solution is to use a cell phone locator service.

Cell phone locator services employ apps that use a phone's cellular signal as well as its GPS to help locate the missing gizmo. These types of apps are available at the Google Play Store. One that I've tried and recommend is Lookout Mobile Security.

Lookout features two different apps. One is free, which you can try to see whether you like it. The paid app offers more features and better locating services. As with similar phone-locating apps, you must register at a website to help you locate your phone, should it go wandering.

Visit Chapter 18 for information about the Google Play Store, where you can obtain copies of the Lookout security app and search for other phone-finding apps.

Visit Task Manager

 If you want to get your hands dirty with some behind-the-scenes stuff on your Galaxy Note, Task Manager is the app to open. It's not for everyone, so feel free to skip this section if you want to use your phone without having to acquire any computer nerd sickness that you have otherwise successfully avoided.

Task Manager is accessed from the Recent apps list; press and hold the Home button to see recent and running apps. Touch the icon in the lower left corner of the screen to run Task Manager, shown in Figure 24-5.

The Task Manager window shows the phone's currently running apps. Tabs at the top of the Task Manager screen display information about downloaded apps, the phone's memory (RAM), and default apps. It's a nerd's paradise of trivial information and meaningless facts.

You can use Task Manager to kill off tasks that are hogging up too much CPU time or memory or that just bug the stuffing from your couch. As illustrated in Figure 24-5, you touch the End button to close an app or touch the End All button to snuff out all running apps.

Running apps

Check memory use.

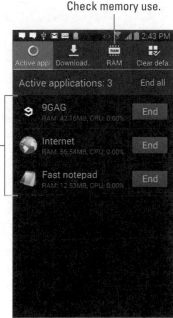

Figure 24-5: Managing tasks.

You can also clear default apps by using Task Manager: Touch the Clear Defaults item to see a list of apps you've selected by touching the Always button on the Complete Action Using menu. Touch the Clear button by an app to remove its associations.

✔ Also see Chapter 23 on killing an app run amok.

✔ The Android operating system does an excellent job of managing apps. If resources are needed for another app, Android automatically closes any open apps as needed. There's no need to futz with Task Manager, unless you just enjoy messing with such a thing.

25

Ten Things to Remember

In This Chapter

▶ Bringing up recent apps

▶ Locking the phone

▶ Using landscape orientation

▶ Saving typing time

▶ Minding activities that consume battery power

▶ Checking for phone roaming

▶ Using the + key to dial international calls

▶ Using a docking stand

▶ Taking a picture of your contacts

▶ Using the Search command

*I*f only it were easy to narrow to ten items the list of all the things I want you to remember when using your Galaxy Note. So even though you'll find in this chapter ten good things not to forget, don't think for a moment that there are *only* ten. In fact, as I remember more, I'll put them on my website, at www. wambooli.com. Check it for updates about your phone, and perhaps even more things to remember.

Return to a Recent App

Apps you run on your Galaxy Note do not quit! They continue to run when you switch to the Home screen or do something else on the phone. To return to a running app, pluck it from the Recent Apps list: Press and hold the Home button to see the list.

I cite this item as something to remember because I always forget that apps are running. So I'll go and hunt down an app on the Applications screen to start it again. That takes too many steps! Instead, it's easier to press and hold the Home button, then pluck out the recent app.

Lock the Phone on a Call

Whether you dialed out or someone dialed in, after you start talking, you should lock your phone: Press the Power/Lock button. By doing so, you ensure that the touchscreen is disabled and the call isn't unintentionally disconnected.

Of course, the call can still be disconnected by a dropped signal or by the other party getting all huffy and hanging up on you, but by locking the phone, you prevent a stray finger — or your pocket — from disconnecting (or muting) the phone.

Use Landscape Orientation

The natural orientation of the Galaxy Note is vertical — the *portrait* orientation. Even so, you don't have to use an app in portrait orientation.

Turning the phone to its side makes many apps appear wider, such as the Internet app and the Maps app. That's often a better way to see things, to see more available items on certain menus; and if you're using the onscreen keyboard, it gives you larger key caps on which to type.

- ✔ Not every app supports landscape orientation.

- ✔ You can lock orientation so that the touchscreen won't flip and flop. The easiest way to do so is by touching the Screen Rotation Quick Action. Also see Chapter 22 to peruse various display settings.

Follow the Keyboard Suggestions

Don't forget to take advantage of the predictive text suggestions that appear above the keyboard when you're typing text. In fact, you don't even need to touch a suggestion: To replace your text with the highlighted suggestion, simply touch the space key. Zap! The word appears.

When predictive text fails you, keep in mind that you can use the keyboard-swipe typing method instead of the old hunt-and-peck. Dragging your finger over the keyboard and then choosing a word suggestion works quickly — when you remember to do it.

See Chapter 4 for information on activating these phone features.

Things That Consume Lots of Battery Juice

Several items on your phone suck down battery power faster than an 18-year-old fleeing the tyranny of high school on graduation day:

- ✔ Navigation
- ✔ Bluetooth
- ✔ The display

Navigation is certainly handy, but because the phone's touchscreen is on the entire time and dictating text to you, the battery drains rapidly. If possible, try to keep the phone connected to the car's power socket when you're navigating. If you can't, keep an eye on the battery meter.

Bluetooth requires extra power for its wireless radio. When you need that level of connectivity, great! Otherwise, turn off your Bluetooth gizmo as soon as necessary to save power.

Finally, the touchscreen display draws a lot of power. You can try using the Auto Brightness setting, but it can get too dark to see or, more frequently, it takes too long to adjust to a high- or low-light setting. So if you avoid the Auto Brightness setting, remember how that bright display can drain the battery.

See Chapter 23 for more information on managing the phone's battery.

Check for Roaming

Roaming can be expensive. The last non-smartphone (dumbphone?) I owned racked up $180 in roaming charges the month before I switched to a better cellular plan. Even though you too may have a good cell plan, keep an eye on the phone's status bar. Ensure that when you're making a call, you don't see the Roaming status icon on the status bar atop the touchscreen.

Well, yes, it's okay to make a call when your phone is roaming. My advice is to remember to *check* for the icon, not to avoid it. If possible, try to make your phone calls when you're back in your cellular service's coverage area. If you can't, make the phone call but keep in mind that you will be charged roaming fees. They ain't cheap.

Use the + Symbol When Dialing Internationally

I suppose that most folks are careful when dialing international numbers. On the Galaxy Note, you can use the + key to replace the country's exit code. In the United States, the code is 011. So whenever you see an international number listed as 011-xxx-xxxxxxx, you can instead dial +xxx-xxxxxxx, where the x characters represent the number to dial.

See Chapter 21 for more information on international dialing.

Get a Docking Stand

I adore my phone's docking stand. Yes, it was horrifically expensive for what it is: The docking stand is a squat little chunk of plastic that props up the phone to a favorable viewing angle. It comes with a charging cord, so the phone charges while it's docked. Yet it has no other features to justify the high price. Well, other than that it was designed specifically for my phone.

Docking stands make excellent bedside holders for your phone. In fact, most phones recognize the docking stand and run a special Home screen app while they're docked. You can use the Clock app, play music, or watch a photo slideshow while the phone is docked.

Snap a Pic of That Contact

Here's something I always forget: Whenever you're near one of your contacts, take the person's picture. Sure, some people are bashful, but most folks are flattered. The idea is to build up your contacts list so that all contacts have photos. Receiving a call is much more interesting when you see the caller's picture displayed, especially a silly or embarrassing picture.

When taking the picture, be sure to show it to the person before you assign it to the contact. Let them decide whether it's good enough. Or, if you just want to be rude, assign a crummy-looking picture. Heck, you don't even have to do that: Just take a random picture of anything and assign it to a contact. A plant. A rock. Your dog. But, seriously, the next time you meet up with a contact, keep in mind that the phone can take that person's picture.

See Chapter 15 for more information on using the phone's camera.

Use the Search Command

Google is known worldwide for its searching abilities. By gum, the word *google* is now synonymous for searching. So please don't forget that your Galaxy Note, which uses Google's Android operating system, has a powerful Search command. Not only that, but the Search command is ubiquitous in the Android environment; just about every app features a Search icon.

Touch the Search icon to look for information such as locations, people, text — you name it. It's handy. It's everywhere. Use it.

Once upon a time, the Search icon was part of the basic navigation icons that appeared at the bottom of an Android phone's touchscreen.

Index

• Symbols and Numerics •

* (asterisk key), 77
+ (plus sign), 77, 285, 338
1X icon, 77
3G networks, 77, 168, 258
4G LTE networks, 13, 77, 168, 176, 258
4G networks, 77, 168, 258
411 abbreviation, 126

• A •

abbreviations for text messages, 126
about:blank as home page, 155
accelerometer, 39, 40
accessories, 19–20
accounts
　corporate e-mail accounts, 137
　Email app
　　setting up, 134–135
　　using multiple, 136
　Facebook, 158
　Google account
　　adding picture to contact, 120
　　backing up phone, 312–313
　　benefits of, 29
　　creating, 28–29
　　importing contacts, 115
　　signing into, 24
　　storing contacts, 113
　online accounts, 30–31
Accuracy Level setting, 303
Action Bar icon, 51
Action Memo app, 54, 55, 236–237
Action Overflow icon, 140
adapting sound to environment, 326
Add icon, 51

address book. See contacts
addresses, searching, 187
Air Command, 54–55
Airplane mode, 282–283
air-travel tips, 284
alarms, 224–225
albums, music, 212
albums, picture, 205, 209
Always On option, 37
Amazon Kindle app, 231
Amazon MP3 app, 219
Android
　overview, 28
　system updates, 313–314
　viruses on, 250
Android Beam, 269
Android File Transfer program, 273
Android Market, 242
answering calls
　overview, 79–80
　two at once, 89–90
　while on another call, 80, 88–89
AOL e-mail, 134
app folders, 48, 294–296
applications. See apps
Applications screen
　changing view, 252
　Clear Cache button, 251
　Clear Data button, 251
　Clear Defaults button, 251
　folders on, 253–254
　Force Stop button, 251
　Move to SD Card button, 251
　Move to Storage Device button, 251
　overview, 47–48, 249–250
　rearranging apps on, 253
　Refund button, 251
　Report button, 251
　Uninstall button, 251

appointments. *See* events, calendar
apps. *See also* Applications screen
  adding to Home screen, 292
  browser versus, 147
  common icons in, 51–52
  default, 328–329
  defined, 242
  determining which are consuming
    battery, 309–310
  displaying all, 42
  Favorites tray, 293
  Google Play Store
    automatic updating of apps, 247
    compatibility, 243
    installing apps, 244–246
    notifications, 245
    overview, 241–243
    purchased apps, 245
    ratings, 243
    refunds, 246
    removing apps, 249
    searching in, 242
    sharing apps, 248
    uninstalling apps, 245
    updating apps, 245, 248
    viewing downloaded, 246–247
    Wish List, 246
  icons for, 42
  importance of, 241
  quitting, 46
  recent, 335
  starting, 46
  switching between, 48–49
  Task Manager app, 332–333
  troubleshooting problems with, 315
Apps icon, 42, 47
Artists view, Music app, 212
assembly
  battery, 11–13
  MicroSD card, 13–14
  rear cover, 11, 15
  SIM card, 13
asterisk (*), 77
AT&T Ready2Go app
  defined, 25
  setting up using, 29–30
  social network contacts, 116
AT&T support, 317
attachments, 129, 142–143

audio, recording, 239–240
Auto Rotate Screen setting, 306
automatic updating of apps, 247

• B •

Back button
  hiding onscreen keyboard, 59
  interface, 18
  quitting apps, 46
  touch buttons, 37
  using, 37
backing up phone, 312–313
battery
  Bluetooth, 267
  car chargers, 15
  charging, 15–16
  compatibility, 13
  determining what is consuming,
    309–310
  disposing of, 12
  extending life of, 311
  flash and, 202
  installing, 11–13
  monitoring, 308
  Navigation mode and, 193
  Power Saving Mode, 310–311
  removing, 12
  tips for, 309, 337
  troubleshooting, 318
  USB connection, 16, 273
BCC field, e-mail, 141
be right back (BRB), 126
birthdays, 229
blank home page, Internet app, 155
Block Offensive Words option, 328
blue dot/triangle in maps, 183
Bluetooth
  activating, 265–266
  Airplane mode and, 283
  extending battery life, 311
  overview, 265
  pairing with device, 266–267
  Power Control widget, 266
  printers, 268
  sharing pictures and videos using, 207
  unpairing with device, 267
  using for phone calls, 76

bookmarks, 150
box, removing phone from, 9–10
BRB (be right back), 126
brightness
  customizing, 306
  for eBooks, 234
  extending battery life, 311
  troubleshooting, 318
BTW (by the way), 126
businesses, searching for on map, 187–188
busy, forwarding calls when, 93
buttons
  Back button
    hiding onscreen keyboard, 59
    interface, 18
    quitting apps, 46
    using, 37
  Home button
    customizing, 290
    doing things during phone calls, 76
    interface, 18
    long-press operation on, 37
    physical buttons, 38
    pressing when on call, 20
    quitting apps, 46
    switching between apps, 48
    unlocking phone, 27
    using, 37
    zooming to center panel, 43
  Menu button
    interface, 18
    using, 37
  Power/Lock button
    functions served by, 23
    interface, 16
    locking phone, 31
    turning off phone, 32–33
    turning on phone, 24
    unlocking phone, 27
    using during call, 20, 336
  S Pen, 53
  touch, 37
  Volume button
    interface, 16
    listening to music, 215
    using, 38–39
    zooming in camera, 197
by the way (BTW), 126

• *C* •

cache, clearing for app, 251
Calculator app, 225–226
calendar
  categories for, 230
  events, 228–230
  notifications, 230
  overview, 226
  S Planner app versus Calendar
    app, 226
  views in, 227–228
  widget for, 226
Call Forwarding status icon, 93
Call In Progress notification icon, 75
call log, 82–83, 113
camera
  deleting immediately after shooting,
    197–198
  Facebook camera app, 162
  flash, 201–202
  focus, 197
  front, 16
  location information, 204
  orientation and, 197
  overview, 196–197
  panoramic pictures, 198–199
  posting pictures on Facebook,
    161–162
  previewing image or video, 197
  rear, 18
  recording video, 197
  resolution, 202–203
  self-portraits, 198
  sending MMS from, 129
  settings for, 200–201
  shooting modes, 199
  storage location, 204–205
  taking for contact, 118
  video quality, 203–204
  zooming in and out, 197
Camera album, 206
Camera setting, USB connection, 272
capturing screen, 199–200
car chargers, 15
car mount, 20
carrier-provided voice mail, 99–101

Cartoon view, video call, 169
cases, 20, 312
CC field, e-mail, 141
cellular data. *See* mobile data network
censored words, 67, 328
charging battery
  overview, 15–16
  troubleshooting, 318
  while phone is off, 33
cleaning phone, 312
clearing app cache, 251
clearing app data, 251
clearing app defaults, 251
Clock app, 223–225
Close icon, 51
cloud
  Google Cloud Printing app, 267
  synchronization using storage in, 277–278
Combined view, Email app, 138–139
Compass app, 183
compatibility of apps, 243
conference calls, 91–92
configuration
  AT&T Ready2Go app, 29–30
  camera
    flash, 201–202
    overview, 200–201
    resolution, 202–203
    video quality, 202–203
  Email app
    default account, 145
    server delete option, 145–146
    setting up account, 134–135
    signatures, 144
    using multiple accounts, 136
  Facebook app, 163
  Google Voice, 102–103
  Internet app
    deleting personal information, 156
    setting home page, 154–155
    text scaling, 155
  online accounts, 30–31
  reject list, 95
  ringtones
    adapting sound to environment, 326
    alarms, 225
    choosing, 95–96
    creating, 97–98

    defined, 80
    Facebook, 163
    setting for contact, 96–97
    for text messages, 96, 131
  silencing phone, 39
  speed dial, 85–86
  turning on for first time, 24–25
  USB connection, 272–273
  volume, 38–39
contacts
  adding
    from call log, 83, 113
    from map, 116–117
    picture for, 118–120, 338
  app for, 109–112
  creating, 114
  creating, from e-mail message, 113
  deleting, 121–122
  dialing, 75, 78
  editing, 118
  favorites, 120
  finding by location, 116–117
  importing, 114–115
  linking identical, 120–121
  locating on map, 112
  merging duplicate, 113
  placing call to, 111
  searching, 112
  searching for on map, 189
  sending e-mail, 111, 142
  sending text message, 111, 125
  sending text message, by swiping, 126
  setting ringtone for, 96–97
  social networking, 115–116
  syncing with Facebook, 159
  unlinking, 121
  video calls, 111
Contextual Action Bar, 69
copying text, 69
corporate e-mail accounts, 137
country-code prefix, 285
cover, removing, 11
cropping images
  for contact photos, 119
  in Gallery app, 207–208
current location
  finding street address, 185–186
  sharing, 186–187

cursor, moving, 67–68
customization
  adapting sound to environment, 326
  censored words, 328
  data limits, 329–331
  Daydream feature, 331
  default apps, 328–329
  display settings, 305–306
  Favorites tray apps, 293
  Home screen
    adding apps, 292
    folders, 294–296
    overview, 290
    panels, 297–298
    rearranging items, 296–297
    removing items, 297
    widgets, 293–294
  lock screen
    changing, 298–299
    disabling, 299
    owner info, 303–304
    Password lock, 300
    pattern lock, 300–302
    PIN lock, 300
    Signature lock, 302–303
    widgets on, 324–325
  motion features, 325–326
  screen fonts, 327–328
  silencing phone, 39
  sound, 304–305
  vibration, 304–305
  volume, 38–39
  wallpaper, 291–292
cutting text, 69
CYA abbreviation, 126

• D •

data connection issues, 315
data surcharges, avoiding
  checking for roaming status, 281–282, 337
  setting limits, 329–331
  using Wi-Fi, 242
Daydream feature, 331
DCIM/Camera folder, 197
default apps, 251, 328–329

Delete icon, 51
deleting
  alarms, 225
  apps, 249
  bookmarks, 150
  contacts, 121–122
  e-mail, 140
  e-mail, server delete option, 145–146
  Google Hangouts conversation, 169
  Home screen items, 297
  picture or video immediately after taking, 197–198
  pictures and videos, 209
  playlists, 221
  text messages, 130–131
dialing phone calls
  contacts, 78
  favorites, 78
  inserting pause, 77, 87–88
  overview, 74
dictating text, 65–66, 328
directions, map, 190–191
disconnecting phone, 274
dock, Home screen, 42
docking stand, 20, 338
Done icon, 52
Done key, 58
doodle button, earphone, 19
double-tap operation
  defined, 36
  selecting text, 68
  web browsing, 149
Download album, 206
downloading
  defined, 153
  files, 154
  image from web page, 153
  notifications for, 153
  viewing downloaded items, 154
Downloads app, 154
Dropbox
  sharing pictures using, 207
  synchronization using cloud storage, 277–278
duplicate contacts, merging, 113

• E •

E networks, 77, 258
earphones, 19, 76
eBooks
  Amazon Kindle app, 231
  brightness, 234
  indexes for, 234
  library, 231–232
  Play Books app, 231
  reading, 232–233
  text size, 234
EDGE networks, 52, 77, 258
editing text
  copying, 69
  cutting, 69
  moving cursor, 67–68
  pasting, 70
  selections, 68–69
e-mail. *See also* Email app; Gmail
  AOL, 134
  attachments, 142–143
  browsing messages, 140
  composing, 141–142
  creating contact from message, 113
  deleting, 140
  drafts, 142
  forwarding, 140
  getting new messages, 137–138
  Gmail app versus Email app, 133–134
  inbox, 138–139
  overview, 133
  reading, 139–140
  replying to, 140
  sending to contact, 111, 142
  sent messages, 142
  sharing pictures using, 207
  signatures, 144
  text messages versus, 128
  Yahoo!, 134
Email app. *See also* e-mail; Gmail
  attachments in, 143
  BCC field, 141
  CC field, 141
  colors in, 139
  Combined view in, 138–139
  corporate accounts, 137
  creating messages, 141–142

default account, 145
Delete icon, 140
Forward icon, 140
Gmail app versus, 133–134
inbox, 138–139
new message notification, 137–138
Reply All icon, 140
Reply icon, 140
saving drafts, 142
sent messages in, 142
server delete option, 145–146
setting up account, 134–135
signatures, 144
using multiple accounts, 136, 142
emergency calls, 27
Enter key, onscreen keyboard, 58
environment, adjusting sound to, 326
events, calendar
  additional reminders for, 230
  creating, 229–230
  notifications, 230
  viewing details, 228–229
exit code, 285
exporting contacts, 115
external storage, 204

• F •

Facebook
  app versus web version, 158
  camera app for, 162
  configuring app, 163
  contact pictures from, 120
  displaying sidebar, 160
  getting app, 158
  Home page widget, 161
  linking identical contacts, 120–121
  logging into app, 158
  Mobile Uploads album, 163
  News Feed, 159, 160
  notifications, 160
  overview, 157
  picture resolution for, 203
  posting pictures, 161–163
  quitting app, 160
  Refresh Interval setting, 163
  ringtone for, 163
  setting status, 160–161

setting up account, 158
sharing pictures using, 207
syncing contacts, 159
favorites
  contacts, 120
  dialing, 78
  playlists, 215, 220
  searching map, 189
Favorites tray apps, 293
fields, adding for contacts, 114
finding lost phone, 332
flash, camera, 201–202
folders
  on Applications screen, 253–254
  on Home screen, 294–296
  view in Music app, 212
fonts, changing for screen, 327–328
for what it's worth (FWIW), 126
for your information (FYI), 126
force stopping apps, 251, 315
form data, remembering, 156
formatting MicroSD card, 280
forwarding
  e-mail, 140
  phone calls
    automatically, 94
    Google Voice and, 102
    overview, 92
    using Android settings, 92–93
    using Verizon network, 93–94
  text messages, 127–128
front camera, 16
full-day events. *See* events, calendar
FWIW (for what it's worth), 126
FYI (for your information), 126

● *G* ●

Gallery app
  changing wallpaper, 291
  cropping images, 207–208
  deleting items, 209
  navigating to location of item, 206
  overview, 205–206
  rotating pictures, 209
  sharing from, 207
games, 234
gang text, 124
gang-video-chat, 175

GB abbreviation, 126
Gear icon, 52
gestures
  browsing e-mail messages, 140
  in Camera app, 197
  on Home screen, 290
  panning web pages, 148
  sending text message, 126
  Turn Over motion, 305
  viewing maps, 183
  zooming web pages, 149
GJ (good job), 126
Global Positioning System. *See* GPS
gloves, and touchscreen, 36
Gmail. *See also* e-mail; Email app
  attachments in, 143
  BCC field, 141
  canceling message, 142
  CC field, 141
  contacts, adding on computer, 114
  creating messages, 141–142
  Delete icon, 140
  Email app versus, 133–134
  Forward icon, 140
  inbox, 138–139
  new message notification, 137–138
  pictures, adding to contacts, 120
  Reply All icon, 140
  Reply icon, 140
  searching in, 139
  sent messages in, 142
  sharing pictures using, 207
  signatures, 144
  voice mail messages in, 101
Go key, 58
good job (GJ), 126
Google, 28
Google account
  backing up phone, 312–313
  benefits of, 29
  creating, 28–29
  importing contacts, 115
  pictures, adding to contacts, 120
  signing into, 24
  storing contacts, 113
Google Calendar, 226
Google Chrome app, 149. *See also* web
    browsing
Google Cloud Printing app, 267

Google Drive, 277–278
Google Hangouts
  deleting conversation, 169
  notifications, 169
  overview, 169
  text chatting, 170–172
  text messages in, 169
  using as text messaging app, 131, 172
  video chat, 172–174
Google Mail. *See* Gmail
Google Now, 235–236
Google Play Store
  automatic updating of apps, 247
  compatibility, 243
  installing apps, 244–246
  music from, 218–219
  notifications, 245
  overview, 241–243
  purchased apps, 245
  ratings, 243
  refunds, 246
  removing apps, 249
  searching in, 242
  sharing apps, 248
  support for, 317
  uninstalling apps, 245
  updating apps, 245, 248
  viewing downloaded, 246–247
  Wish List, 246
Google Search widget, 152
Google Voice
  adding second line, 103–104
  configuring, 102–103
  forwarded calls, 93
  overview, 101–102, 104–105
  text transcription in, 105
  using app, 104–105
Google Voice Typing, 65
Google+, 166
got to go (GTG), 126
GPS (Global Positioning System)
  activating during initial setup, 25
  activating location services, 184
  location information in pictures, 204
  Maps app, 182
GPS Tag, 204
GR8 abbreviation, 126
GSM cellular networks, 13, 77
GTG (got to go), 126

• *H* •

H+ icon, 77
Hangouts app. *See* Google Hangouts
hardware support, 317
headphone jack, 16
headset, 176, 267
help. *See also* troubleshooting
  Help app and command, 314
  support contacts, 316–317
hiding onscreen keyboard, 59
history, clearing web browsing,
    150, 156
HOAS (hold on a second), 126
hold, putting calls on, 88
Home button
  customizing, 290
  doing things during phone calls, 76
  interface, 18
  long-press operation on, 37
  physical buttons, 38
  pressing when on call, 20
  quitting apps, 46
  switching between apps, 48
  unlocking phone, 27
  using, 37
  zooming to center panel, 43
home page, Internet app, 154–155
Home screen
  apps, adding to, 292
  bookmarks on, 150
  folders, 294–296
  items on, 41–42
  notifications on, 43–45
  overview, 41
  panels
    accessing, 43
    index display, 42
    managing, 297–298
  phone orientation and, 40
  Quick Actions on, 45
  rearranging items, 296–297
  removing items, 297
  widgets
    adding, 293–294
    defined, 42
    overview, 46–47
    removing, 297
    resizing, 294

HootSuite app, 166
HSPA networks, 77, 258
human engineering, 156

● **/** ●

IC abbreviation, 126
icons commonly used in apps, 51–52
IDK abbreviation, 126
ignoring calls, 80
IMO (in my opinion), 126
importing contacts, 114–115
initial configuration, 24–25
installing
  apps, 244–246
  battery, 11–13
  MicroSD card, 13–14
  rear cover, 15
  SIM card, 13
interface
  Back button
    hiding onscreen keyboard, 59
    interface, 18
    quitting apps, 46
    using, 37
  Home button
    customizing, 290
    doing things during phone calls, 76
    interface, 18
    long-press operation on, 37
    physical buttons, 38
    pressing when on call, 20
    quitting apps, 46
    switching between apps, 48
    unlocking phone, 27
    using, 37
    zooming to center panel, 43
  Home screen
    adding apps to, 292
    bookmarks on, 150
    folders, 294–296
    items on, 41–42
    notifications on, 43–45
    overview, 41
    panels, 42, 43, 297–298
    phone orientation and, 40
    Quick Actions on, 45
    rearranging items, 296–297

    removing items, 297
    widgets, 42, 46–47, 293–294, 297
  Menu button
    interface, 18
    using, 37
  Multi Window tab feature
    activating, 49
    controls for, 51
    defined, 38
    exiting, 50
    on Home screen, 42
    tray for, 50
    using, 49–50
  navigation icons, 37–38
  onscreen keyboard
    displaying, 59
    Enter key changes, 58
    hiding, 59
    Keyboard Swipe feature, 63
    overview, 57–58
    predictive text, 61–62, 336
    S Pen, 64–65
    special characters, 60–61
    special keys on, 58–59
    typing one character at a time, 59
    voice input, 65–67
  orientation of phone, 39–40
  overview, 16–18
  Power/Lock button
    functions served by, 23
    interface, 16
    locking phone, 31
    turning off phone, 32–33
    turning on phone, 24
    unlocking phone, 27
    using during call, 20, 336
  S Pen button, 53
  touch buttons, 37
  touchscreen operations, 36
  Volume button
    interface, 16
    listening to music, 215
    using, 38–39
    zooming in camera, 197
  volume settings, 38–39
internal storage
  defined, 204
  moving apps to/from, 251

international usage
  call failure, 285
  dialing, 77, 284–285
  replacing exit code, 338
  using phone abroad, 286–287
  using Skype, 286
Internet app. *See also* web browsing
  multiple windows in, 151–152
  overview, 148–149
  setting home page, 154–155
  text scaling, 155
ISP (Internet service provider), 134
iTunes, 218

• J •

JK (just kidding), 126
JPEG image format, 197

• K •

K abbreviation, 126
keyboard, onscreen
  displaying, 59
  Enter key changes, 58
  hiding, 59
  Keyboard Swipe feature, 63
  overview, 57–58
  predictive text, 61–62, 336
  S Pen, 64–65
  special characters, 60–61
  special keys on, 58–59
  typing one character at a time, 59
  voice input
    activating, 65
    censored words, 67
    dictating text, 65–66

• L •

L8R abbreviation, 126
Labyrinth app, 40
Landscape mode, 319, 336
language, setting, 24
laugh out loud (LOL), 126
laughing my a** off (LMAO), 126
layers, map, 183–184
let me know (LMK), 126

library, music, 211–213
LinkedIn, 166
linking identical contacts, 120–121
links, Internet, 149, 151
live wallpaper, 43, 291
LMAO (laughing my a** off), 126
LMK (let me know), 126
location
  activating services, 184
  finding contact by, 116–117
  storing information in pictures, 204
Lock Automatically setting, 299
Lock Instantly with Power Key
      setting, 299
lock screen
  automatic locking, 299
  changing, 298–299
  disabling, 299
  emergency calls and, 27
  notices on, 26
  owner info, 303–304
  Password lock, 300
  pattern lock, 300–302
  PIN lock, 300
  Signature lock, 302–303
  timeout for, 299, 306
  types of, 26
  unlocking, 26
  Volume button and, 39
  widgets on, 324–325
locking phone
  automatic screen lock, 31–32
  overview, 31
  turning off phone versus, 31
LOL (laugh out loud), 126
long-distance calls, 73–74
long-press operation
  defined, 36
  on Home screen, 290
  selecting text, 68
lost phone, finding, 332
low-battery warnings, 309

• M •

Mac
  exporting contacts, 115
  USB connection on, 273–274

maintenance
  backing up phone, 312–313
  cleaning phone, 312
  system updates, 313–314
maps
  adding contact from, 116–117
  blue dot/triangle in, 183
  Compass app, 183
  current location
    finding street address, 185–186
    sharing, 186–187
  directions, 190–191
  displaying sidebar, 183
  GPS and, 182
  Internet access and, 186
  layers
    adding, 183
    removing, 184
  locating contact on, 112
  Maps app, 182–183
  navigating, 191–193
  overview, 182
  panning, 183
  perspective, changing, 183
  rotating, 183
  searching
    addresses, 187
    businesses and points of interest,
      187–188
    contacts, 189
    favorites, 189
    recent places, 189
  Street View, 186
  zooming in and out, 183
Media Device setting, USB
    connection, 272
Media Transfer Protocol (MTP), 272
Meebo, 166
meetings. *See* events, calendar
megapixel, 203
Menu button
  interface, 18
  touch buttons, 37
  using, 37
merging
  contacts, 113
  phone calls, 89

Messages app, 124–125. *See also* text
    messages
microphone, 18
Microphone icon, 52, 65
MicroSD card
  adapters for, 14
  battery removal and, 11
  copying music from computer, 216
  formatting, 280
  installing, 13–14
  moving apps to/from, 251
  removing, 14
  SIM card and, 13
  storing pictures and videos, 204–205
  unmounting, 280
Microsoft Exchange Active Sync accounts,
    137, 230
Microsoft Live, 137
Microsoft SkyDrive, 277
missed calls
  forwarding, 93
  notice on lock screen, 26
  overview, 82
MMS (Multimedia Messaging Service)
  attaching media, 128–129
  e-mail versus, 128
  limits on, 129
  roaming and, 282
  saving media from, 130
  text messages versus, 128
mobile data network, 258
Mobile Hotspot feature, 262–263
More Notifications icon, 45
Most Played playlist, 220
motion features, 40, 325–326
MPEG4 video format, 197
MTP (Media Transfer Protocol), 272
Multi Window tab feature
  activating, 49
  controls for, 51
  defined, 38
  exiting, 50
  on Home screen, 42
  tray for, 50
  using, 49–50
multimedia dock, 20

Multimedia Messaging Service. *See* MMS
multipurpose jack, 18
music
  adapting sound to environment, 326
  browsing library, 211–213
  copying from computer, 216–218
  from Google Play Store, 218–219
  identifying music heard, 215
  Internet radio, 221–222
  motion features for, 326
  notifications, 215
  onscreen controls, 212–213
  playing, 213–214
  playlists
    creating, 220–221
    deleting, 221
    overview, 219–220
  repeat options, 214
  shuffle options, 214
  Sound Search widget, 215
  volume for, 215
muting
  motion features for, 326
  phone calls, 76, 168
  voice navigation, 193
My Files app, 280
My Music website, 221
Myspace, 166

• *N* •

navigation
  icons for, 37–38
  to location of picture of video, 206
  using Maps app, 191–193
NC (no comment), 126
Near Field Communications (NFC), 269
Nearby Devices view, Music app, 213
network communication
  Bluetooth
    activating, 265–266
    Airplane mode and, 283
    extending battery life, 311
    overview, 265
    pairing with device, 266–267
    Power Control widget, 266
    printers, 268
    sharing pictures and videos using, 207

    unpairing with device, 267
    using for phone calls, 76
  mobile data network, 258
  NFC, 269
  roaming, 281–282, 337
  tethering Internet connection, 264
  Wi-Fi
    activating, 259
    Airplane mode and, 283
    avoiding data surcharges, 242
    connecting to network, 260–261
    extending battery life, 311
    Internet radio and, 222
    location services, 184
    Mobile Hotspot feature, 262–263
    overview, 259
    Quick Action for, 259
    status icon, 261
    turning off, 259
    using phone abroad, 287
    video chat, 176
    WPS, 261–262
network icons, 77
New Voicemail notification icon, 101
Next key, 58
Nextel support, 317
NFC (Near Field Communications), 269
no comment (NC), 126
no problem (NP), 126
no reply needed (NRN), 126
notifications
  app updates, 248
  downloads, 153
  e-mail messages, 137–138
  event reminders, 230
  Facebook, 160
  Google Hangouts, 169
  Google Play Store, 245
  on Home screen, 43–45
  missed calls, 82
  Music app, 215
  Skype, 176
  text messages, 127
  USB connection, 272
  voice mail, 101
NP (no problem), 126
NRN (no reply needed), 126

• O •

offensive words, 328
OMG (oh my goodness), 126
online accounts, adding, 30–31
onscreen keyboard. *See* keyboard, onscreen
orientation of phone
camera and, 197
customization, 306
locking, 336
overview, 39–40
using Landscape mode, 336
Overflow icon, 52
overheating, troubleshooting, 318–319
overseas usage. *See* international usage
owner info, 303–304

• P •

pairing Bluetooth devices, 266–267
Pandora Radio, 222
panels, Home screen
accessing, 43
index for, 42
managing, 297–298
panning maps, 183
panoramic pictures, 198–199
Password lock, 26, 300
passwords, 59, 156
pasting text, 70
pattern lock, 26, 300–302
pauses, dialing, 77, 87–88
pausing music, 326
Pen Window command, 55
people in room (PIR), 126
person over shoulder (POS), 126
perspective, changing in maps, 183
Phone app, 42
phone calls
answering incoming while on call, 80, 88–89
Bluetooth headsets, 267
call log, 82–83
conference calls, 91–92
dialing, 74
doing things during, 76

ending, 76
forwarding
automatically, 94
Google Voice and, 102
overview, 92
using Android settings, 92–93
using Verizon network, 93–94
ignoring incoming, 80
inserting pause, 77
international
dialing, 284–285
using +, 338
using phone abroad, 286–287
using Skype, 286
locking phone during, 336
long-distance, 73–74
merging, 89
missed calls, 82
motion features for, 325
muting, 76
placing, 75
placing, for contacts, 111
putting on hold, 88
receiving, 79–80
rejecting
automatically, 94
list for, 95
with text message, 80–82
returning to, 76
speaker option, 76
speed dial
adding pauses, 87–88
configuring, 85–86
swapping multiple, 89
two at once, 89–90
phone jacket, 20
phone status icons, 42
photos. *See* pictures
Picasa Web albums, 206
Picture Transfer Protocol (PTP), 272
pictures
adding for contact, 118–120, 338
attaching to MMS, 128–129
Camera app, 196–197
cropping, 207–208
deleting, 197–198, 209
file format for, 197
Gallery app, 205–206

pictures *(continued)*
 navigating to location of, 206
 panoramic, 198–199
 posting on Facebook, 161–163
 posting to Twitter, 165
 resolution, 202–203
 rotating, 209
 saving from web page, 153
 screen shot, 199–200
 sharing, 207
 storage location, 204–205
 using as wallpaper, 291
PIN lock
 as backup, 302, 303
 overview, 26
 setting, 300
pinch operation, 36, 149
PIR (people in room), 126
Play Books app, 231
Play Music app, 219, 221
Play Store app. *See* Google Play Store
playing music, 213–214
playlists
 creating, 220–221
 defined, 212
 deleting, 221
 favorites, 215
 overview, 219–220
plus sign (+), 77, 285, 338
PNG image format, 200
points of interest on map, 187–188
POP3 (Post Office Protocol 3), 135
pop-up windows, blocking, 156
POS (person over shoulder), 126
posting pictures
 on Facebook, 161–163
 to Twitter, 165
Power Control widget, 266
Power Saving Mode, 310–311
power up process, 23
Power/Lock button
 functions served by, 23
 interface, 16
 locking phone, 31
 pressing when on call, 20
 turning off phone, 32–33
 turning on phone, 24

unlocking phone, 27
 using during call, 336
predictive text, 61–62
preinstalled apps, 249
press. *See* touch operations
Previous Image icon, 197
primary Home screen panel, 298
printers
 Bluetooth, 268
 Google Cloud Printing app, 267
privacy for web browsing, 156
proximity sensor, 20, 31
PTP (Picture Transfer Protocol), 272
punctuation, speaking, 66
purchased apps, 245

QT abbreviation, 126
Quick Actions, 45, 46
quitting apps, 46

R

RAM (random access memory), 332
ratings, app, 243
reading eBooks, 232–233
rear camera, 18
rear cover, 11, 15
recent apps, 37, 335
Recently Accessed Places, Maps app, 189
Recently Added playlist, 220
Recently Played playlist, 220
recording audio, 239–240
Refresh icon, 52
Refresh Interval setting, Facebook app, 163
refunds on purchased apps, 246, 251
Reject Messages screen, 81
rejecting calls
 forwarding automatically, 94
 ignoring, 80
 reject list, 95
 with text message, 80–82
reloading web page, 149
reminders, event, 230
removable storage, 13
repeat music, 214

replacement batteries, 13
reporting apps, 251
resetting phone, 316
resolution for camera, 202–203
restarting phone
  accessing command, 33
  fixing general problems, 314–315
restaurants, searching for, 187–188
ringtones
  adapting sound to environment, 326
  alarms, 225
  choosing, 95–96
  creating, 97–98
  defined, 80
  Facebook, 163
  setting for contact, 96–97
  for text messages, 96, 131
roaming, 281–282, 337
ROFL (rolling on the floor, laughing), 126
rotate operation, 36
rotating maps, 183
Route icon, 188
running apps, 250

● *S* ●

S Finder search app, 37, 55
S Memo app, 236–237
S Note app, 119
S Pen
  Air Command, 54–55
  button on, 53
  following links on web page, 149
  interface, 18
  overview, 53
  replacing, 318
  screen shot using, 200
  scribbling
    Action Memo app, 236–237
    on screen shot, 238–239
  tricks using, 55
  typing with, 64–65
  unlocking phone, 27
Samsung keyboard. *See* keyboard, onscreen
Samsung Kies program, 276–277, 313
Saved Places, Maps app, 189

Scrap Booker command, 54
screen protectors, 312
Screen Rotation feature, 40
screen shot
  capturing, 199–200
  defined, 54
  file format for, 200
  scribbling on, 55, 238–239
  selective portion of screen, 55
Screen Timeout setting, 32, 306
Screen Write command, 54
Screenshots album, 206
scribbling
  Action Memo app, 236–237
  on screen shot, 55, 238–239
SD card. *See* MicroSD card
search
  contacts, 112
  finding text on web page, 152
  Gmail app, 139
  Google Now, 235
  Google Play Store, 242
  Google Search widget, 152
  icon for, 52
  Internet app, 149
  Maps app
    addresses, 187
    businesses and points of interest, 187–188
    contacts, 189
    favorites, 189
    recent places, 189
  music, 218
  overview, 339
  Sound Search widget, 215
Search key, 58
security
  unlock pattern versus password lock, 302
  viruses, 250
  web browsing, 156
  Wi-Fi, 261
selecting text, 68–69
self-portraits, 198
server delete option, Email app, 145–146
Service Set Identifier (SSID), 261
Settings icon, 52
Share icon, 52, 143

sharing
  apps, 248
  with cloud storage, 277–278
  current location, 186–187
  with Facebook app, 163
  from Gallery app, 207
  printing to Bluetooth printer, 268
  web pages, 152–153
  Wi-Fi, using Mobile Hotspot feature,
    262–263
Shift key, 59
Short Message Service. *See* text messages
shortcuts, Home screen, 292
Show Song List button, 213
shuffle music, 214
Shutter icon, 196
Signal Strength icon, 77
Signature lock, 26, 302–303
signatures, e-mail, 144
silencing phone
  overview, 39
  Turn Over motion, 305
SIM (Subscriber Identity Module) card
  battery removal necessary, 11
  installing, 13
  purpose of, 13
Simple Mail Transfer Protocol
    (SMTP), 135
Skype
  international calls, 286
  notifications, 176
  overview, 174–175
  pros and cons, 175
  text chatting, 175–176
  text message alternative, 132
  video calls, 176–177
Smart Rotation feature, 306
Smart Screen feature, 306
Smart Stay feature, 32
SMS (Short Message Service). *See* text
    messages
SMTP (Simple Mail Transfer Protocol), 135
social networking
  contact pictures from, 120
  contacts from, 115–116
  Facebook
    app versus web version, 158
    camera app for, 162

configuring app, 163
displaying sidebar, 160
getting app, 158
Home page widget, 161
logging into app, 158
Mobile Uploads album, 163
News Feed, 159
notifications, 160
overview, 157
posting pictures, 161–163
quitting app, 160
Refresh Interval setting, 163
ringtone for, 163
setting status, 160–161
setting up account, 158
syncing contacts, 159
updating News Feed, 160
Google+, 166
HootSuite app, 166
LinkedIn, 166
linking identical contacts, 120–121
Meebo, 166
Myspace, 166
Twitter
  Home screen widgets, 164
  logging into app, 164
  overview, 163–164
  posting pictures, 165
  reading tweets, 165
  setting up account, 164
  tweeting, 165
  viewing contact info, 112
SOS (someone over shoulder), 126
Sound Picker app, 97
Sound Search widget, 215
speaker, 16, 18
Speaker button, 76
special characters, typing, 60–61
speed dial
  adding pauses, 87–88
  configuring, 85–86
spread operation, 36
Sprint support, 317
SSID (Service Set Identifier), 261
Star icon, 52, 120
starred contacts, 78
status bar, 41
stopwatch, 224

storage
  cloud, 277–278
  external, 204
  internal
    defined, 204
    moving apps to/from, 251
  MicroSD card
    adapters for, 14
    battery removal and, 11
    copying music from computer, 216
    formatting, 280
    installing, 13–14
    moving apps to/from, 251
    overview, 280
    removing, 14
    SIM card and, 13
    storing pictures and videos, 204–205
    unmounting, 280
  pictures and videos location,
    204–205
  removable, 13
  statistics, 278–279
storing phone, 21
streaming music, 222
Street View, Maps app, 186
stylus. *See* S Pen
Subscriber Identity Module card.
    See SIM card
sunlight, 21
support contacts, 316–317
swapping phone calls, 89
Swipe lock
  overview, 25–26
  removing S Pen and, 53
swipe operation
  defined, 36
  Keyboard Swipe feature, 63
switching between apps, 48–49
symbols, typing, 60–61
Sync Contacts option, 116
synchronization
  e-mail account options, 135
  Facebook contacts, 159
  Samsung Kies program, 276–277
  social network contacts, 115–116
  transferring files, 274–276
  using cloud storage, 277–278
system updates, 313–314

● T ●

talk to you later (TTYL), 126
tap. *See* touch operations
Task Manager app, 332–333
ta-ta for now (TTFN), 126
TC (take care), 126
tethering Internet connection, 264
text
  copying, 69
  cutting, 69
  finding on web page, 152
  moving cursor, 67–68
  pasting, 70
  selecting, 68–69
text chatting
  using Google Hangouts, 170–172
  using Skype, 175–176
text messages
  alternatives to, 131
  carrier apps, 132
  common abbreviations, 126
  deleting, 130–131
  e-mail versus, 128
  forwarding, 127–128
  Google Hangouts, as app for, 131, 172
  landlines and, 127
  limitations of, 128
  limits on, 124
  MMS
    attaching media, 128–129
    e-mail versus, 128
    limits on, 129
    saving media from, 130
    text messages versus, 128
  notice on lock screen, 26
  opting out of, 132
  overview, 123–124
  receiving, 127
  rejecting call with, 80–82
  ringtone for, 96, 131
  roaming and, 282
  sending
    from Contacts app, 111, 125
    from Google Hangouts, 171
    from Messages app, 124–125
    by swiping contact, 126
Skype, 132

thank you (TY), 126
THX abbreviation, 126
TIA (thanks in advance), 126
timer, 224
TMI (too much information), 126
T-Mobile support, 317
toll roads, 191
touch buttons, 37
touch operations, 36
touchscreen
  automatic timeout for, 31–32
  cleaning, 312
  defined, 2
  disabling during call, 336
  gloves and, 36
  interface, 16
  touch operations, 36
  troubleshooting, 317, 318
transferring files, 274–276
travel tips, 284
troubleshooting
  app problems, 315
  battery, 318
  data connection issues, 315
  general problems, 314–315
  Help app and command, 314
  Landscape mode, 319
  phone overheating, 318–319
  resetting phone, 316
  screen too dark, 318
  touchscreen, 317, 318
TTFN (ta-ta for now), 126
TTYL (talk to you later), 126
TuneIn Radio app, 222
Turn Over motion, 305
turning off phone, 31–33
turning on phone, 24–25
turning pages in eBooks, 232
Twitter
  Home screen widgets, 164
  linking identical contacts, 120–121
  logging into app, 164
  overview, 163–164
  posting pictures, 165
  reading tweets, 165
  setting up account, 164
  tweeting, 165
TY (thank you), 126
typing
  Enter key changes, 58
  Keyboard Swipe feature, 63
  one character at a time, 59
  passwords, 59
  predictive text, 61–62, 336
  with S Pen, 64–65
  special characters, 60–61
  special keys, 58–59
  voice input, 65, 67, 328

• U •

U2 abbreviation, 126
Unhold icon, 88
uninstalling apps, 245, 249, 251
unlinking contacts, 121
unlock pattern, 300–302
unlocking phone, 26–27
unmounting MicroSD card, 280
updating Android, 313–314
updating apps, 245, 248
uploading, 153
UR abbreviation, 126
USB connection
  advantages of 3.0, 10
  charging battery, 15–16
  configuring, 272–273
  connecting cable, 272
  copying music from computer, 216
  disconnecting phone, 274
  importing contacts, 115
  on Mac, 273–274
  MicroSD card mounted, 273
  multipurpose jack, 18
  notification, 272
  Samsung Kies program, 276–277
  tethering Internet connection, 264
  transferring files, 274–276
  uniqueness of, 18

• V •

vCard format, 115
Verizon
  forwarding phone calls using, 93–94
  support from, 317
Vibration mode
  customizing, 305
  extending battery life, 311
  using Volume button, 39
video calls
  Enable Cartoon View, 169
  making, 167–169
  muting, 168
  phone compatibility, 168
  placing for contacts, 111
  Skype, 176–177
video chat
  Google Hangouts, 172–174
  Skype, 176–177
videos
  deleting, 209, 197-198
  file format for, 197
  navigating to location of, 206
  playing, 240
  posting on Facebook, 162
  recording, 196–197
  resolution, 202–203
  setting quality, 203–204
  sharing, 207
  storage location, 204–205
viruses on Android, 250
voice input
  activating, 65
  censored words, 67, 328
  dictating text, 65–66
voice mail
  carrier-provided
    overview, 99
    retrieving, 101
    setting up, 100
  Google Voice
    adding second line, 103–104
    configuring, 102–103
    text transcription in, 105
    using app, 104–105
  greeting for, 100

voice navigation, 191–193
Voice Recorder app, 239–240
volume
  adapting to environment, 326
  setting, 38–39
  silencing phone, 39
Volume button
  listening to music, 215
  using, 38–39
  zooming in camera, 197

• W •

W8 abbreviation, 126
wallpaper, 43, 291–292
web browsing
  blocking pop-up windows, 156
  bookmarks, 150
  double-tap operation, 149
  downloading
    files, 154
    images, 153
    overview, 153
    viewing downloaded items, 154
  finding text on page, 152
  Google Chrome app, 149
  Google Search widget, 152
  history of previous pages, 150
  Internet app
    deleting personal information, 156
    overview, 148–149
    setting home page, 154–155
    text scaling, 155
  Landscape mode, 149
  mobile devices and, 147
  multiple windows, 151–152
  navigating back and forward, 150
  panning web page, 148
  privacy, 156
  reloading page, 149
  saving image from page, 153
  searching using Address box, 149
  security, 156
  sharing web page, 152–153
  stop loading page, 149
  visiting web page, 149
  zooming web page, 149

web sites for book, 5–6
webmail, 134
widgets, Home screen
  adding, 293–294
  defined, 42
  overview, 46–47
  removing, 297
  resizing, 294
widgets, lock screen, 324–325
Wi-Fi (wireless fidelity)
  activating, 259
  activating location services, 184
  Airplane mode and, 283
  avoiding data surcharges, 242
  connecting to network, 260–261
  extending battery life, 311
  Internet radio and, 222
  Mobile Hotspot feature, 262–263
  overview, 259
  Quick Action for, 259
  status icon, 261
  turning off, 259
  using phone abroad, 287
  video chat, 176
  WPS, 261–262
Wi-Fi Protected Setup (WPS), 261–262
Windows Live Mail, 115
Windows Mail, 115
Windows Media Player, 216–217

wireless fidelity. *See* Wi-Fi
Wish List, Google Play Store, 246
world clocks, 224
WPS (Wi-Fi Protected Setup), 261–262

XOXO abbreviation, 126

Y abbreviation, 126
Yahoo! e-mail, 134
YouTube
  sharing videos using, 207
  watching videos, 240
YW (you're welcome), 126

Zedge app, 96, 292
zooming
  in camera, 197
  to center panel of Home screen, 43
  maps, 183
  motion features for, 326
  web pages, 149
ZZZ abbreviation, 126

About the Author

Dan Gookin has been writing about technology for over 25 years. He combines his love of writing with his gizmo fascination to create books that are informative, entertaining, and not boring. Having written over 130 titles with 12 million copies in print translated into over 30 languages, Dan can attest that his method of crafting computer tomes seems to work.

Perhaps his most famous title is the original *DOS For Dummies,* published in 1991. It became the world's fastest-selling computer book, at one time moving more copies per week than the *New York Times* number-one bestseller (though, as a reference, it could not be listed on the *Times'* Best Sellers list). That book spawned the entire line of *For Dummies* books, which remains a publishing phenomenon to this day.

Dan's most popular titles include *PCs For Dummies, Word For Dummies, Laptops For Dummies,* and *Android Phones For Dummies.* He also maintains the vast and helpful website www.wambooli.com.

Dan holds a degree in Communications/Visual Arts from the University of California, San Diego. He lives in the Pacific Northwest, where he enjoys spending time with his sons playing video games indoors while they enjoy the gentle woods of Idaho.

Publisher's Acknowledgments

Acquisitions Editor: Katie Mohr

Senior Project Editor: Mark Enochs

Copy Editor: Rebecca Whitney

Editorial Assistant: Annie Sullivan

Sr. Editorial Assistant: Cherie Case

Project Coordinator: Lauren Buroker

Cover Image: Background image ©iStockphoto.com/Attila445; Device and Screenshot images courtesy of ©Dan Gookin.

Apple & Mac

iPad For Dummies,
6th Edition
978-1-118-72306-7

iPhone For Dummies,
7th Edition
978-1-118-69083-3

Macs All-in-One
For Dummies, 4th Edition
978-1-118-82210-4

OS X Mavericks
For Dummies
978-1-118-69188-5

Blogging & Social Media

Facebook For Dummies,
5th Edition
978-1-118-63312-0

Social Media Engagement
For Dummies
978-1-118-53019-1

WordPress For Dummies,
6th Edition
978-1-118-79161-5

Business

Stock Investing
For Dummies, 4th Edition
978-1-118-37678-2

Investing For Dummies,
6th Edition
978-0-470-90545-6

Personal Finance

Personal Finance
For Dummies, 7th Edition
978-1-118-11785-9

QuickBooks 2014
For Dummies
978-1-118-72005-9

Small Business Marketing
Kit For Dummies,
3rd Edition
978-1-118-31183-7

Careers

Job Interviews
For Dummies, 4th Edition
978-1-118-11290-8

Job Searching with Social
Media For Dummies,
2nd Edition
978-1-118-67856-5

Personal Branding
For Dummies
978-1-118-11792-7

Resumes For Dummies,
6th Edition
978-0-470-87361-8

Starting an Etsy Business
For Dummies, 2nd Edition
978-1-118-59024-9

Diet & Nutrition

Belly Fat Diet For Dummies
978-1-118-34585-6

Mediterranean Diet
For Dummies
978-1-118-71525-3

Nutrition For Dummies,
5th Edition
978-0-470-93231-5

Digital Photography

Digital SLR Photography
All-in-One For Dummies,
2nd Edition
978-1-118-59082-9

Digital SLR Video &
Filmmaking For Dummies
978-1-118-36598-4

Photoshop Elements 12
For Dummies
978-1-118-72714-0

Gardening

Herb Gardening
For Dummies, 2nd Edition
978-0-470-61778-6

Gardening with Free-Range
Chickens For Dummies
978-1-118-54754-0

Health

Boosting Your Immunity
For Dummies
978-1-118-40200-9

Diabetes For Dummies,
4th Edition
978-1-118-29447-5

Living Paleo For Dummies
978-1-118-29405-5

Big Data

Big Data For Dummies
978-1-118-50422-2

Data Visualization
For Dummies
978-1-118-50289-1

Hadoop For Dummies
978-1-118-60755-8

Language &
Foreign Language

500 Spanish Verbs
For Dummies
978-1-118-02382-2

English Grammar
For Dummies, 2nd Edition
978-0-470-54664-2

French All-in-One
For Dummies
978-1-118-22815-9

German Essentials
For Dummies
978-1-118-18422-6

Italian For Dummies,
2nd Edition
978-1-118-00465-4

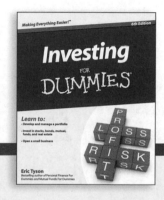 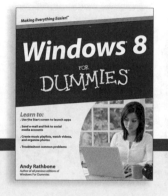  

e **Available in print and e-book formats.**

Available wherever books are sold. **For more information or to order direct visit www.dummies.com**

Math & Science

Algebra I For Dummies,
2nd Edition
978-0-470-55964-2

Anatomy and Physiology
For Dummies, 2nd Edition
978-0-470-92326-9

Astronomy For Dummies,
3rd Edition
978-1-118-37697-3

Biology For Dummies,
2nd Edition
978-0-470-59875-7

Chemistry For Dummies,
2nd Edition
978-1-118-00730-3

1001 Algebra II Practice
Problems For Dummies
978-1-118-44662-1

Microsoft Office

Excel 2013 For Dummies
978-1-118-51012-4

Office 2013 All-in-One
For Dummies
978-1-118-51636-2

PowerPoint 2013
For Dummies
978-1-118-50253-2

Word 2013 For Dummies
978-1-118-49123-2

Music

Blues Harmonica
For Dummies
978-1-118-25269-7

Guitar For Dummies,
3rd Edition
978-1-118-11554-1

iPod & iTunes
For Dummies, 10th Edition
978-1-118-50864-0

Programming

Beginning Programming
with C For Dummies
978-1-118-73763-7

Excel VBA Programming
For Dummies, 3rd Edition
978-1-118-49037-2

Java For Dummies,
6th Edition
978-1-118-40780-6

Religion & Inspiration

The Bible For Dummies
978-0-7645-5296-0

Buddhism For Dummies,
2nd Edition
978-1-118-02379-2

Catholicism For Dummies,
2nd Edition
978-1-118-07778-8

Self-Help & Relationships

Beating Sugar Addiction
For Dummies
978-1-118-54645-1

Meditation For Dummies,
3rd Edition
978-1-118-29144-3

Seniors

Laptops For Seniors
For Dummies, 3rd Edition
978-1-118-71105-7

Computers For Seniors
For Dummies, 3rd Edition
978-1-118-11553-4

iPad For Seniors
For Dummies, 6th Edition
978-1-118-72826-0

Social Security
For Dummies
978-1-118-20573-0

Smartphones & Tablets

Android Phones
For Dummies, 2nd Edition
978-1-118-72030-1

Nexus Tablets
For Dummies
978-1-118-77243-0

Samsung Galaxy S 4
For Dummies
978-1-118-64222-1

Samsung Galaxy Tabs
For Dummies
978-1-118-77294-2

Test Prep

ACT For Dummies,
5th Edition
978-1-118-01259-8

ASVAB For Dummies,
3rd Edition
978-0-470-63760-9

GRE For Dummies,
7th Edition
978-0-470-88921-3

Officer Candidate Tests
For Dummies
978-0-470-59876-4

Physician's Assistant Exam
For Dummies
978-1-118-11556-5

Series 7 Exam For Dummies
978-0-470-09932-2

Windows 8

Windows 8.1 All-in-One
For Dummies
978-1-118-82087-2

Windows 8.1 For Dummies
978-1-118-82121-3

Windows 8.1 For Dummies,
Book + DVD Bundle
978-1-118-82107-7

𝑒 Available in print and e-book formats.

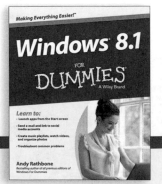

Available wherever books are sold. **For more information or to order direct visit www.dummies.com**

Take Dummies with you everywhere you go!

Whether you are excited about e-books, want more from the web, must have your mobile apps, or are swept up in social media, Dummies makes everything easier.

Leverage the Power

For Dummies is the global leader in the reference category and one of the most trusted and highly regarded brands in the world. No longer just focused on books, customers now have access to the For Dummies content they need in the format they want. Let us help you develop a solution that will fit your brand and help you connect with your customers.

Advertising & Sponsorships

Connect with an engaged audience on a powerful multimedia site, and position your message alongside expert how-to content.

Targeted ads • Video • Email marketing • Microsites • Sweepstakes sponsorship

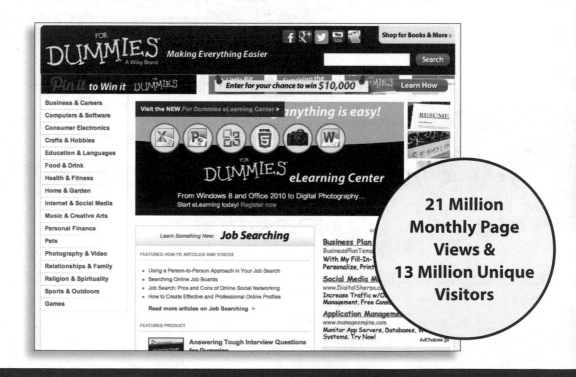